P9-CLP-159

SOUTHERN WRITERS

Appraisals in Our Time

SOUTHERN WRITERS

Appraisals in Our Time

EDITED BY

R. C. SIMONINI, JR.

LONGWOOD COLLEGE

THE UNIVERSITY PRESS OF VIRGINIA

CHARLOTTESVILLE

This collection first published 1964

THE UNIVERSITY PRESS OF VIRGINIA

Library of Congress Catalog Card Number: 64-13719

Printed in the United States of America by
THE WILLIAM BYRD PRESS, INC.

FOREWORD

THE South today is the most dynamic region of our country. Far from being an economically and socially depressed tobacco road, the South at mid-century is experiencing prosperity and at the same time a cultural revolution which has already made it a focal point of renascence in American literature. Thus, the South is being forced more than ever before to understand itself—the relevance of its historical traditions to its present ideals, the integrity of its "regionalism," the potentiality of its human and natural resources. The South must, in effect, try to find out what it has been and what it is in order to discover what it should be. Fortunately, Southern writers have left an impressive and illuminating record of this search.

The Institute of Southern Culture at Longwood College was established in 1956 to promote the study of traditional aspects of Southern civilization through academic course work, special lectures, and publication of research. The essays of this collection have been selected from previous publications of the Institute: *Virginia in History and Tradition* (1958), *The South in Perspective* (1959), and *The Dilemma of the Southern Writer* (1961). They have been particularly well received and deserve wider attention. As arranged, they have the unity of dealing with important aspects of Southern literature from its beginnings to the present day.

The theme of the collection is clear: Southern literature was born in a struggle of the creative artist for recognition in an indifferent society; it has flourished as its writers reacted with varied inspiration to their environment—its traditions, aspirations, achievements, and failures.

In the leading essay, Professor Thorp of Princeton University examines the status of the writer in the Old South and finds that before the Civil War not one author could earn a living entirely by writing. Southern agrarian society was epitomized by the practical plantation owner, who was content to import his books from the North or from England just as he imported machinery and manufactured products. The only art cultivated in the Old South was the art of "living," and writing was a poorly regarded avocation.

Professor Jacobs of the University of Kentucky finds Edgar Allan Poe projecting a "slightly schizoid" double image as he tried at once to be businessman and gentleman, journalist and poet. Poe's dilemma in the twilight years of the Old South was "in being caught between two worlds and trying to live in both." Southern tradition could appreciate the image of the melancholy Byronic poet, but the rising middle class rejected anyone who lived a disreputable, useless private life. Conversely, the aristocratic South still thought itself too genteel to admire hard-hitting, professional journalistic practices. Ironically, Professor Jacobs concludes, "As time went on, the canny journalist was forgotten, and the South wept over the memory of the melancholy poet."

In the tragedy of the Civil War, one would expect the South to find both the inspiration and the content for great literature, perhaps even a Southern counterpart to Tolstoy's *War and Peace.* But Professor Rubin of Hollins College finds little really good fiction written about "The War." Unlike the Napoleonic army in Russia, the Confederate army gets almost no introspective treatment, and the war in Southern fiction is seen mostly in its impact on the regional social pattern. Southern war novels lack a great protagonist whose personal crisis is brought into moving interplay with his country's crisis. In short, loyal Southern writers have been inspired to defend the Confederacy but not to analyze and understand it.

One possible exception to the disappointing literary achievement of Civil War novels is the work of Mary Johnston. After reviewing her long career as a historical novelist, Professor Nelson of Sweet Briar College cites *The Long Roll* and *Cease Firing* as the prose epic of the Confederacy, "the nearest thing we have in American literature to *War and Peace.*" Here in these underrated masterpieces is the true historical novel, a well-organized mixture of history and romance, tragedy and comedy, pastoral and folk tale, fable and legend, and, as Professor Nelson says, "probably the completest and the most authentic embodiment of the Southern Myth."

In the case of the more celebrated Ellen Glasgow, Professor Holman of the University of North Carolina observes that the best Southern writers are often placed "outside" the Southern literary tradition by critics. Because of accidents of residence, concentration on man's inner rather than outer landscape, and use of "foreign" literary subjects and techniques, Poe, Wolfe, Faulkner, and many contemporary Southern writers, as well as Miss Glasgow, are said to work in a non-Southern literary tradition. But Professor Holman asserts that there are a fairly consistent Southern view of life and literary characteristics peculiar to Southern writing, and that Ellen Glasgow's work is in the best of this tradition.

The relation of James Branch Cabell to the South—and particularly to Southern romanticism—is another neglected topic in that most of his critics have considered him to be hostile toward his environment. But Professor Schlegel of Longwood College describes how the South's chivalric attitude toward life and its reversion to the immediate past nourished the genius of Cabell, who saw himself as a knight in shining armor fighting for a cause and who took the neoclassical period as his artistic milieu. Moreover, both the South and Cabell adopted a poetic attitude toward life in that they created the worlds they wanted out of the raw materials of life about them. In spite of certain obvious sharp departures from the Southern tradition by Cabell, Professor Schlegel feels that Southern romanticism furnished him with the initial dynamics governing his philosophy of life and of art.

William Faulkner is one of the most discussed yet least understood of modern Southern writers. Professor Meriwether of the University of North Carolina believes that the sectional prejudice and personal bias of Northern critics have given Faulkner an unsympathetic reading, whereas in the South he is hardly read at all. Early critics of Faulkner were often Marxist, placing social values before literary values; other critics have censured him for historically muddled or "wrong-headed" thinking, which they automatically associate with poor writing. Professor Meriwether pleads for a critical judgment of a novelist based on literary standards alone.

Professor Meeker, formerly of Longwood College and now of the State University College at Potsdam, New York, brings our survey of Southern literature down to the contemporary scene with his study of the youngest generation of Southern fiction writers, who now find it is a definite asset to their careers to be Southerners. In his reading of the work of thirty-four novelists, he finds three general groups: those who approve of the South, those who are critical of it, and those who ignore it. Taking the criteria for the Southern literary tradition established by Professors Holman and Rubin, he concludes that the youngest literary generation in the South retains a love of rhetoric, a sense of style, and a consciousness of evil; but racial and family pride clearly and significantly diminishes as do regional pride and the deep awareness of the past related to the Civil War. If, as Professor Meeker states, "the tragic vision has been replaced by a guilt complex," this represents an important revision of the prevailing concept of the Southern literary tradition.

Although the critics represented here worked independently on their assigned topics at different times, they come to some striking agreements concerning Southern literature: (1) the struggle by the Southern writer for judicious recognition and approval—especially in his own region—has been characteristic of his career from Poe to Faulkner; (2) the South's tragic vision of war and reconstruction did not, ironically, inspire great literature; (3) the now-neglected Mary Johnston was the only writer to approach epic greatness in her "historic imagination" of the great conflict; (4) the best Southern writers—such as Glasgow, Cabell, and Faulkner—are curiously misunderstood in modern criticism, particularly in the way each related himself to a clearly defined Southern literary tradition; and (5) the next generation of important Southern writers is modifying its relation to the Southern literary tradition and to the reading public in several significant aspects.

To students and scholars of Southern literature, we wish these essays to be illuminating, if not heretical; and if the breeze blowing through the magnolia trees becomes momentarily heady, we would be happy that the Institute of Southern Culture has served its purpose.

R. C. SIMONINI, JR.

Farmville, Virginia
December 1963

CONTENTS

SOUTHERN WRITERS

Appraisals in Our Time

1

THE WRITER AS PARIAH IN THE OLD SOUTH

WILLARD THORP

PARIAH is a strong word. Strictly, a pariah is a member of a low caste in southern India where its members supply, or once did supply, most of the domestics in the service of Europeans. So far as I know there were no antebellum writers in our South who worked as house servants, though they often had to resort to distasteful hackwork of various kinds in order to gain spare time for their verses and essays. Nor were they forbidden the company of their social equals or superiors. But writers were not respected in Southern society as were doctors, lawyers, and other professional people. Some of them resorted to pseudonymity or to anonymity, if they had a worldly position to maintain. And in their private correspondence they complain bitterly of their lot. Frequently they also spoke up in public and berated their society for its indifference and even its hostility to the arts. Here is one such public rebuking. I shall let it stand for many which I might summon as witnesses. The author of it is one of the best poets of the Old South, Henry Timrod, called rather quaintly the South Carolina Petrarch. He is writing on "Literature in the South" in *Russell's Magazine*. The year is 1859.

We think that at no time, and in no country, has the position of an author been beset with such peculiar difficulties as the Southern writer is com-

A LECTURE given for the Institute of Southern Culture at Longwood College, April 21, 1961.

pelled to struggle with from the beginning to the end of his career. In no country in which literature has ever flourished has an author obtained so limited an audience. In no country, and at no period that we can recall, has an author been constrained by the indifference of the public amid which he lived, to publish with a people who were prejudiced against him. It would scarcely be too extravagant to entitle the Southern author the Pariah of modern literature. . . .

The truth is, it must be confessed, that though an educated, we are a provincial, and not a highly cultivated people. At least, there is among us a very general want of a high critical culture. The principles of that criticism, the basis of which is a profound psychology, are almost utterly ignored. There are scholars of pretension among us, with whom Blair's Rhetoric is still an unquestionable authority. There are schools and colleges in which it is used as a textbook. With the vast advance that has been made in critical science since the time of Blair few seem to be intimately acquainted. The opinions and theories of the last century are still held in reverence. Here Pope is still regarded by many as the most *correct* of English poets, and here, Kaimes [*sic*], after having been everywhere else removed to the top shelves of libraries, is still thumbed by learned professors and declamatory sophomores. Here literature is still regarded as an epicurean amusement; not as a study, at least equal in importance, and certainly not inferior in difficulty, to law and medicine. Here no one is surprised when some fossil theory of criticism, long buried under the ruins of an exploded school, is dug up, and discussed with infinite gravity by gentlemen who know Pope and Horace by heart, but who have never read a word of Wordsworth or Tennyson, or who have read them with suspicion, and rejected them with superciliousness.

In such a state of critical science, it is no wonder that we are prudently cautious in passing a favourable judgment upon any new candidates for our admiration. It is no wonder that while we accept without a cavil books of English and Northern reputation, we yet hesitate to acknowledge our own writers, until, perhaps, having been commended by English or Northern critics, they present themselves to us with a "certain alienated majesty."[1]

I should say at once that writers, through the ages, have often felt themselves alienated from their society and indeed have occasionally been cast out for one reason or another. Socrates was put to death for introducing new deities and corrupting youth with new ideas. Shelley was in trouble in England from the time he was dismissed from Oxford for publishing *The Necessity of Atheism.* Byron left England under a cloud of infamy at the age of twenty-eight, never to return.

[1] *The Essays of Henry Timrod,* ed. by Edd Winfield Parks (Athens, 1942), pp. 83, 85-86.

In the period after our Civil War, an era aptly termed the Gilded Age by Mark Twain, an alarming number of artists and writers left this country, thinking to find a more congenial society abroad. Among these expatriates were John Singer Sargent, Edwin Abbey, Mary Cassatt, Whistler, Henry James, Edith Wharton, and Logan Pearsall Smith. To many of them the words of Henry Adams seemed the ghastly truth:

> The American character showed singular limitations which sometimes drove the student of civilized man to despair. Crushed by his own ignorance—lost in the darkness of his own gropings—the scholar finds himself jostled of a sudden by a crowd of men who seem to him ignorant that there is a thing called ignorance; who have forgotten how to amuse themselves; who cannot even understand that they are bored.[2]

I shall readily grant, therefore, that some of the sense of alienation felt by these early Southern writers is a variant of the malady from which writers have suffered from time to time in various countries and in many ages. Nevertheless, there was something remarkable about the literary situation in the Old South, and the degree of its remarkableness can be measured.

One way to measure and judge what was happening—or, better, not happening—is to consider what was going on in the North. Perhaps it is enough to say that by 1861 Northern writers had succeeded in creating an American literature. The efforts of Charles Brockden Brown, Irving, Cooper, Emerson, Thoreau, Hawthorne, Melville, Whitman, and Longfellow had brought them fame not only in their own country but in England and Europe as well. Among the creators of this new-world literature only two Southern names of importance can be found: Poe and the novelist William Gilmore Simms. It would be wrong to infer that this wonderful flowering, so gratifying to Americans who wanted us to excel in every activity of the mind, was a spontaneous outburst, one of those accidents of civilization by which Holland was endowed with many painters and few poets, Germany with composers and philosophers, England with poets and novelists but few painters and composers.

[2] *The Education of Henry Adams: An Autobiography* (Boston, 1927), p. 297.

The fact is that this great burst of creativity in the North was to a considerable degree willed and planned.

We may smile, now, at the remark of Samuel Lorenzo Knapp, who said in his 1829 *Lectures on American Literature,* "Whenever a nation wills it, prodigies are born." Yet there was some truth in this grandiloquent prophecy. As soon as the Republic was established, the call went out for a national literature. The poets strove to produce an American epic because the epic was still considered the greatest test of poetic genius, since its rules are immutable. (We got our epics almost at once. They were not great epics but they were American at least and some English reviewers admired them.) The dramatists ransacked our history for American themes. Lyric poets like Freneau ousted English larks and nightingales and found birds nearer home to take their place. With the publication of Cooper's *The Spy* in 1821 and *The Pioneers* in 1823, two great themes for our novelists got their first run-through, the American Revolution and the frontier. This determination to be free of England, to discover native themes and new forms, has its amusing aspects, of course. A great deal of chauvinistic prose and poetry was written and much of it was dutifully read. Yet the fact remains that a course was laid out and a faith established. What Hawthorne and Melville achieved in the 1850's would not have been possible if there had been no pioneers before them.

What about the South? There are no names there to match Emerson and Melville and Whitman. The best were, as I have said, Poe and Simms, and Poe became an expatriate in Philadelphia and New York. Then come, farther down the scale, the poets St. George Tucker, Edward Coote Pinkney, Thomas Holley Chivers, Philip Pendleton Cooke, Henry Timrod, and Paul Hamilton Hayne; the essayist William Wirt; the novelists Nathaniel Beverley Tucker, J. P. Kennedy, W. A. Caruthers, and John Esten Cooke. This is a short roll call. We could add to it if we descended to the poetasters or included historians and theologians. Comparisons on the ground of quality I do not care to make. What concerns us here is that the list is so short. The question is: Why did the South produce so few writers in comparison with the North?

We could find a ready answer in the fact that apart from the writers themselves there was little interest in the South in the need for creating a national literature for America. There was, indeed, considerable hostility to this Yankee notion. This hostility is at the center of the argument advanced by Edward W. Johnston, writing on "American Literature" in the *Southern Review* for August 1831. Johnston was reviewing Knapp's *Lectures* and Samuel Kettell's *Specimens of American Poetry* (1829), the first extensive anthology of American verse. "We do," says Johnston, "in the name of the good people of the planting States, utterly disclaim having even the humblest part, which is assigned us, in a separate school of writers, dignified with the title of 'American.'"[3] American literature was to Johnston still a part of English literature and should be proud to remain so. To attempt to create a separate American literature would be "the most singularly bold effort to advance the kingdom of Dullness that the world has yet ever beheld." He then advances an argument which will shock you as much as it does me, but this would not be the last time it would be heard in the South. "The general feeling of aversion to authorship" in the South may be said to prevail, "for the greater part, precisely in proportion to good education and cultivated taste." Johnston advises young Southerners to give up ambitious schemes for a writing career and seek rather to perfect themselves in eloquence. One of the most powerful of Southern orators, William Lowndes Yancey, who would later write the ordinance for secession, gave the final twist to this argument. It is not only that men of education and good taste have a proper aversion to authorship. They cannot suppose that the South has any need for authors at all. "Our poetry is our lives," Yancey declared; "our fiction will come when truth has ceased to satisfy us; and as for our history, we have made about all that has glorified the United States."[4] Incidentally this argument of Yancey's that the South does not need the artist because living is an art was invented anew in our time by Stark Young and Donald Davidson.

But we should not be content with this one possible explanation for the short roll call of antebellum writers—the explanation that

[3] Quoted in Jay B. Hubbell, *The South in American Literature, 1607-1900* (Durham, 1954), p. 217.

[4] Hubbell, pp. 342-43.

the South generally wanted no part in the campaign for a national or even a regional literature. Other reasons were advanced then and still others can be proposed at this distance in time. It has often been said, for example, that the very nature of Southern society militated against the writer. The Old South was agrarian and in no agrarian society had the arts ever flourished. This argument would be difficult to sustain. How much more agrarian was the South in 1830 than the North? The great landowners of England in the eighteenth century, to whom Virginia and South Carolina plantation owners liked to compare themselves, were often notable encouragers of the arts. But there is undoubtedly some truth in the argument, though it must be qualified. It would be more accurate to say that there were certain features of the Southern agrarian society which crowded out the artist and poet. The plantation owner was often a hard-pressed man. Nature was frequently against him in crop failures, sudden frosts, a rapidly depleted soil, sickness among his slaves. He had to be a good manager and a very practical one. His labor force was inefficient and illiterate and must be kept illiterate lest education induce thoughts of rebellion. When he was not tending to the thousand and one things which must be kept in working order, he sought recreation in field sports or the race track. Once a year he took his family to the Springs of Virginia or north to Saratoga, if possible, or to some resort nearer home if he had to watch expenses. The lawyer was needed to settle land claims and defend him in court. The doctor was needed for his ever-breeding wife and when the yellow fever struck. The artist was needed once in a generation to do the portraits of the whole family. The poet or novelist was not needed. Let the North supply reading matter for his wife and daughters or, better still, let the English do it. Pope, Goldsmith, and especially Sir Walter Scott sufficed.

This willingness to import from the North or from England what books were needed, just as one imported farm machinery or calico, was the crux of the matter. The Southern writer's commodity was not a staple nor were the institutions and agencies needed which support and encourage and train writers, publish and disseminate and review their work.

Of all the arts music, I suppose, is most dependent on a favorable cultural environment to support it. It cannot flourish without orchestras, singing societies, and conservatories. Painters need ateliers to study in and dealers to promote their work. The writer can write alone, in the garret or on his island. But even he needs some institutional support in the form of publishing houses and literary journals. As we might expect, the antebellum South was lacking in this regard. As the important publishing firms came into existence in the North—Mathew Carey in Philadelphia, Wiley and Putnam and Harper and Brothers in New York, Ticknor and Fields in Boston—there was no corresponding development in the South. Local printers there, as in the North, contrived to issue books occasionally but their presswork was poor and they had no means for distributing books over a wide area. Thus the Southern writer was forced to make publishing connections in the North and work hard to keep them strong. On the whole the Northern firms were receptive to the work of Southern authors, as letters which passed back and forth clearly show. It is pleasant to remember that the first volume of an ardent young Charleston poet, Paul Hamilton Hayne, was taken by Ticknor and Fields in 1855 and that Simms's many novels bear various famous Northern imprints—Carey and Hart, Harper and Brothers, Baker and Scribner, Redfield, Wiley and Putnam. Of course the arrangements with Northern publishers were terminated during the Civil War, though in many instances they were renewed as soon as hostilities ceased.

The literary history of the Old South is strewn with ill-fated attempts to foster magazines which could compete with Philadelphia's *Port Folio* (1801-27) and the august Bostonian *North American Review* (1815-39). Even the longest lived of the Southern journals, *The Southern Literary Messenger* (1834-64), which had Poe for its editor during 1836, was constantly on the edge of failure. In 1851 John R. Thompson, its editor, wrote to a Northern literary friend:

> *The Messenger* is almost "gone." I look into the future to see nothing but diseases. . . . Four years of hard labor find me in debt, my small patrimony almost exhausted. . . . I have followed the will-o'-the-wisp, literary fame, into the morass, and it has gone out, leaving me up to the armpits in mud.[5]

[5] Quoted in Frank Luther Mott, *A History of American Magazines, 1741-1850* (Cambridge, 1939), p. 647.

Four years later he said publicly in an editorial:

Harper's Magazine has probably five times as many subscribers south of the Potomac . . . and even *Putnam's Monthly*, which has recently outraged the entire slaveholding portion of the Union by lending itself to the extremist views of the abolitionists, has a larger circulation among slaveholders. . . . For years past the *Messenger* has met with only the most meagre patronage and now stands in need of enlarged means, or it must share the fate of other similar works which preceded it and perished.[6]

Even the tireless William Gilmore Simms was not able to give long life to the several magazine ventures he engaged in. His most ambitious attempt, *The Southern and Western Monthly Magazine and Review*, lasted just one year, from January to December 1845. We can understand why Simms gave up so soon if we glance at the table of contents of the March issue. No fewer than nine (possibly eleven) of the items Simms wrote himself, using various pseudonyms or leaving them unsigned. Here was a backbreaking job which might kill a man of even Simms's vigor.

This, then, was the literary situation in the Old South. Not one author before the Civil War made his living entirely by writing. The writing of novels and verse could be only an avocation. Most of the would-be writers were lawyers—like William Wirt of Richmond, Philip Pendleton Cooke of Martinsburg, Virginia, J. P. Kennedy and Edward Coote Pinkney of Baltimore. William A. Caruthers was a busy physician. Simms tried the law briefly but depended on his plantation to give steady support to his family, though he probably made more by his writing than any Southern author.

What did the writers think about the situation they found themselves in? How did they vent their frustration? The answers are as various as the men themselves. William Caruthers, for instance, wasted little time in recrimination. He found the necessary hours in a busy professional life to turn out three novels, *The Kentuckian in New-York* (1834), *The Cavaliers of Virginia* (1834-35), and *The Knights of the Horse-Shoe* (1845), and he was pleased with their success. He regretted, as he once said, that "no man in this country can afford to write, unless he pursues some lucrative employment

[6] *Ibid.*, p. 648.

at the same time."[7] But that was the reality and he was too busy with his patients and his work for the Whig party to spend time trying to reform an impossible situation. Once, only, do we hear him express regret for the other career he might have had. The Introduction to his last novel, a tale of Governor Spotswood's exploration of the western borders of Virginia, ends with these nostalgic words:

> Would that we could do justice to the vast field which our explorations have barely entered! Nowhere in this country is there such an unexplored storehouse of materials for the novelist as may be found still clustering around the hearthstones of the old cocked-hat gentry. In many of these old mansions there are still preserved genealogical trees, and the family pictures of all the generations from the landing of their forefathers down to the present time. There may be learned at one and the same time the histories of the old people, and the various costumes, from the hoops and farthingales down to the republican simplicity of Thomas Jefferson's era. This alone might form an interesting study to one sufficiently imbued with the true antiquarian spirit. But, alas! few in this country have the fortune or the elegant leisure necessary to pursue these matters uninterruptedly; such is the fate of the author of the following imperfect and crudely-digested effort, and he must offer it in extenuation of his many shortcomings.

At the other end of the scale there are laments and diatribes, a few of them uttered publicly, most of them reserved for the privacy of letters to friends. The novelist Simms, for example, was in and out of love with his native Charleston because it did not buy his works. In his black moments he could speak with this degree of violence: "Charleston . . . would generally prefer to elevate a [chimney] sweep rather than myself"; "they would as soon think of making a statesman out of whipt syllabub as out of a Poet."[8] In 1858 when Simms jotted down the fragment of an intended autobiography, he recalled his father's advice that he should seek his fortune on the Mississippi frontier, and went on to say:

> Thirty odd years have passed, and I can now mournfully say the old man was right. All that I have [done] has been poured to waste in Charleston, which has never smiled on any of my labors, which has steadily ignored my claims, which has disparaged me to the last, has been the last place

[7] Quoted in Curtis C. Davis, *Chronicler of the Cavaliers: A Life of the Virginia Novelist Dr. William A. Caruthers* (Richmond, 1953), p. 323.

[8] *The Letters of William Gilmore Simms,* coll. and ed. by M. C. S. Oliphant, A. T. Odell, and T. C. Duncan Eaves (Columbia, 1952), I, lxxxi.

to give me its adhesion, to which I owe no favor, having never received an office, or a compliment, or a dollar at her hands; and, with the exception of some dozen of her citizens, who have been kind to me, and some scores of her young men, who have honored me with a loving sympathy and something like reverence, which has always treated me rather as a public enemy, to be sneered at, than as a dutiful son doing her honor.[9]

In a detailed account of how Southern writers reacted to the situation they found themselves in, it would seem natural to begin with Poe. But, as I have said, although he was immensely loyal to the South, Poe was a voluntary expatriate in the North. His first public recognition came to him in Baltimore, largely through the encouragement of J. P. Kennedy, the author of the first novel about plantation life, *Swallow Barn* (1832). Kennedy secured Poe an editorial post on the *Southern Literary Messenger* of Richmond. Within a year occurred one of those inevitable explosions in Poe's life. He drank too much and he could not get on with his employer. Soon he was on his way to Philadelphia where the same troubles overtook him. By 1844 he was starting again in New York. But Poe, in spite of his calamity-ridden life, was an extremely able editor and was often in a position to aid his fellow writers in the South. The story of the behind-the-scenes encouragement he gave them has yet to be written. When it is told, the record will be impressive.

In some instances we can only infer what kind of struggle was going on in the minds of the would-be writers. Such is the case with Edward Coote Pinkney, a poet of promise, who died at the age of 26. Having served some time in the Navy, where he was frequently in trouble for defying what he considered arbitrary authority, he made the usual Southern compromise for a literary man and tried the law. His biographers tell us, on what authority I do not know, that "his reputation as a poet is said to have been a decided drawback to his rapidly gaining a large clientele."[10] Pinkney must have thought he had found a way out when in 1826 he was appointed Professor of Rhetoric and Belles-Lettres at the University of Maryland. The catch was that no salary was attached to the chair and Pinkney naturally enough soon relinquished it. The irony

[9] William P. Trent, *William Gilmore Simms* (Boston, 1899), pp. 238-39.

[10] *The Life and Works of Edward Coote Pinkney*, prepared by Thomas Olive Mabbott and Frank Lester Pleadwell (New York, 1926), p. 34.

deepens when one remembers that Longfellow's most productive period as a poet was from 1836 to 1854, during which time he enjoyed the salary and the leisure which went with the Smith Professorship of French and Spanish at Harvard. James Russell Lowell succeeded him as Smith Professor. Professing literature was one way for a Northern poet to earn his keep.

In the case of another Southern poet who also died young, Philip Pendleton Cooke, we have more evidence to show how ardently he longed for a career in literature. Cooke was graduated from Princeton in 1834. There he had come under the influence of a young instructor in ancient languages, John S. Hart, the ideal kind of college teacher who tries to find what a young man's bent is and makes him stretch himself in order to prove just how great his talent is. Cooke was already in college a maker of verses, and when he returned to his native Virginia, the desire for literary fame would not be kept down. Inevitably he drifted into law. For a time he thought of emigrating to Missouri. He also toyed with the idea of entering politics by the usual route of the district attorney's office. But we can be certain that what Cooke really wanted to do was to write. And this we know from a revealing letter written to his father in the summer of 1844. Young Cooke had sent off to the *Southern Literary Messenger* a poem entitled "To My Daughter Lily." The elder Cooke thought it unsuitable for publication and had evidently taken his son to task for persisting in his hope of being a poet. Here is Philip Pendleton's answer.

What you say about my poetic vein being exhausted was a mistake. [But] I agree with you entirely, however, in believing that poetical composition gains a man neither wealth nor honours in this country. It is in the maturity of countries that the harp is listened to—or rather in the old age of countries, when energy has given way to ease and indulgence, and men have leisure to delight in the arts. The Anglo-Saxon who is pressing towards California with a knapsack on his back, has no leisure for scholarly indulgence; and he is a type of our population. I *know* that six months of continuous composition, such as that at Glengary[11] in my nineteenth year, would develope my "poetical vein"; and that any apparent poverty in its present yield is owing not to exhaustion but to the fact that the shaft has been, in years of disuse, choked with rubbish.[12]

[11] The family place, near Winchester, Virginia.
[12] John D. Allen, *Philip Pendleton Cooke* (Chapel Hill, 1942), pp. 60-61.

The struggle ended six years later with the poet's death, but not before some measure of fame had come to him. The poem his father had disparaged circulated widely after its appearance in *Graham's Magazine* and was even reprinted abroad in *Chambers's Edinburgh Journal.* Encouraged by Poe and other editors in the North, Cooke had managed to publish one volume before his death, *Froissart Ballads, and Other Poems* (1847). Whether the father and the law or Poe and poetry would have won in the end we cannot say, but we can admire Philip Pendleton Cooke for putting up a brave fight.

When we come to consider William Wirt of Virginia, we must again conjecture. Outwardly his life was most respectable and conformist. Orphaned at the age of eight, he was a bright lad in school and evidently read voraciously. In the many places he lived as a boy and young man he always contrived to have access to a library he could read his way through. Settling in Culpeper County, he began to practice law as soon as he came of age. He quickly made friends with some of the ablest men of the state, including Madison and Monroe. Jefferson, who knew him well, wrote of him in 1799 (Wirt was then 27): "He is a person of real genius and information, one of the ablest at the bars in this part of the country, amiable and worthy in his private character, and in his republicanism most zealous and active."[13] Wirt became a successful lawyer in Norfolk and in Richmond. In 1817 he entered Monroe's cabinet as Attorney General, and continued to hold the post through the administration of John Quincy Adams. In 1832 he ran for the Presidency on the Anti-Masonic ticket. In the election he carried one state, Vermont.

That Wirt wanted to write we know from the fact that he did write, though what he published was issued in disguise. His first attempt was a series of essays called *The Letters of the British Spy,* printed anonymously in the *Virginia Argus* (1803) and then collected. Wirt's Spy is not investigating anything more secret than the state of culture in America and particularly in Virginia. The disguise permitted Wirt to speak freely about many matters which were on his mind, including, as it happened, the vagaries of some of his associates at the bar. The mark of the literary mind is seen on

[13] Quoted in Hubbell, p. 235.

nearly every page of *The British Spy*. If Wirt were not so clearly enjoying his readiness in alluding to scores of authors, we could accuse him of parading his learning. What interests us most are his adroitly spaced attacks on the low state of culture and of civic pride in Virginia. Here is one typical passage. Wirt is speaking of the lack of public improvements in Virginia. The state is rich but its guardians are wanting in "that attention and noble pride, wherewith it is their duty to consult her appearance." He goes on to say:

[Our] highest officers are sustained with so avaricious, so niggardly a hand, that if they are not driven to subsist on roots, and drink ditch-water, with old Fabricius, it is not for the want of republican economy in the projectors of the salaries; and, above all, the general culture of the human mind, that best cure for the aristocratic distinctions which they profess to hate, that best basis of the social and political equality, which they profess to love: this culture, instead of becoming a national care, is intrusted merely to such individuals, as hazard, indigence, misfortunes or crimes, have forced from their native Europe to seek an asylum and bread in the wilds of America.[14]

The British Spy was enormously and strangely successful. By 1832 it had reached a tenth edition. There had been a London edition in 1812. No wonder, then, that Wirt wished to try again. In 1814, with the help of Virginia friends who also had literary ambitions, he published *The Old Bachelor,* ostensibly the lucubrations of a worldly-wise old gentleman who receives (and publishes) letters and communications from friends and interested readers. In the *Old Bachelor* essays the theme of Virginia's neglect of genius is strong and persistent. One imagines that Wirt and his scribbling companions discussed it often in their convivial meetings. Here is one of his severest passages, from a communication by "Timothy Lovetruth."

Wo, say I! wo to those nations whose rulers think, that nothing grand, nothing transcendantly useful can be accomplished without gold! Whose chiefs do not know how to seize, how to vibrate the mysterious chords of the human heart! Were *they* founded upon gold; those civil and political institutions of Greece and of Rome, whose effects still astonish us?—The Olympick Wreathe was a single laurel; the Civick Crown, a bough of verdant oak. What supernatural influence, then, rendered both so desirable, so productive of sublime emulation, of efforts scarcely to be

[14] *The Letters of the British Spy* (New York, 1875), p. 193.

credited? Legislators, if your coffers are empty, have you no similar rewards to bestow? Have you no smile for virtue and science? no frown for vice and brutality? Cannot one solitary day of each legislative session be devoted to the rising generation, to those youths, so precious to our common country? Ah! what germs of native genius and worth might be developed by your parental care! In you, resides the majesty of the people; but you would become the images of God himself, upon earth, by ascending to such a height of creative wisdom and beneficence![15]

In Wirt's case the usual word of disapproval filters through to us. His law partner in Norfolk feared that the *British Spy* essays would give him "a light and idle appearance, in the eye of the world, and might, therefore, injure him in his profession." We know, too, that Wirt, even at the height of his career in the law, longed for a different sort of life. In 1819 he wrote to a close friend (Wirt was then Attorney General): "I had always hoped to be able to retire from active pursuits at fifty and to spend the evening of my days . . . in literature and a preparation for futurity—But now I have little hope of any thing better than to toil on until actual decrepitude, or the superior vigor of the rising generation drives me from the bar."[16]

One distinguished member of William Wirt's group of friends serenely defied the prevailing opinion against men of position who indulged in creative writing. This is George Tucker who, after a career in law and politics, was called to the Professorship of Moral Philosophy in the first faculty at the University of Virginia. He was a prolific and well-informed writer on various economic subjects. No one could say that he neglected his clients in his earlier years as a lawyer or his professorial duties at the University, but he had dared to publish two novels, *The Valley of Shenandoah* in 1824 and *A Voyage to the Moon* in 1827. He had also scandalized many respectable people by his satirical essays in *Letters from Virginia, Translated from the French* (1816). One distinguished scientific colleague of his wrote that

if there is anything which has detracted more than another from the reputation of Mr. Tucker, it is the fact of his having written works of this character [he is alluding to the novels]. Wherever I travel, I hear this

[15] *The Old Bachelor* (Baltimore, 1818), I, 141-42. There were two Baltimore editions in this year. The edition I have used was that issued by Fielding Lucas, Jr.

[16] Quoted in Hubbell, pp. 241-42.

objected to him, and find him underrated, for his merits are very far beyond his reputation. Of these objections, he does not seem aware, although the want of success in the production of what he has issued, ought to have warned him of it.[17]

Incidentally this colleague was inaccurate as well as churlish. Tucker's *The Valley of Shenandoah* was brought out in London and there was a German translation of it.

Though Professor George Tucker went his own way and defied Virginia mores by stooping to the production of novels, there is something to be read out of the fact that when he retired at seventy, he left the state and went to live in Philadelphia. There he persisted in his odd ways. He left unpublished at his death a series of verses entitled *Pleasures Left to Old Age.*

I should not leave this matter without noting that in the 1850's there was a sudden shift of opinion in the South as regards the question of a need for a literature which would represent the region fairly. As the struggle between North and South grew more acrimonious and the possibility of armed conflict loomed, the South found itself in need of apologists to praise the distinctive Southern way of life. At last the poets and novelists were wanted and they were exhorted from many platforms and editorial pages to go to work. Typical of these exhortations is an address before the Society of Alumni, of the University of Virginia, delivered in 1853.

We can no longer cover the salient points of our institutions through the halls of Congress. The voice of the statesman and the orator can not reach the masses, with whom lie the issues of life and death. Literature alone can dispossess the demon of fanaticism by its "sweet compulsion." Let us appeal to her varied forms, of poem, drama, novel, history, and essay, to enter every cottage in the land, and disperse the delusions which invest this whole subject of domestic slavery.[18]

One event in particular was largely responsible for this shift in attitude, the enormous success of Mrs. Stowe's *Uncle Tom's Cabin,* published in 1852. It was practically a banned book in the South, but Southerners read it surreptitiously and quickly surmised the fateful influence it would have in Europe as well as the North. In

[17] Philip Alexander Bruce, *History of the University of Virginia, 1819-1919* (New York, 1920), II, 22-23.

[18] Quoted in Jay B. Hubbell, "Literary Nationalism in the Old South," *American Studies in Honor of William Kenneth Boyd* (Durham, 1940), p. 202.

the year of its publication six proslavery novels were written in an attempt (vain, as it proved) to counteract Mrs. Stowe's inaccuracies and distortions. George Frederick Holmes, who reviewed *Uncle Tom's Cabin* in the *Southern Literary Messenger,* could not resist an "I-told-you-so" passage addressed to his fellow Southerners.

> The Southern population have checked and chilled all manifestations of literary aptitudes at the South; they have discouraged by blighting indifference, the efforts of such literary genius as they may have nurtured; they have underrated and disregarded all productions of Southern intellect; and now, when all the batteries of the literary republic are turned against them, and the torrent of literary censure threatens to unite with other agencies to overwhelm them, it is in vain that they cry in their dire necessity, "Help me, Cassius, or I sink."[19]

We should not leave this subject without a word of praise for the writers in the South who persisted in spite of the general belief that they could be better employed than in scribbling verses or writing novels. We do not yet know enough about this antebellum Southern literature. There is a great deal of it which can still give pleasure and tell us what life was like between the Potomac and the Mississippi. Details of plantation life are charmingly recorded in J. P. Kennedy's *Swallow Barn.* At his best William Gilmore Simms is as good as Cooper or Scott. The poets have less to offer, but there are fine anthology pieces to be found in Pinkney, Philip Pendleton Cooke, Henry Timrod, and Paul Hamilton Hayne. But the glory of Southern antebellum literature, to my mind, is the humorous writing to be found in A. B. Longstreet's *Georgia Scenes,* J. J. Hooper's *Some Adventures of Captain Simon Suggs, Late of the Tallapoosa Volunteers,* and George Harris' *Sut Lovingood Yarns.* Scarcely thought of as literature at all, in its time, and certainly not fit reading for refined and well-bred females, these rough tales of gander pullings, quarter races, gouging fights, coon hunts, bear hunts, and gargantuan practical jokes are as native and as savory as cracklin' bread and burgoo. But I venture to say that if Professor Tucker or Attorney William Wirt had attempted anything as racy as Harris' "Old Burns' Bull Ride" or T. B. Thorpe's "The Big Bear of Arkansas," the University of Virginia might have lost a professor and the state its illustrious United States Attorney General.

[19] *Ibid.,* pp. 202-3. I am much indebted to this essay by Professor Hubbell.

2

POE IN RICHMOND: THE DOUBLE IMAGE

Robert D. Jacobs

On a spring day in 1833 John H. B. Latrobe, one of the judges of a literary contest held by the *Baltimore Saturday Visiter,* received a courtesy call from the winner of the first prize for fiction. Forty-four years later Latrobe described his guest at the Poe Memorial Exercises in Baltimore:

> He was dressed in black, and his frock coat was buttoned to the throat, where it met the black stock, then almost universally worn. Not a particle of white was visible. Coat, hat, boots, and gloves had very evidently seen their best days, but so far as mending and brushing go, everything had been done, apparently, to make them presentable. On most men his clothes would have looked shabby and seedy, but there was something about this man that prevented one from criticizing his garments, and the details I have mentioned were only recalled afterwards.[1]

Thus at twenty-four Poe already presented to the world the image of a melancholy poet, all in funereal black, seedy, but so obviously a gentleman that his shabbiness appeared only as an afterthought. This was the image to be cherished by the South in later years, particularly after 1865, when gentlemanly shabbiness became more

A Lecture given for the Institute of Southern Culture at Longwood College, July 26, 1961.

---

[1] Quoted in Arthur Hobson Quinn, *Edgar Allan Poe* (New York, 1941), p. 204.

the rule than the exception. The South was not quick to claim Poe as her own, but when she did she sought evidences of his allegiance in the qualities of his temperament, and sometimes in his mind and art.

The "Southernness" of Poe's temperament and his poetry is deceptively easy to locate; the Southern quality of his mind is more difficult to ascertain. If it is peculiarly Southern to consider oneself a gentleman, in spite of poverty and a somewhat desiccated family tree; if it is Southern to demonstrate overtly one's chivalry toward "females"; if it is Southern to be quick-tempered and sensitive to slights; then Poe was Southern to the core. Yet such attitudes could exist anywhere, particularly in an age that cherished the behavior patterns set by the heroes of romantic fiction. Furthermore, it would be difficult to ascertain which of Poe's stances were determined by the attitudes admired in the South and which were temperamental idiosyncrasies.

I use the word "stances" advisedly, because, in spite of all the biographical attention that has been devoted to Poe, it is still impossible to say whether his conduct in any given instance is justified by the circumstances or is simply a self-dramatization calculated to produce an effect upon an audience. In fact, an entire book has been written to prove that Poe, consciously or unconsciously, was an actor, and that much of his behavior and his creative work "are quite clearly theatrical performances."[2]

More recently Professor Edward Davidson has said that Poe's poems are like masks through which the poet's real concerns can be traced only with difficulty. Yet there is nothing strange about this. In a sense all poems are masks. Ezra Pound even called a series of his poems *Personae,* or "masks." Every art work is a mask, for the formal demands of art, the artistry, intervene between the conception and its realization. Modern critics, recognizing the accommodation that any artist must make to his craft, no longer expect the art work to make a direct statement of belief or of emotion. Critics in Poe's time called for "sincerity" of expression,[3] and they tended to be suspicious of any direct evidence of craft or artiness

[2] N. Bryllion Fagin, *The Histrionic Mr. Poe* (Baltimore, 1949), p. x.
[3] M. H. Abrams, *The Mirror and the Lamp* (New York, 1958), p. 298.

in the art work; but we know now that probably the most sincere expression of emotion in the romantic sense may be an inarticulate cry of joy or a grunt of pain. And we are likely to think today that the most sincere expression of belief is one that is qualified by all the doubts and uncertainties that have plagued the believer.[4] Consequently many modern literary critics condemn the work that makes an unqualified statement and have sought virtues of irony and ambiguity in even the most elementary lyric poems. Poe comes off badly under such an examination, and some critics have concluded that his achievement has been vitiated by sentimentality and a calculated appeal to stereotyped emotions.

Thus in dealing with Poe in the South we must somehow manage to keep in a corner of our minds the fact that Poe was given to self-dramatization both in his life and in his creative work. We are never quite sure whether an attitude expressed at a given time is fully representative of belief or is simply a stance assumed for a given audience. But even the failure of sincerity should not invite complete condemnation. All of us, like Eliot's Prufrock, put on faces to meet the faces that we meet; and we must remember that Poe lived in an age when an overt expression of sensibility was simply the outward sign of the inward grace of the poet born, just as the side-of-the-mouth reticence of the Hemingway hero is symbolic of the toughness of the age of disillusion, in which sentimentality and self-deception are among the worst of sins.

Our problem—and also Poe's—is that he alternated between the stance of the sensitive, aristocratic poet and that of the shrewd, somewhat unscrupulous, journalist; and, as we shall see, neither image was completely satisfactory to the Southern mind, which was in the 1830's, as it is today, slightly schizoid.

Everyone knows the story of how Edgar Poe, the son of wandering actors, came to the South; how his mother, Elizabeth Arnold Poe, died in Richmond on December 10, 1811, only sixteen days before the old Richmond Theater burned with a loss of seventy-two lives; and how Poe was taken into the family of a Scottish merchant, John Allan.

[4] Cf. I. A. Richards' discussion of sincerity in *Practical Criticism* (New York, 1929), pp. 263-74.

Possibly the fact that Poe was the child of professional actors caused a lingering prejudice in the mind of Allan that was to appear many years later in his relationship with the young man. Actors and actresses were supposed to be dissolute and immoral. Even the drama itself in its modern form was not highly respected in the South as a form of literary endeavor. The famous lawyer, William Wirt, who later became Attorney General of the United States, wrote to his friend Dabney Carr in 1813, asking whether the production of a sentimental drama he had written would injure his reputation with such men as Jefferson, Madison, Monroe, Marshall, and Littleton Tazewell.[5] Wirt's fears were well grounded, for Tazewell, his law partner, even objected to the essays which Wirt published in the Richmond newspapers, saying that they gave him "a light and idle appearance, in the eye of the world, and might, therefore, injure [him] in [his] profession."[6]

The only evidence that John Allan might have been prejudiced against the profession of Elizabeth Arnold Poe, other than some hints from Poe himself, is in a letter Allan wrote to Poe's brother Henry in 1824. In it he expresses doubt about the legitimacy of Poe's sister Rosalie, saying, "At least She is half your Sister & God forbid my dear Henry that We should visit upon the living the Errors & frailties of the dead."

In the same letter Allan revealed a great deal of animosity toward the fifteen-year-old Poe. "The boy possesses not a Spark of affection for us not a particle of gratitude for all my care and kindness toward him," Allan complained. Furthermore Poe, according to Allan, was "miserable, sulky & ill-tempered to all the family."[7]

With this background of ill-feeling, which Poe's biographers have been able to explain only conjecturally, Allan could be expected to react very badly two years later when Poe's behavior at the new University of Virginia seemed to confirm his foster father's suspicion of bad blood.

John Allan, though he had experienced serious financial difficulties

[5] John Pendleton Kennedy, *Memoirs of the Life of William Wirt* (Philadelphia, 1860), I, 307.

[6] Quoted in Jay B. Hubbell, *The South in American Literature* (Durham, 1954), p. 235.

[7] Quoted in Quinn, p. 89.

in 1822, became a rich man in 1825, when he inherited from his uncle, William Galt, a fortune estimated at $750,000. More wealthy than many of the planters whose sons kept horses and servants at the University, Allan sent Poe to enroll with only $110, which according to Poe's account was $39 less than had to be paid in advance for fees, room rent, and furniture.[8] Thus, Poe said, he "was immediately regarded in the light of a beggar."

We know enough about the first years of the University of Virginia to realize that in this case Poe was speaking the truth. Students at Jefferson's new university were recruited from some of the most affluent families in the state, which meant, of course, that many of them had plantation backgrounds. They were accustomed to the so-called gentlemanly pastimes—riding, hunting, and, no doubt, drinking and gambling. A number of them carried pistols, in violation of the rules of the university. Thomas Jefferson had hoped that student self-government would be sufficient to establish control, but he was entirely too optimistic. Discipline broke down almost completely before the end of the year. Riots were frequent and dangerous. Professors were sometimes threatened, and, in fact, Professor J. A. G. Davis was killed some years later when he was exerting his authority to quell a student disturbance.

Into this undisciplined group came young Edgar Poe, and if we may believe his words, he was forced into the company of the drunkards and gamblers who were paupers because of their extravagance. He did not have the means to associate with the better sort.[9] This situation explains Poe's actions, but it does not excuse them. Apparently he chose to live in the style of his companions. Though only the foster son of a Scottish merchant, he must have cultivated the habits of the wealthiest and the most dissipated of the students, for during his nine and a half months at the university, he ran up debts amounting to between $2,000 and $2,500. Most of these were gambling debts, but not all. One merchant from Charlottesville sent John Allan a bill for a suit of "Super Blue Cloth," ornamented with the "Best Gilt Buttons."[10]

[8] See Poe's letter to Allan dated January 3, 1831, in John Ostrom, *The Letters of Edgar Allan Poe* (Cambridge, 1948), I, 40.

[9] *Ibid.* [10] Quinn, p. 112.

At least on the face of it, Poe was determined to dress like a Virginia gentleman's son and to behave like one even if he had to do it on credit. What might have happened had Poe gone to school among the "pious young monks" of Harvard or Yale, we cannot say, but we do know that his first assumption of the stance of a wild young Virginia gentleman ended in disaster. The code of a Scottish merchant was different from the code of the planter aristocracy, and in the incompatibility of the two Poe met misfortune.[11] Allan evidently refused to pay the debts that Poe had incurred without his sanction, even the legitimate ones;[12] and this must have been especially galling to a young man who was trying to establish at least the outward signs of honor as he understood them.

Thus leaving the University of Virginia in financial though not scholastic disgrace, Poe was for the moment forced to return to Richmond; but back in Allan's home the actuality was a far cry from the life of grace and dignity that Poe knew existed in at least some of the Virginia families. His letter to Allan early in 1827 reveals a situation that would have been intolerable to a young Southerner far more stolid than Poe. He writes:

> You have . . . ordered me to quit your house, and are continually upbraiding me with eating the bread of idleness, when you yourself were the only person to remedy the evil by placing me to some business—You take delight in exposing me before those whom you think likely to advance my interest in this world—You suffer me to be subjected to the whims & caprice, not only of your white family, but the complete authority of the blacks—these grievances I could not submit to; and I am gone—.[13]

Perhaps regretfully we may conclude that, given Poe's temperament and the nature of the family with which he was involved, his early life in Virginia was unfortunate. Virginia still glorified the past and the plantation tradition which represented it. Some Virginians cherished aristocratic ideals and were willing to excuse a certain lordly sowing of wild oats if it were done in the approved manner. Byronic behavior, because it was lordly, could be condoned if not exactly recommended. The businessman's code of John Allan was

[11] On this point see Edward H. Davidson, *Poe, A Critical Study* (Cambridge, 1957), p. 208.

[12] Quinn, pp. 112-13.

[13] Ostrom, I, 7-8.

quite different. The merchant spirit was common enough in the North, but it was only beginning to manifest itself in the Old Dominion. Poe, a young romanticist, chose the pattern that appealed to his imagination; but he lived with the wrong family, and his pretensions collapsed against the hard wall of the businessman's common sense.

A good many Virginians sensed what they took to be a decline long before Poe became involved in the change. William Wirt, an acquaintance of the Allans, as early as 1812 had published a series of essays designed to awaken the spirit of Virginian youth to emulate the qualities of the leaders of the past.[14] Beverley Tucker, prominent lawyer and novelist-to-be, thought that the election of Jackson in 1828 signaled that "Virginia was sunk in a slough of Democracy, which has no sense of Honor." Philip Pendleton Cooke, whose poetry Poe was to admire in later years, wrote to his father, "It is lamentable to see the old families of the land, the first in gentility and caste *reduced;* to see their descendants gradually sinking by marriage and association into humbler classes, and to see mine thus would break my heart."

This self-consciously aristocratic stance with its antipathy to democratic leveling—and, we might add, commercialism—was very appealing to young Poe. It was romantic, and it was attuned to the attitude of lordly pride to be found in the poetry of Byron and the feeling for chivalry that glowed in the pages of Sir Walter Scott. For Edgar Poe, more than for most, life copied fiction; and we can see behind his quarrels with John Allan his desperate attempts to live in a pattern shaped by his imagination.

Even Poe's flight from Richmond cannot be blamed unconditionally on his quarrel with Allan; for it was the fictionally approved mode of behavior for a disappointed lover. Before he enrolled at the University of Virginia he had been in love, or at least thought he was in love, with Elmira Royster, who was then fifteen or sixteen. Elmira's father objected, even going so far as to intercept Poe's letters. Then at seventeen Elmira was married to a Mr. Shelton, and Poe was free to act the role of the rejected lover. Although only one poem written by Poe during this early period can be

[14] *The Old Bachelor,* 3rd ed. (Baltimore, 1818), I, 135.

realistically attributed to his disappointment over Elmira's marriage,[15] the behavior expected of a brokenhearted lover was quite clear: he was supposed to wander over the face of the earth, with a brow of agony and a heart of stone. Ladies' albums all over the South during the 1820's and 1830's were stuffed with verses inscribed in them by discarded sweethearts; and some of these verses were to be published in the *Southern Literary Messenger.* Almost invariably they invoked Byronian despair. The lover, either drinking from "Sorrow's cup" or whatever passed for the Southern version of Samian wine, left his "native haunts" and roamed the wide world in never-ending woe. This is a typical example of such verse:

> Then fare thee well! An exile now,
> Without a friend or home,
> With anguish written on my brow,
> About the world I'll roam.
> For all my dreams are sadly o'er,
> Fate bade them all depart,—
> And I will leave my native shore,
> In brokenness of heart.[16]

If the rhyming words *roam* and *home, o'er* and *shore, heart* and *depart,* had been eliminated from the language before 1820, Southern albums would have been deprived of some of their treasures of poetic heartbreak. But most of these Southern lovers remained in Winchester, or Tuscaloosa, or Charleston. Poe was different. He was trying to *live* the fictional role approved by his imagination. This may account for some of the legends that he had joined the revolution in Greece and that he had wandered as far as St. Petersburg, Russia. In fact it is said that letters to his foster mother were dated from St. Petersburg. A young Byronic hero, disappointed in love and turned out by his family, *should* have gone to Greece or St. Petersburg, but Poe got no farther than Boston. There, in the early summer of 1827, a printer named Calvin F. Thomas, a former resident of Norfolk, brought out his *Tamerlane and Other Poems, by a Bostonian.* Why "by a Bostonian"? Various reasons have been advanced for this anonymity, but here only one need be mentioned. Anony-

[15] Edward Davidson suggests others, but only one, "I Saw Thee on Thy Bridal Day," seems precisely on the subject.

[16] *Southern Literary Messenger,* I, 12.

mous publication was frequent in both England and America; but in the South it was almost obligatory. As we shall see, it was the only gentlemanly thing to do. Thus at eighteen Poe had committed himself as a poet, but not quite publicly.

Though he did not join the Greek Revolution, Poe did enlist in the United States Army. This, too, was something in the Southern mode. When he was fifteen he had been a lieutenant in the Richmond Junior Volunteers, who had served as General Lafayette's bodyguard during his visit to Richmond in 1824. The gentlemanly profession of the military was very much approved of in Virginia, as the North was to find out at Manassas thirty-odd years later. But Poe, though he may have been a gentleman, was certainly not an officer. For this reason, perhaps, he enlisted under an assumed name, Edgar A. Perry. To the astonishment of some of his biographers, Poe was a good soldier, for he rose from private to regimental sergeant major in little over a year.

In November of 1827 Poe's battery of artillery was sent to Fort Moultrie, on Sullivan's Island in Charleston Harbor. Here he remained until December, 1828, when the battery was ordered to Fortress Monroe in Virginia. But Poe had already written to John Allan attempting a reconciliation. Evidently the life of a soldier, even that of a sergeant major, offered few attractions to a young man who had announced in his first volume of verse,

> I wrapp'd myself in grandeur then
> And donn'd a visionary crown.

It is dangerous, of course, to attempt to make biographical readings of most poetry. Yet Poe, more than most poets, was *living* the attitudes expressed in his early verse. His first long poem, "Tamerlane," was clearly in the Byronic mode in its subject of the loss of love through unbridled ambition. Other poems in the volume lament the wane of pride and power, the loss of the visions and dreams of youth, and the possession of a "sear'd and blighted heart."

Such attitudes may seem ridiculous in a boy of eighteen, but we must remember that they were perfectly standard in the poetry of the Byronic age in the South. In Poe's case we are justified in assuming a more deeply personal significance. Within two years Poe had lost his sweetheart, his chance at a university education, and had been dismissed from the home of a wealthy and influential protector. The mere fact that he was willing to humble himself enough to approach Allan again indicates that he had to swallow his pride if he was to regain a respectable position in the world. Yet his first letter to Allan after joining the army does not reveal humility by any means. Poe wrote,

> You will perceive that I speak confidently—but when did ever Ambition exist or Talent prosper without prior conviction of success? I have thrown myself on the world, like the Norman conqueror on the shores of Britain &, by my avowed assurance of victory, have destroyed the fleet which could alone cover my retreat—I must either conquer or die—succeed or be disgraced.[17]

This is fairly bombastic, to say the least; and we do not know whether John Allan was more impressed by Poe as William of Normandy than he had been by Poe as Tamerlane. Again and again in his next few letters Poe sounds the note of ambition to Allan, and the wary Scotchman was led to believe that this ambition was military. What Poe wanted was a reconciliation that would enable him to be discharged from the army, which in turn would permit him to apply for an appointment to West Point.[18] *This* Allan could understand and approve. Within two months after his first appeal Poe was writing him confidently that the appointment "could easily be obtained either by your personal acquaintance with Mr. Wirt—or by the recommendation of General Winfield Scott."[19] Other influential friends of Allan, Judge John J. Barber, Major James Gibbon, and Colonel James P. Preston were to write letters in Poe's behalf.

That Allan bestirred himself to obtain the recommendations of these influential Virginians for a foster son whom he had formerly

[17] Ostrom, I, 10.

[18] Poe did not mention the possibility of an appointment to West Point until two letters had failed to gain the desired response. Poe's second letter to Allan is revealing. He says, "I only beg you to remember that you yourself cherished the cause of my leaving your family—ambition. If it has not taken the channel you wished it, it is not the less certain of its object." Allan certainly did not approve of Poe's ambition to become a writer, so Poe brought up the West Point plan, which succeeded.

[19] Ostrom, I, 13.

characterized as a worthless and ungrateful wretch speaks volumes. At last it appeared that Poe was going to acquire status on terms which Virginians could understand. He was going to be an officer and a gentleman instead of a melancholy poet with an anguished brow and a seared and blighted heart. In fact, he wrote Allan, "I have long given up Byron as a model—for which, I think, I deserve some credit." What he did not tell Allan—for that would have been fatal—was that he had not the slightest interest in a military career.

Between February, 1829, when Poe wrote to Allan that he wished to be appointed to the Military Academy, and May of the same year a reconciliation was effected. On May 20 Poe wrote Allan a warm note acknowledging receipt of $100 but only nine days later he wrote again, making a request that he should have known would infuriate the Scotchman. Poe wanted Allan to back financially the publication of his second book of poems by making a guarantee to the firm of Carey, Lea & Carey, in writing, to the extent of $100.[20] This was a serious tactical error for Poe to make. Not only did it touch the Scotch merchant in a tender spot—his moneybag—but it also awakened his suspicion about the sincerity of Poe's desire to go to West Point. Allan had gone to a good bit of trouble to secure letters of recommendation for Poe and had been sending the young man an allowance. Now to be called upon to support him in a publishing venture was too much to be borne. His reaction to this request is clearly revealed by a note he made on Poe's letter, "replied to Monday 8th June 1829 strongly censuring his conduct—& refusing any aid."[21] Poe's next two letters to Allan were apologetic in tone, but he received no answer, even though he went so far as to say that he would not publish his poems without Allan's approval. Finally, on the 19th of July Allan did write Poe, sneering that "men of genius ought not to apply" for aid. Poe explained carefully his handling of the money Allan had given him, and gradually the affair was smoothed over, though not till Allan had fully voiced his grievances and Poe had reassured him that he was making every effort to get into West Point. On November 18, Poe acknowledged the receipt of $80 and made the proud announcement that his poems were to be printed by Hatch and Dunning of Balti-

[20] *Ibid.*, p. 20. [21] *Ibid.*, p. 21.

more, without expense to Allan, of course, and that he was sending a copy of the book to Allan by Mr. Dunning, who was going to Richmond.[22] We can assume both by the contents and the tone of this letter that Allan was mollified. Apparently it was all right to have a publishing poet in the family as long as his publications didn't cost anything and if he didn't make poetry his primary concern.

Allan was reassured that Poe was going to make himself into the image proper for a Virginia youth of good familly—a West Point cadet.

The image of a Byronic poet was another thing. Contrary to what some historians have said, poetry was not held in contempt in Virginia. However, it was not considered respectable as a *profession.* Virginians were supposed to be lawyers or military men or—at least if they were recent Scottish immigrants—businessmen. It was quite proper to inscribe verses in young ladies' albums, or even to publish them if you did it pseudonymously; but it was not proper to proclaim that poetry was your life's work. Philip Pendleton Cooke, the best Virginia poet of the period other than Poe, was trained for the law. Cooke once wrote Rufus Griswold that a good friend of his said gravely to him, "I wouldn't waste time on a damned thing like poetry." This crude comment has received undue attention as being representative of Virginia opinion. It was not. However, it *was* expected that a Virginian of good family should do something to justify his breeding and education. This usually meant public service other than the writing of love poems or mortuary verse. Edward Coote Pinkney, the best poet of the South before Poe, had been commissioned in the Navy and had studied law, though his law practice was pretty much of a fiasco. Richard Henry Wilde, author of the famous but long anonymous "My Life Is Like the Summer Rose," was a successful lawyer, state attorney general, and member of Congress. Even Henry Timrod, whose passion for poetry was as great as Poe's, made an attempt to be a lawyer before he dwindled into a tutor for the children of plantation families. Paul Hamilton Hayne, born to wealth and social position, studied law in the office of James Louis Petigru before he committed himself fully to a literary career.

[22] *Ibid.*, p. 34.

The pattern is quite clear. In the South a young man must try to be something useful to society. If he wished to write poetry, he must toss it off with bold abandon in careless moments; and if he wished to be completely respectable, he should show elaborate unconcern about its publication.[23] Philip Pendleton Cooke was being quite déclassé when he sent a number of his poems to the *Southern Literary Messenger* and argued hotly in print about their merits. Even then, he did it under the pseudonym, Larry Lyle. On the other hand, a number of poems appeared in the first two volumes of the *Messenger* signed boldly, Edgar A. Poe. This was disgraceful professionalism for a Virginian.

But we are getting ahead of the story. In 1829 Poe was maneuvering more or less earnestly to get into West Point, with Allan's help; but almost to a certainty he had no intention of pursuing a military career. Why, then, we may ask, did he make an effort that stretched out for nearly two years? (1) It could be expected to rehabilitate him in the eyes of John Allan and, we suppose, in the eyes of the Virginians. (2) It might bring him some support from Allan that would provide leisure for writing. And, as we have seen, the plan worked. Allan did send him some money from time to time, and the fruit of his leisure appeared in the aforementioned volume of verse, *Al Aaraaf, Tamerlane, and Minor Poems.*

The long-delayed appointment to West Point finally came in March, 1830, through the efforts of Powhatan Ellis, senator from Mississippi and brother of T. H. Ellis, Allan's former business partner. Poe took the entrance examinations in June and went to summer camp during July and August. He began his academic work in September. But the old problem of finances returned to plague him. More serious, an indiscretion that was clearly his own fault came to the attention of Allan.

Poe had been able to get out of the army in 1829 only by hiring a substitute, one Sergeant Samuel "Bully" Graves. Allan had sent

[23] A letter to the editor of the *Messenger* accompanying a contribution entitled "Beauty without Loveliness" exhibits the typical attitude: "The writer of the above throws off such scraps at idle times, without effort and without pretension. With so much of the inspiration of poetry, he has nothing of its madness, and will never consent to be known to the world as an author" (*Southern Literary Messenger,* I, 255).

money to Poe for the purpose, but apparently it went for something else[24] and Graves continued to dun him. On May 3, 1830, Poe wrote Bully Graves that it was difficult to depend upon Mr. Allan, for he "is not very often sober." He went on to say that he had tried to get money from Allan for Graves a dozen times but "he always shuffles me off."[25] Graves kept the letter for some months and then, failing to receive his money, sent it to Allan after Poe had gone to West Point. Then the situation became rather sticky, to say the least. In response to Allan's recriminations, Poe defended himself by making a countercharge, saying that he had written the defamatory letter within a half hour after "you had embittered every feeling of my heart against you by your abuse of my *family*, and myself, under your own roof—and at a time when you knew my heart was almost breaking."[26]

Poe went on to rehearse the whole history of Allan's injustices to him and announced, "From the time of writing this I shall neglect my studies and duties at the institution—if I do not receive your answer in 10 days—I will leave the point without—for otherwise I should subject myself to dismission."[27] Poe had made up his mind to resign—in fact it is hard to see what else he could do. Allan had sent him to West Point with scarcely enough money to pay his book deposit and other expenses; and his salary as a cadet was not enough to maintain him without an allowance from home. Now Allan was enraged, this time with quite good cause. Poe permitted himself the luxury of salvaging his pride with the famous letter of January 3, 1831, and requested only that Allan, as nominal guardian, give permission for his resignation, which would enable him to draw mileage pay to his place of residence.

Allan made a fairly lengthy endorsement on this particular communication:

> I recd this on the 10th & did not from its conclusion deem it necessary to reply. I make this note on the 13th & can see no good Reason to alter my opinion. I do not think the Boy has one good quality. He may do or act as he pleases, tho' I wd have saved him but on his own terms & conditions since I cannot believe a word he writes. His letter is the most barefaced one sided statement.[28]

[24] See Quinn, pp. 166-67, for a discussion of this matter.
[25] Ostrom, I, 36. [26] *Ibid.*, p. 42. [27] *Ibid.* [28] Quinn, p. 173.

Sentimental biographers of Poe have succeeded in making John Allan out as some sort of monster, but this description is hardly fair. In the statement above he was telling the truth according to his own lights. It is clear now that Poe was determined to have a literary career. Allan had wanted to commit him to a profession he considered suitable for the foster son of a wealthy and influential Virginian. These aims were irreconcilable, as were the temperaments of the two men. Only sentimental pity for Poe can place the blame entirely on Allan.

Poe did not wait for Allan's reply before he carried out his threat to neglect his duties. A general court-martial tried Cadet E. A. Poe on January 28 for "Gross neglect of Duty" and "Disobedience of Orders." The court found him guilty of both charges and sentenced him to be dismissed, effective March 6, 1831.

After this, we would expect the break between Poe and his foster father to be final. Poe's often paraded pride should have prevented him from making further appeals; but five times during the remainder of 1831 he wrote to Allan for a reconciliation. These letters are no credit to Poe, because his pleas for affection alternate with pleas for funds; and he does not hesitate to use every device to arouse pity. He is sick, he says; he is alone with no friends to aid him; he is going to be imprisoned for debt if Allan does not come to his assistance. To Allan's credit, he did respond to this last appeal. His endorsement on Poe's letter reads as follows: "Wrote on the 7th Decr. 1831 to John Walsh to procure his liberation & to give him $20 besides to keep him out of further difficulties & value on me for such amt as might be required—neglected sending it on till the 12th Jany 1832 Then put in the office myself."[29]

Professor Arthur Hobson Quinn, the most careful of the Poe biographers, was able to find no evidence that Poe was actually confined for debt. This may have been simply one more instance of his histrionics.

After 1831 there was only one more letter to John Allan. In April, 1833, Poe made a last appeal, saying, "I am perishing—absolutely perishing for want of aid. . . . For God's sake pity me, and save me from destruction." But Allan had heard it all before, and there is no

[29] *Ibid.*, p. 191.

record of any answer. Eleven months later John Allan died, leaving nothing in his will to his foster son. For some reason this came as a surprise to Poe, or at least he said it did, for in a letter dated November, 1834, he wrote to John P. Kennedy as follows:

> Since the day you first saw me my situation in life has altered materially. At that time I looked forward to the inheritance of a large fortune, and, in the meantime, was in receipt of an annuity sufficient for my support. This was allowed me by a gentleman of Virginia (Mr Jno Allan) who adopted me at the age of two years (both my parents being dead) and who, until lately, always treated me with the affection of a father. But a second marriage on his part, and I dare say many follies on my own at length ended in a quarrel between us. He is now dead, and has left me nothing.[30]

The kindest thing we can say about this letter is that Poe's imagination was running away with him. Allan had never legally adopted Poe. Relations between them had been continually strained between 1824 and 1831 and had been broken completely before 1833, when Poe first met Kennedy. If Poe really expected to inherit a large fortune from Allan, he was sanguine to the point of idiocy; and Poe was never an idiot. Probably this letter is one more example of his romancing. He was posing as a disappointed heir of a "gentleman of Virginia," an heir who, after youthful indiscretions, was disinherited because of the intrigues of a second wife. This was a standard romantic role, far more appealing than that of an unsuccessful writer who had to resort to literary contests when the magazines and publishers rejected his work. Thus with Poe we must always try to distinguish between what appears to be the actuality of a situation and the part that his imagination required him to play. More than most of us Poe continually created and recreated the image that he wished to present to the world.

Poe's brief stay at West Point had had only one result that related to his future career. He had succeeded in circulating a subscription list among the cadets for a new volume of poems. This list contained enough names to induce a publisher, Elam Bliss of New York, to bring out Poe's third book of verse, the *Poems* of 1831, dedicated to "The U. S. Corps of Cadets." Even with three volumes of verse to his credit, Poe at twenty-two was still an unknown writer, but

[30] Ostrom, I, 54.

at least he had taken the plunge. All pretensions toward a career that would look respectable to Allan and the Virginians had been given up. In 1831 he wrote a number of short stories and submitted five of them to a contest held by the *Philadelphia Saturday Courier.*

Although Poe did not win the prize, his tales were published by the *Saturday Courier.* "Metzengerstein," the first to appear, was admittedly an imitation of the popular German terror tale. The other four were what Poe called "Grotesques." One was a burlesque of the sensational type of fiction that had been appearing in the enormously successful *Blackwood's Edinburgh Magazine,* two were comic versions of contests with the devil, a subject which had been popular since the Middle Ages, and the last, "A Tale of Jerusalem," gained its questionable humor at the expense of the Jews.

These tales are quite obviously journalistic. Poe was trying to write something that would sell. Yet this professionalism ran directly counter to the Southern code of the amateur, the gentleman who tossed off his effusions in careless moments of inspiration while devoting his energy to a profession dignified by public service.

But does this transformation into a hard-working if as yet unsuccessful journalistic writer mean that Poe has given up the stance of the Byronic poet? Not at all. The melancholy gentleman in black who appeared before John Latrobe in 1833 presented an image that would be understood by romantic Southerners; and it was this personal image as much as Poe's virtuosity as a writer that won him the sympathy and aid of John Pendleton Kennedy, a Baltimore lawyer who had published the sketches of Virginia life called *Swallow Barn.*

John H. Hewitt, a Baltimore writer who knew Poe well during this period, says that the young man "wore Byron collars and a black stock, and looked the poet all over." Thus it was not as a hack writer of journalistic fiction that Poe appealed to Kennedy, but as a sensitive, gentlemanly genius, buffeted by fate in an unkind world. When Kennedy invited Poe to dinner, Poe replied in terms that sustained the image of pride, even in poverty:

Dr. Sir,—Your kind invitation to dinner today has wounded me to the quick. I cannot come—and for reasons of the most humiliating nature in my personal appearance. You may conceive my deep mortification in making this disclosure to you—but it was necessary. If you will be my friend so far as to loan me $20, I will call on you to-morrow—otherwise it will be impossible, and I must submit to my fate.[31]

Kennedy's reaction was immediate. Later, he wrote,

I gave him clothing, free access to my table and the use of a horse for exercise whenever he chose; in fact brought him up from the very verge of despair. I then got him employment with Mr. White, in one department of the *Southern Literary* newspaper at Richmond.[32]

The Southern quality of Kennedy's assistance to Poe is unmistakable. Poe was not given money, but clothing, so that he could dress as a gentleman; access to the table, so that charity could appear under the guise of hospitality and good company; and a horse, so that he could exercise in a gentlemanly fashion. An Emerson or a Thoreau might have preached Poe a sermon on the virtue of long walks in the open air with probably a few footnotes about self-reliance and economy; but Kennedy, a Southerner, gave Poe the tactful kind of help that could be accepted by a gentleman down on his luck.

More important, Kennedy gave Poe his first opportunity to become a professional editor, and as fortune would have it, in Richmond, Virginia.

Thomas Willis White, publisher and owner of the new journal, the *Southern Literary Messenger,* desperately needed the assistance of someone as clever as Poe. A printer by trade but with great ambition, White was handicapped by a limited education and a reluctantly acknowledged incapacity to make intelligent decisions about matters of literary taste. From the very beginning of his enterprise he sought advice and contributions from his literary friends; and without their help the *Messenger* would probably have foundered before Poe arrived to make it famous—or notorious, as some contemporaries would have it.

To understand what Poe actually confronted when he assumed the assistant editorship of the *Southern Literary Messenger,* we should take a brief look at the magazine before his pen—and authority, limited though it was—began to make themselves felt.

[31] *Ibid.,* p. 56. [32] Quoted in Quinn, p. 208.

When White undertook in 1834 to publish a magazine in the South, he knew that the odds were against him. Magazines had not flourished, even in Charleston, the most literary of the Southern cities. Hugh Swinton Legare's *Southern Review,* a somewhat ponderous quarterly modeled after the famous *Edinburgh Review,* had survived four years, 1828-32; but it had been only a review, impressive in its learning and dignity, but about as likely to succeed with the general public as the *Publications of the Modern Language Association.* White wanted to establish a monthly "variety" magazine, with articles, stories, poems, and a few reviews. That such a magazine could have tremendous popularity had already been proved by *Blackwood's.* Then, too, White hoped to gain subscriptions by appealing to the South's sensitivity to its literary backwardness in comparison with that of the North. His very first issue, August, 1834, issued the call for a "Southern literature" on page one.

And the call was answered, though many times White might have wished that it had not been. The ladies' albums began to yield their treasures, presumably over the dead bodies of the protesting authors. An attempt at anonymity was usually made, some contributors allowing their effusions to be sent in by "a friend," others modestly concealing themselves behind single or multiple initials or pseudonyms. Frequently the disguises were quite transparent, however. John Collins M'Cabe signed his verse "M'C," and Alexander Beaufort Meek went so far as to give his home address, "A.B.M. of Tuscaloosa."

Although White had invited contributions from friends and acquaintances in Virginia, he must have found himself handicapped by his personal loyalties. One correspondent, from Shepherdstown, Virginia, thought it a mystery that so much bad verse got into the *Messenger,* unless it was through personal acquaintanceship with the publisher. Perhaps a little surprising to us, many of the poems published in the early numbers of the *Messenger* are similar to Poe's poetry in theme and subject matter. I have already given a brief sample of the wail of the brokenhearted lover which Poe attempted once or twice. Other poems in the *Messenger* treated the death of women—beautiful, of course—that subject which Poe eventually proclaimed the most poetic of all. Philip Pendleton

Cooke, the most accomplished of the Virginia poets, contributed "Rosalie Lee," a lament for the death of a beautiful girl that does not hesitate to follow the corpse into the grave in a manner that would cause the literary psychoanalysts to cry "necrophilia." A number of other less gifted contributors followed the same pattern much less tactfully than either Poe or Cooke.

We all know that the literary psychoanalysts, such as Mme. Marie Bonaparte, have analyzed the morbidity in Poe's poems and have come to some startling conclusions about his sexual nature. But it seems to me that our chief concern in this matter should be historical rather than psychological. Morbid poems about heartbreak at the loss of a sweetheart, either by death or desertion, were the kind that Southerners were writing in the 1820's and 1830's. These, plus effusions about the obvious beauties of mountain peak and waterfall, were standard subjects for amateur writers in the South. Probably the reason that a high percentage of the poems in the South during this period were on these subjects was simply that the South had practically no one deliberately setting out to be a professional writer, no one who could break new ground. Poe and William Gilmore Simms were almost the only exceptions, and even these two were strongly influenced by the existing tastes of the South. It was quite natural for Poe, who had written most of his poetry by 1831, to imitate Byron and Moore, beloved in the South. Poe was ahead of his compatriots only in his admiration for Coleridge, Keats, and Shelley. Thus the resemblance of Poe's early verse to the verse published in the *Messenger* can hardly be termed accidental. Poe shaped himself into the image of a certain type of romantic poet, a type well known and often admired in the South—the poet-aristocrat, driven by pride and ambition, moody, agonized, guilt-ridden; somber, sensitive, and heartbroken. These attitudes were reflected in his poetry and his stories. Of course these attitudes are subject to psychological interpretation, but the psychological interpretation is incomplete without the historical. Had Poe lived in another age, and had he been brought up in a different region, his imagination would have required him to play a different part.

Unfortunately for Poe, to maintain the image of a poet-aristocrat, one needed a private income; and without an estate from which to draw funds, he had to take his Byronic collar into the ink-stained office of Thomas Willis White over Anchor's shoe store on Fifteenth Street in Richmond.

Poe's poetry apparently did not impress the subscribers to the *Southern Literary Messenger*—they were used to that kind of poetry; but his tales and his criticism did—these they were not used to. Yet here his difference caused him trouble. Even before he came to Richmond to assist White, Poe received protests from his future employer about the nature of his fiction. Early in 1835 White objected to Poe's short story "Berenice" as being far too horrible. Poe wrote in return that the "history of all Magazines shows plainly that those which have attained celebrity were indebted for it to articles *similar in nature*—to *Berenice. . . .*"[33]

The implications of this little *contretemps* are not too difficult to unravel. From the time that Poe had dedicated himself to journalistic work back in 1831, he had studied magazine writing. In particular, as several investigators have shown, he studied *Blackwood's Edinburgh Magazine.* This was the most popular monthly magazine that he knew. In spite of his public image as the melancholy poet Poe had made himself into a professional journalist before he came to work for White. In comparison, Thomas Willis White was an amateur, assisted by amateurs. White's first editor, James E. Heath, was a minor Virginia writer, but he served White without pay, and, we can conclude, without much imagination. It is evident from his editorial comments that Heath was representative of the middle-class morality that was beginning to supplant the aristocratic attitude in Virginia. Both White and Heath could have understood a John Allan better than an Edgar Allan Poe or a Philip Pendleton Cooke. Heath announced in the pages of the *Messenger* that he was opposed to fairy tales and to German diablerie. He reviewed harshly Beckford's *Vathek,* which Byron had admired, saying that its author preferred all that "was diabolical and monstrous, rather than what was beautiful and good."[34] Heath, like most of the editors of Northern magazines, wanted "good sense, sound morality, and correct taste." If a tale or a poem did not show a proper concern for morality and piety, Heath condemned it. He was quite stern with a certain

[33] Ostrom, I, 57. [34] *Southern Literary Messenger,* I, 189.

contributor who signed himself "Fra Diavolo" because "Brother Devil's" poems violated the common decency. "We regret," Heath wrote, "that he should thus fancy to imitate such vicious models as Byron, Shelly [*sic*] and other gentlemen of 'the Satanic School,' as it has been called, who, we think, have had their day."[35]

If Byron and Shelley had had their day, they were replaced by someone to the modern taste infinitely more appalling: Mrs. Lydia Huntley Sigourney, frequently called the "American Hemans," after that refulgent star of the British female poets, Felicia Hemans. Mrs. Sigourney appears more often in the first numbers of the *Messenger* than any other poet. Her forte was gentle melancholy warmed over with religion and moral earnestness. The titles of her poems are sufficient to indicate their tone: "The Death of the Motherless," "To Hope," "To the Bible," and this intriguing specimen—"On the Deaf, Dumb, and Blind Girl of the Asylum at Hartford, Connecticut."

We cannot say whether such poems represented the taste of Heath or of Thomas Willis White; but it is easy to see that both preferred religio-moral melancholy over Byronic despair or Shelleyan Satanism. My own opinion is that White was guided by Heath in his objection to Poe's "German horror" but that he probably liked Mrs. Sigourney on his own. When in January, 1836, Poe criticized the divine Lydia mildly for her imitation of Mrs. Hemans' subjects, he was required by White to write a letter of apology. Apparently Mrs. Sigourney went into a huff at Poe's criticism and wrote that she would be unable to send any more contributions. Poe answered, "That we have evinced any 'severity amounting to unkindness' is an accusation of which you will, I sincerely hope, unhesitatingly acquit us."[36]

I have dwelt on this matter because it helps explain why Thomas Willis White was willing to discharge his brilliant editor after only a year's service. The poems Poe published in the *Messenger* were neither Byronic nor Satanic enough to ruffle the feathers of either White or Heath. His tales, on the other hand, lacked the moral earnestness demanded by both. "Berenice" had been too horrible; and "Morella," according to Heath, blended "the shadows of the

[35] *Ibid.*, p. 324. [36] Ostrom, I, 89.

tomb with the clouds and sunshine of life."[37] Middle-class morality was the controlling ethic of Thomas Willis White and his magazine.

Yet it was neither his tales nor his poems that made Poe famous as editor of the *Southern Literary Messenger*. It was his criticism. We have already seen that a mildly censorious review of Mrs. Sigourney caused White difficulties with his most prolific contributor; but some of Poe's other reviews were anything but mild.

White's first editor, Heath, had objected to severe criticism editorially, comparing severe critics to the snapping and barking "curs which infest our streets, and annoy the by-ways."[38] Heath was not alone in his opinion; in fact, it was quite customary to think of a harsh reviewer as a bad-tempered, ill-mannered hack. Heath's own reviews were completely innocuous, except for his condemnation of Beckford's *Vathek* for immorality. This kind of condemnation was perfectly safe, for it was in accord with the middle-class ethic; and, after all, *Vathek* had been published in 1786 by an Englishman!

Heath was succeeded in the editorial post of the *Messenger* by Edward Vernon Sparhawk in May of 1835, but apparently he did not get along with White and left after he had edited three numbers. It is difficult to make an estimate of Sparhawk's attitude toward fiction and criticism, for his reviews during these three months, when they can be identified, are brief and perfunctory; they are more professional than Heath's but less detailed than either Beverley Tucker's or Poe's. Poe may have been contributing reviews since February, 1835, but those that have been attributed to him between February and April are fairly commonplace and may have been someone else's.

It was in April, 1835, that the first criticism by Poe for which there is definite external evidence appeared. This was a review of an anonymous book called *Confessions of a Poet*. Reading this review, subscribers to the *Messenger* must have realized that something odd had happened to the mild-mannered journal. For Poe ridicules a ridiculous book without mercy. We do not have to search far for the origins of Poe's method. He had been studying the reviews in the British magazines, particularly those in *Blackwood's*. The famous John Wilson of *Blackwood's* had for many years demolished the

[37] *Southern Literary Messenger*, I, 460. [38] *Ibid.*, p. 322.

works he did not like with wit, humor, and sometimes savage ridicule. We know that Poe had studied Wilson's criticism. In fact he defended himself against the charge of undue levity in a letter to Beverley Tucker, one of White's trusted advisers, by citing a review from *Blackwood's* that demolished "an Epic Poem by a Cockney tailor."[39] Wilson was notorious for his attacks upon the Cockney school of writers, and his favorite symbol of vulgarity was a Cockney tailor. Tucker, however, was not convinced. He answered, "As to Blackwood; I admire Wilson, but he is an offence unto me by the brutal arrogance of his style of criticism. I have no doubt he demolished the poor tailor. But 'who breaks a butterfly upon the wheel?' "[40]

Now White depended upon Tucker heavily for advice, and undoubtedly Tucker's opinion of the satirical method Poe was using had its effect on the publisher. Furthermore Poe was going against the editorial policy in book reviewing announced by Heath and presumably supported by White. But the *Messenger* had seen nothing yet. Poe assumed the chief responsibility for the critical department in December of 1835. Immediately we notice that the number of pages devoted to literary criticism is tripled, and in this issue appeared the review which was to make Poe notorious as the hatchet man of the *Southern Literary Messenger*. This was the review of a silly novel called *Norman Leslie*. Poe tore the book apart, scattered the pieces, and sowed salt where they lay in the pungently satirical manner of John Wilson. The book had been written by Theodore S. Fay, one of the editors of the *New York Mirror*, a pretentious gentleman who belonged to a powerful New York literary clique. White must have quaked in his boots as he realized the kind of antagonist Poe was challenging in the name of his young magazine. To make things worse, two months later Poe did it again, this time destroying *Paul Ulric*, by Morris Mattson of Philadelphia. Poe wrote, "When we called Norman Leslie the silliest book in the world we had certainly never seen Paul Ulric . . . [it] is too purely imbecile to merit an extended critique."[41]

[39] Ostrom, I, 77.

[40] Quoted in James A. Harrison, *The Complete Works of Edgar Allan Poe* (New York, 1902), XVII, 23.

[41] *Ibid.*, VIII, 178.

Such reviews as these were comparatively unusual in America although frequent in England; and, as Poe had undoubtedly figured, they made the *Messenger* famous. Comments on the critical department of the Southern magazine appeared all over the country, and Poe carefully copied them down and published them in supplements to the January and April and July numbers of the *Messenger.* Demonstrably Poe had become a professional journalist; he knew the value of publicity, and he did not scruple as to the means he used to gain it. The subscriptions to the *Messenger* doubled, tripled, quadrupled, and quintupled, but was Thomas Willis White happy? Apparently not.

Criticism by the method Poe was using seemed ungentlemanly if not unscrupulous to many literary Southerners. Even Thomas Jefferson had written to William Wirt back in 1816 that he might expect to be "hacked and hewed, with tomahawk and scalping knife" by the Quarterly Reviewers when he published his biography of Patrick Henry. Francis Walker Gilmer, another literary man of Virginia, once wrote to his young niece that he disliked the "shallow, surly, presumptuous and malignant criticism" of Samuel Johnson. William Wirt was thrown into something of a rage by a fairly mild criticism of his essays by Robert Walsh in the *Analectic;* Walsh was one of the few harsh American critics. Philip Pendleton Cooke reacted violently to a criticism of his poetry in the *Messenger* by a correspondent from Shepherdstown, Virginia.

Perhaps if Southern writers had been more professional in their attitude they would have taken harsh criticism more philosophically, but they all remembered Byron's reaction to the castigation given his *Hours of Idleness* by the *Edinburgh Review,* and some of them knew that poor John Keats had been allegedly "killed" by a malignant review of his *Endymion.* Although the opinions of the *Messenger* Poe printed in his supplements were generally favorable, the *Norfolk Beacon* thought the critical notices were in bad taste; the *Lynchburg Virginian* thought the criticism "too dogmatical and flippant," and the *Newbern Spectator* issued an editorial warning to the *Messenger.* Poe was succeeding, but White must have thought at too great a cost. At any moment the headstrong young critic might turn on someone who could do the magazine great damage, a valued contributor or an influential journalist. Furthermore, White thought, Poe could not be trusted because he drank.

Poe, as he put it later, surrendered to Virginian conviviality now and then and apparently suffered from the most abominable hangovers. White had written to him even before he became editor condemning this habit. In his own house, White averred, liquor was not used.[42] So once again the Byronic poet-cum-editor became a victim of middle-class morality. Drinking might have status among the sons of the Virginia aristocracy, but it had no place in the sober editorial office of a sober publisher.

Thus Poe, in spite of his brilliance as a short story writer and a critic, became increasingly obnoxious to Thomas Willis White. His pungent reviews, even when their severity was justifiable, seemed ungentlemanly; and they came ever closer to home. His most satirical reviews, the two which I have previously mentioned, were of books by Northerners; but in January, 1836, he abused *The Partisan,* by William Gilmore Simms of Charleston, South Carolina. We do not have any record of White's reaction to this particular review, but we should be able to reconstruct it. The *Messenger* had publicly dedicated itself to the cause of Southern literature. Simms was already one of the most promising of Southern writers, with four novels and some poetry to his credit. To White it must have seemed that Poe was deliberately alienating a possible contributor; and indeed Simms did contribute some poetry to the *Messenger* later that year. It was bad enough for Poe to take exception to Mrs. Sigourney, already a contributor, but to hamper future contributions with a scurrilous review was sheer perversity, White must have thought. And Poe's review of Simms *was* scurrilous. He spent two pages making fun of Simm's four line dedication of the novel to a friend, and then proceeded to damn the book for lack of plot, for vulgarity of language, for bad taste in characterization, and for "shockingly bad English," concluding finally that Simms had the eye of a painter and might do better in sketching a landscape than in writing a novel. Simms's reaction, which we find in a letter to Evert Duyckinck some years later, was quite understandable:

[42] *Ibid.,* XVII, 20. White went on to say that no man who drank before breakfast could attend to business properly!

> Poe is no friend of mine. . . . He began by a very savage attack on one of my novels—The Partisan. . . . he was rude & offensive & personal, in the manner of the thing, which he should not have been, in the case of anybody,—still less in mine. My deportment had not justified it. He knew, or might have known, that I was none of that miserable gang about town, who beg in literary highways. I had no clique, mingled with none, begged no praise from anybody, and made no condition with the herd. He must have known what I was personally—might have known—& being just should not have been rude.[43]

Poe began increasingly to have to defend himself against charges of hypercriticism. In the supplement to the July, 1836, number of the *Messenger* he printed at length a reproof from the *Newbern Spectator* which made the point that there simply was not enough talent in the South for Poe to "assume the tone of a Walsh, a Blackwood, or a Jeffries [*sic*]; and to attempt it, without the means to support the pretension, tends to accelerate the downfall of so indiscreet an attempt."[44]

Poe's reply to the *Newbern Spectator* began by making fun of the editor, saying that probably he was the "identical gentleman who once sent us from Newbern an unfortunate copy of verses. It seems to us that he wishes to be taken notice of, and we will, for the once, oblige him with a few words—with the positive understanding, however, that it will be inconvenient to trouble ourselves hereafter with his opinions."[45]

Again White must have shuddered. Not content with alienating possible contributors, now his young assistant was abusing Southern newspaper editors. Actually Poe was following a pattern of journalism that had been highly successful in England and was frequently practiced in the North, the pattern of stirring up a feud. The *Edinburgh Review*'s attacks on the Lake school of poetry; *Blackwood's* constant ridicule of the "Cockney school"; and the notorious rivalry between the two journals themselves brought in subscriptions. "To kick up a bobbery," as Poe phrased it, was a sure formula for journalistic success. But the South was no more ready for this kind of professionalism than it was for the sharp practices of Yankee businessmen. It is true that the aristocratic tradition with its antipa-

[43] Quoted in Hubbell, p. 599.
[44] *Southern Literary Messenger*, II, 517. [45] *Ibid.*

thy to trade was in decline; but the business ethic had not yet replaced it. The image of an aristocratic poet in the Byronic tradition would fail to impress such middle-class citizens as John Allan and Thomas Willis White; but when Poe went to the other extreme and tried to don the mantle of John Wilson, he found that the South was not yet ready for journalism in the British manner. Still a qualification must be made. Poe's criticism *was* frequently admired in the South. Most of the Southern newspapers spoke with respect of his independent, fearless judgment. But White and his advisers, such as Beverley Tucker, were not prepared to engage in magazine warfare—competitive journalism.

White, as revealed by his letters, thought of himself as a man with a holy mission. After he had discharged Poe, he wrote to Tucker, "I feel proud of the *Messenger*. I feel proud to believe that I have been the humble instrument of rearing up a publication which shall be a credit to my native State and Country."[46] He was not proud, however, of the literary criticism of Edgar Allan Poe. In another letter to Tucker he said, "The truth is, Poe seldom or ever done [*sic*] what he knew was just to any book. He read few through—unless it were some trashy novels,—and his only object in reading even these, was to ridicule their authors."[47]

This was unfair to Poe, but probably White was in no mood to be fair. Poe had come to him as an assistant and had challenged his authority again and again. Poe had paraded his learning, and White was an uneducated man. In fact, some years later Poe asserted in a letter that his "best energies were wasted in the service of an illiterate and vulgar, although well-meaning man, who had neither the capacity to appreciate my labors, nor the will to reward them."[48] Surely White was aware of this attitude of contempt. Furthermore Poe had alienated friends and contributors and had gained for the *Messenger* a reputation for severe criticism that, however remunerative it was in terms of subscriptions, White did not like. Thus on December 27, 1836, the publisher wrote to Beverley Tucker summing up his grievances against Poe:

[46] Quoted in David K. Jackson, *Poe and* The Southern Literary Messenger (Richmond, 1934), p. 114.
[47] *Ibid.*, p. 115. [48] Ostrom, I, 141.

> Highly as I really think of Mr. Poe's talents, I shall be forced to give him notice, in a week or so at farthest, that I can no longer recognize him as editor of my *Messenger*. Three months ago I felt it my duty to give him a similar notice,—and was afterwards overpersuaded to restore him to his situation on certain conditions—which conditions he has again forfeited.
>
> Added to all this, I am cramped by him in the exercise of my own judgment, as to what articles I shall or shall not admit into my work. It is true that I neither have his sagacity, nor his learning—but I do believe I know a handspike from a saw. Be that as it may, however,—and let me even be a jackass, as I dare say I am in his estimation,—I will again throw myself on my own resources—and trust my little bark to the care of those friends who stood by me in my earlier, if not darker days.[49]

White made good his threat, and the January, 1837, issue of the *Messenger* contained a notice of Poe's resignation. Never again was White's magazine so famous. The year after Poe's resignation the critical notices almost disappeared. The journal continued to survive, but it subsided into the condition of a respectable but innocuous family magazine. Poe was to contribute to the *Messenger* again, late in life, when it was edited by John R. Thompson, but henceforth he had no influence over its destinies.

After Poe left Richmond in January of 1837, he never returned to the South except for brief visits. Yet the attitudes that had been fostered in the South remained with him. The few poems that he was to write in later years were still the poems of love and death—the favorite themes of the Virginia poets. His greatest tales, such as "Ligeia," "The Fall of the House of Usher," and "William Wilson," depict the degeneracy of the descendants of aristocratic families, themes that might have been suggested to him by the common complaint that Virginia was losing its aristocracy and its sense of honor. Even the personal stance of the melancholy poet remained, but it was effective in the North only in fluttering the hearts of innumerable literary ladies. As for the un-Virginian professionalism that had been disliked by White and his advisers, Poe should have found more scope for it in the North; but he was always handicapped by his temperament and by the fact that he never achieved real editorial authority until it was too late. When Poe finally got control of the *Broadway Journal* in 1845, he was harassed by poverty

[49] Jackson, pp. 109-10.

and the illness of his wife. His old technique of "kicking up a bobbery" won him more enemies than friends; and he made the mistake of picking on the institutionalized grandeur of Henry Wadsworth Longfellow, who chose to ignore his attacks.

Finally, toward the end of his life, Poe came back to Richmond trying to raise funds to establish a magazine. Throughout his struggles in the North, he had always looked to the South and the West for backing for this projected journal; and in 1849 it looked as if he had found it. E. H. N. Patterson, a gentleman from Illinois, had agreed to finance a literary magazine, and Poe was to make a trip through the South to arouse interest. In Richmond Poe made public lectures which were well attended. He says in a letter to his aunt, Maria Clemm, "I *never* was received with so much enthusiasm. The papers have done nothing but praise me before the lecture and since."[50] So it appeared that the poet was returning home with public honor.

Even more pleasant, Poe, a widower, met in Richmond his old sweetheart, Elmira Royster, now the Widow Shelton. They became engaged to be married. It seemed as if Poe were at last going to reestablish himself in Richmond on terms that would be acceptable to the South; but, as everyone knows, he left Richmond on Thursday, September 27, 1849, on the boat for Baltimore and was found there in the street, semiconscious, on October 3. He died the next morning.

What can we say then of Poe in the South? Dismissing the question of personal temperament, which cannot be debated in this paper, we can say that Poe's great predicament was in being caught between two worlds and trying to live in both. The South could understand and sympathize with the fictional image of a melancholy, despairing poet; but the rising middle class had little patience with anyone who attempted to follow such a pattern in his private life. On the other hand, the South still professed to be too gentlemanly to admire a professional journalist who used shrewd practices to gain public success. As time went on, the canny journalist was forgotten, and the South wept over the memory of the melancholy poet.

[50] Ostrom, II, 458.

Actually Poe was both; each stance represented an element of his personality. His professional ambition sent him North, but like a later Southerner who invaded New York, Thomas Wolfe, he never forgot his origins. Had he lived, he might have found, again like Wolfe, that "you can't go home again."

3

THE IMAGE OF AN ARMY
THE CIVIL WAR IN SOUTHERN FICTION

LOUIS D. RUBIN, JR.

AT THE close of the War between the States, Father Abram Ryan, the poet laureate of the Confederacy, penned some verses which were set to music. The song was called "The Conquered Banner," and it has remained one of the best known of Confederate hymns. One of its stanzas ran as follows:

> Furl that banner! True, 'tis gory,
> Yet 'tis wreathed around with glory,
> And 'twill live in song and story,
>   Though its folds are in the dust;
> For its fame on brightest pages,
> Penned by poets and by sages,
> Shall go sounding down the ages . . .
>   Furl its folds though now we must.

Father Ryan's was a fairly common expectation: that future generations of Southerners would be able to draw the inspiration and the material for great literature from the tales of their warring forefathers. An army such as the Confederacy's, and a chieftain such as Robert E. Lee, could scarcely fail to provide the image by which poets and novelists could create a heroic literature, commensurate with the loftiness of the subject matter. A young Vir-

A LECTURE given for the Institute of Southern Culture at Longwood College, April 26, 1957.

ginian, John Hampden Chamberlayne, expressed the idea quite well in a letter to his sister, written in the autumn of 1862 when he was an artilleryman in the Army of Northern Virginia:

> When by accident I at any time see Gen. Lee, or when I think of him whether I will or no, there looms up to me some king-of-men, superior by the head, a Gigantic figure, on whom rests the world,
>
> With Atlantean shoulder, fit to bear
> The weight of empire.
>
> Was it a King Henry whose son was lost at sea, whereafter he never smiled? In the weight he carried to suppress all joy forever, he was but a fool to this Lee. When you and I are white haired and tell huge stories about these times to awe struck youngsters white haired around us then the shadow of Lee lengthening through the years behind him will mark a continent with a giant form.[1]

In the nine decades that have elapsed since the Civil War, there has been no dearth of attempts to tell the story of the Confederate army in fiction and verse. More than a thousand novels have been written about the war by Southerners alone, and the poems must surely number in the tens of thousands. In a recent study entitled *Fiction Fights the Civil War*, Dr. Robert A. Lively waded through some five hundred novels of the war in order to show how the changing attitudes of Northern and Southern writers provided an important index to American social and political history. Each season produces a new crop. Some few Civil War novels—Margaret Mitchell's *Gone with the Wind*, Allen Tate's *The Fathers*, Andrew Nelson Lytle's *The Long Night*, Stark Young's *So Red the Rose*, William Faulkner's *The Unvanquished*, Caroline Gordon's *None Shall Look Back*, Evelyn Scott's *The Wave*, Ellen Glasgow's *The Battle-Ground*, Thomas Nelson Page's *Meh Lady*, Mary Johnston's *The Long Roll*, Clifford Dowdey's *Bugles Blow No More*, George Washington Cable's *The Cavalier* and *Kincaid's Battery*, to name a baker's dozen—are interesting work, often of high literary excellence, and well worth reading.

Most of the South's Civil War fiction, however, is wretched stuff. Only the fiercest chauvinism can make *Surry of Eagle's Nest*,

[1] C. G. Chamberlayne, ed., *Ham Chamberlayne, Virginian* (Richmond, 1932), p. 126.

Macaria, Tiger-Lilies, The Little Shepherd of Kingdom Come, The Clansman, and shelfload after shelfload of novels of similar caliber into palatable literature. Professor Lively assures us, after reading five hundred novels, that "my own experience with a mass of second-rate novels suggests that the effort would be more than an adventure among the Philistines. The rapid achievement of technical proficiency by historical novelists has guaranteed a certain quality to their efforts which is fairly impressive."[2] A kind judgment, surely, and perhaps it comes because Professor Lively is a historian rather than a literary scholar (though his critical analysis of various novels would seem to belie it), and he may be a bit timid about making final critical judgments in a field of scholarship foreign to his own training. Either that, or Mr. Lively's earlier researches in economic history made even second-rate fiction seem interesting by comparison.

What with the fascination that the Civil War has exerted on the South's writers ever since the 1860's, it seems strange that so little really good fiction has been produced about the Confederate army. There has surely been no shortage of good writers, especially in recent decades when Southern novelists have been producing work of the first importance. Yet the fact is that from a region that has produced Faulkner, Wolfe, Warren, Welty, Cable, Lytle, Glasgow, and others, and which possesses so vivid a historical symbol as the Civil War, there has not been really outstanding work of fiction written about the Confederate soldier and his times.

There have been good novels, interesting novels, competent novels. Yet in their best books, most of the South's outstanding writers have not been primarily concerned with the Confederacy. Soldiers and statesmen and battles have figured in their work, but no single Confederate war novel exists which we can read and then say with satisfaction and admiration, *That* was the Lost Cause; *that* was Lee's army.

William Faulkner, perhaps the contemporary South's finest novelist, illustrates this point. He has written one novel, *The Unvanquished,* primarily about the war as such. It is an interesting, well-written narrative. But it is not comparable in scope or artistry to the

[2] Chapel Hill, 1957, p. 193.

same writer's *Absalom, Absalom!* Indeed, in *Absalom, Absalom!* there are a few scattered war sequences which despite their brevity and secondary role in the novel present far more of what a Confederate military historian has called "the inspiration of personalities, humble and exalted, who met a supreme test and did not falter,"[3] than the entire narrative of *The Unvanquished.* Likewise, Ellen Glasgow's *The Battle-Ground* is a poor thing compared with *The Sheltered Life* or others of her best novels. Robert Penn Warren's only Civil War novel has to do with Yankee soldiers. George Washington Cable's Civil War romances are neither so amusing as *The Grandissimes* nor so socially perceptive as his fine Reconstruction novel, *John March, Southerner.* Caroline Gordon's *None Shall Look Back* has not the strength or scope of several of her novels about the modern South. And so on.

"Where the plowshare of war cut deepest," Chancellor Kirkland of Vanderbilt wrote several decades after Appomattox, "the first fruits of tradition and of story ought to grow. The burden of Southern sorrow and suffering ought to elicit a burst of Southern song."[4] But his prediction has not come true. The effect of the South's history on its literature has been profound, but the war itself awaits its fictional chronicler. There is no *War and Peace* about the South and its army. There is not even *A Farewell to Arms.* All we have is *Gone with the Wind,* a novel comparable only in physical size. We have no Prince Andrew; only Ashley Wilkes. Instead of Natasha, we have only Scarlett O'Hara. Above all, we have no Bezukhov, no fictional protagonist for whom, as Andrew Lytle has said of him, "his own ordeal and his country's can become one."[5]

Discussing the fiction of the South, Herbert Marshall McLuhan remarks that

> the impersonal social code which permits a formal expression of inward emotion makes it quite pointless for people to interpret one another constantly, as they do in most 'realistic' novels. There is thus in the Southern

[3] Douglas S. Freeman, *The South to Posterity* (New York, 1939), p. 193.

[4] James H. Kirkland, "The Intellectual Tendencies of the South," in John Bell Henneman, ed., *The South in the Building of a Nation,* VII (Richmond, 1909), xxxix.

[5] "The Image as Guide to Meaning in the Historical Novel," *Sewanee Review,* LXI (1953), 423.

novel a vacuum where we might expect introspection. . . . The stress falls entirely on slight human gestures, external events which are obliquely slanted to flash light or shade on character.[6]

Though Mr. McLuhan's diagnosis fits some Southern novelists better than it does others (surely Quentin Compson, Jack Burden, and Eugene Gant are introspective characters of a most extraordinary kind), it is certainly true of a writer such as Caroline Gordon. Here for example is Rives Allard, the chief male character of *None Shall Look Back,* looking on at a crucial moment in Southern destiny, when General Nathan Bedford Forrest pleads in vain with Braxton Bragg to let him seal the Confederate success at Chickamauga by cutting off the Union army from Chattanooga. Rives listens to them arguing, and then follows as the irate Forrest rides off with an aide:

Riding behind the two dark figures he raised his clenched hand in impotent fury. When he had first heard the conversation between the two generals he had been excited to think that he, a private, was receiving information about important maneuvres. That emotion seemed trivial now. The incidents of the morning seemed trivial, too, and vain. He thought of George Rowan, dead and buried on the field. He had felt pity for the dead man as he laid him in his grave but now he knew envy. If the Confederate cause failed . . . and for the first time he felt fear for its outcome . . . there could be no happiness for him except in the grave.[7]

That is all. The chapter ends there. There is no introspection, no meditation upon what Rives Allard has seen, and what he thinks of it. There is no opportunity for us to explore, whether through Rives's eyes or Miss Gordon's, the impact of a Confederate soldier's first realization that the war might be lost. All we get is a clenched fist and a half-dozen terse sentences. Nor would an intense reverie on Rives's part be appropriate in Miss Gordon's novel. In her fiction, it would seem forced, didactic. The meaning of that moment, and of the entire war, must be resolved entirely in terms of symbol, in what Mr. McLuhan describes as "slight human gestures, external events." There is no room for self-revelation at all.

What might seem an opposite extreme to Miss Gordon's almost

[6] "The Southern Quality," in Allen Tate, ed., *A Southern Vanguard* (New York, 1947), p. 117.
[7] New York, 1937, p. 286.

complete externality is the technique of a novel such as Stark Young's *So Red the Rose*. Here is Sallie Bedford of that novel as she thinks about her husband and the war:

She saw that the suspense of the Vicksburg siege was always at the back of Malcolm's mind. She herself had been busy with the children and with the managing of the place. Somebody had to do that, for children must eat . . . and now, talking with her husband in the solitude of the bedroom sometime past midnight, she understood more profoundly what it meant if Vicksburg fell. Vicksburg was the last Confederate stronghold on the Mississippi. Its fall meant that the North would possess the river from St. Louis to New Orleans; that the Confederate territory would be cut in half, the eastern and western; that the Northern men now in this country would be freed to be used elsewhere in the war against the South. If the Southern leaders were not mad, Malcolm Bedford said over and over, they would know that the fall of Vicksburg would mean defeat and the end of the war. "No use trying to speak of the ruins that would follow," he said to his wife. "Oh, no use speaking of it."

"Darlin,' don't put your hands up to your head like that," she said, and turned away to find something she could do about the room.[8]

And there follows a lengthy exposition of the progress of the Federal campaign against Vicksburg.

Where Miss Gordon's characters were mostly silent about the events of the war, Stark Young's people spend a great deal of time discoursing on it and thinking about it. They do so almost exclusively in historical terms, however. There is almost no interpolation of the historical events into the more subjective consciousness of individual characters. Mr. Young's people deal with the events of the Civil War with complete objectivity, as if they were spectators who, from a distant vantage point, watch the coming and going of foreign armies on a battle map. His approach to characterization and dialogue is reminiscent of that of a wartime novelist, August Jane Evans Wilson, in *Macaria*, who has two female characters discuss the progress of events as follows:

"A long, dark vista stretches before the Confederacy. I can not, like many persons, feel sanguine on a speedy termination of the war."

"Yes . . . a vista lined with the bloody graves of her best sons; but beyond glimmers Freedom . . . Independence. In that light we shall walk without stumbling. Deprived of liberty we cannot exist, and its price was fixed when the foundations of time were laid. I believe the termina-

[8] New York, 1953, p. 244.

tions of the war to be contingent only on the method of its prosecution. Agathocles, with thirteen thousand men, established a brilliant precedent, which Scipio followed successfully in the Second Punic War; and when our own able generals are permitted to emulate those illustrious leaders of antiquity, then, and I fear not until then, shall we be able to dictate terms of peace."[9]

Seventy years of literary history and aeons of literary judgment save Mr. Young's dialogue from that, but actually the notion of what fictional characters ought to say and think is similar in both novels. It is Mr. Young's taste and intelligence, not his method, that make the difference. The characters of both novels speak, and think, with mannered formality and propriety. They react to events in quite conventional, literal fashion, exemplifying the official point of view, so to speak, of the South, and they thus serve as their author's commentary on the events of the war. So while at first glance their loquaciousness may seem to contrast with Caroline Gordon's externalized male protagonist of *None Shall Look Back,* actually they are the other side of the same literary coin. They are designed for defense of the Southern Way. The picture of the war is not predicated on individual terms. The characters serve as spokesmen for the region's attitudes, as the authors conceive of them. Despite Rives Allard's failure to enlarge on his thoughts on the subject of the Confederate cause, he is nevertheless intended by the author to exemplify a social system, a school of character, the region. At bottom the author's intention is patriotic; Rives Allard is the prototype of a society. His death is intended to symbolize the failure of his cause. Primarily he exists to embody the cause. We see Rives from the outside, and we see the Bedfords and the McGehees of *So Red the Rose* from the outside. The limits of their characterization are defined by their role as symbols of what for their author is an essentially noble and praiseworthy society.

It is this attitude toward the Civil War on the part of many Southern novelists, I think, that determines the form that numerous Southern war novels have taken. It is admirably summed up in a statement by Mr. Walter Sullivan in an essay on Southern war fiction. "In the Old South," he says,

[9] New York, 1868, p. 413.

the honor and the pride were there, not as individual virtues in isolated men, but as part of the public consciousness, the moral basis on which the culture was constructed. This is the reason that the War has been used so often by so many Southern writers. It is the grand image for the novelist, the period when the 'ultimate truths,' with which Mr. Faulkner says the writer must deal, existed as commonly recognized values within a social framework. It is the only moment in American history when a completely developed national ethic was brought to a dramatic crisis.[10]

Mr. Sullivan thus ascribes to Civil War fiction an essential basis in social commentary. It is written in order to pay homage to a society, and to demonstrate the moral values which characterize that society.

Similarly, Donald Davidson notes of *So Red the Rose* that "the Bedfords and McGehees, in their histories, dwellings, and personal peculiarities, represent different and complementary aspects of Southern life," and he remarks that in the characterization of Hugh McGehee "Southern society has produced an example of the unified personality, in tune with its environment while also commanding it," so that therefore we may assume "that Southern society at the outbreak of the war was tending toward such an ideal."[11]

In conceiving of the Civil War as the testing ground for the virtues of antebellum society, as well as the occasion of its destruction by materialism, the novelists heretofore mentioned are in effect striving to fulfill a charge given to young Southern writers by Thomas Nelson Page. Addressing an audience of college students in the late 1880's, Page took for his topic the Old South. "What nobler task," he asked, "can [the young Southern writer] set himself than this . . . to preserve from oblivion, or worse, from misrepresentation, a civilization which produced as its natural fruit Washington and Lee!"[12] That was precisely what Page himself sought to do . . . in *Meh Lady*, in *Red Rock*, in *Two Little Confederates*, and in every other story he wrote about the Civil War in Virginia.

For better or for worse, Page has spoken for the vast majority of Southern writers who have taken the war for their subject mat-

[10] "Southern Novelists and the Civil War," in Louis D. Rubin, Jr., and Robert D. Jacobs, eds., *Southern Renascence* (Baltimore, 1953), p. 125.

[11] "Theme and Method in *So Red the Rose*," in *Southern Renascence*, pp. 267, 269.

[12] *The Old South* (New York, 1919), p. 51.

ter. For while individual writers may differ greatly on how best to preserve and honor the image of antebellum Southern society, behind their novels rests the same attitude toward the war as the climax of a social system which, for all its faults, was far preferable to that which followed it. From *Macaria* to *None Shall Look Back,* the Southern war novel has usually been concerned with portraying the social structure of Southern society, with the individuals, and has been intended primarily for that purpose.

So important has that social ideal been that in many Southern war novels little attention has been paid to the actual war itself. Ellen Glasgow, for example, saw the war almost exclusively as an event in a social history. She has written that "in *The Battle-Ground* I have tried to portray the last stand in Virginia of the aristocratic tradition," and, again,

> What I tried to do in *The Battle-Ground* was to write, not literally a novel of war, but a chronicle of two neighboring families, the Amblers and the Lightfoots, who had lived through a disastrous period in history. If I used the Civil War as a background, it was merely as one of several circumstances which had moulded the character of the individual Virginian, as well as the social order in which he made a vital, if obscure, figure.[13]

The war as such constitutes only a small portion of the text; Miss Glasgow's emphasis is on prewar life. This existence she portrays in almost idyllic hues. In its time *The Battle-Ground* was shocking in its harsh realism; times have long since changed, and now the book seems merely a conventional love story. Miss Glasgow was impressed by her boldness in daring to make a Southern mountaineer, who did not own slaves or landed estates, one of her Confederate soldiers. Actually, however, Pine Top, her "common man," is treated with much condescension by Miss Glasgow, who sees him entirely through aristocratic eyes. Today one finds little impressive realism in *The Battle-Ground,* and the devastating social irony Miss Glasgow thought she was composing now seems mild and inoffensive. Her prewar society is probably romantic, her plantation belles glamorous, her Confederate soldiers cavaliers all. She seems much closer to

[13] Preface to *The Battle-Ground,* in *A Certain Measure* (New York, 1943), pp. 13, 19.

Thomas Nelson Page than to Thomas Wolfe or William Faulkner. Her picture of the life "before de wah" is in roseate colors, and the war is important only as it destroys the old society.

The Civil War scenes of George Washington Cable are actually much more realistic than Miss Glasgow's, for all their light touch and for all Cable's unwillingness to take life very tragically in his fiction. As seen in *Kincaid's Battery* and *The Cavalier,* Cable's war is a time of adventure and romance. But despite his melodramatic love stories, there is a certain realistic honesty to his characters, a flesh and blood quality that makes them into believable people in their own right instead of exemplars of Southern social patterns. Occasionally there is a flash of real emotion and pathos, as in *The Cavalier* when Cable depicts a Confederate troop riding back after an engagement:

> And yet a lovely ten miles it was, withal. You would hardly have known this tousled crowd for the same dandy crew that had smiled so flippantly upon me at sunrise, though they smiled as flippantly now with faces powder-blackened, hair and eyelashes matted and gummed with sweat and dust, and shoulders and thighs caked with grime. Yet to Ned Ferry as well as to me . . . I saw it in his eye every time he looked at them . . . these grimy fellows did more to beautify those ten miles than did June woods beflowered and perfumed with magnolia, bay and muscadine, or than slant sunlight in the glade or grove.[14]

The fine understatement and tangible quality of that passage, however, with its touching image of the Confederate soldiers, is one of the few serious looks that Cable casts at the Confederate army-as-army in his novel. The social muse has pervaded his aesthetic, too . . . not in an idealized presentation of prewar society, to be sure, but in his inability to take the Confederates seriously for very long at a time. The Creoles are missing in *The Cavalier,* though present in *Kincaid's Battery,* but this is still the world of *Old Creole Days,* in which highborn Southerners play idly at life, in this case the war. Earlier in Cable's life, as Jay B. Hubbell has said, he had "felt a certain scorn for luxury-loving Creoles and easygoing Southern planters."[15] *Kincaid's Battery* and *The Cavalier* date from the later period, and Cable is no longer scornful. Nevertheless, he still con-

[14] New York, 1901, p. 107.
[15] *The South in American Literature* (Durham, N.C., 1955), p. 806.

siders the South's aristocracy essentially frivolous creatures, and this attitude usually prevents him from viewing the war with sufficient seriousness to make possible anything beyond the limits of comedy.

The social approach to the war, of course, is completely dominant in Stark Young's *So Red the Rose,* which takes the war quite seriously. There are no scenes of Confederate armies in full combat, however; the book is a story of the war on the home front and its effect on Southern plantation life. Donald Davidson rightly sees the novel as drawing into focus "the battle between tradition and anti-tradition that has been waged with increasing bitterness since the Renaissance." *So Red the Rose,* he says, "is a large-scale narrative in which events of national importance exert catastrophic force upon the life of the Bedfords, the McGehees, and their kin, friends, visitors, slaves . . . the whole complex of plantation life and, by implication, of Southern life in general."[16] The novel is a story of the downfall of traditional Southern society before the onslaught of anti-traditional Northern materialism, and the war is merely the device by which this social tragedy is effected.

Caroline Gordon's *None Shall Look Back* is more of the same, done by a different kind of artist but one who shares the same essential purpose. "At the end of the book," Walter Sullivan points out, "every single character who has remained constant to the Southern ethic has either been killed or sadly broken. Of all the immediate Allard kin, only Jim, who represents the spirit of commerce, is seen to thrive in the end."[17] A staunch advocate of the well-planned novel, Miss Gordon has carefully constructed her characters and her plot to accomplish that result. The dissolution of antebellum Southern plantation society provides *None Shall Look Back* with its form, and its limitations as well. The whole purpose is to show the downfall of a society before superior force and internal weaknesses, and her characters are not permitted to develop in any direction not contributing to that end. This rules out such themes as the personal impact of war on an individual sensibility, the hammering out of the individual soul on the anvil of conflict, the growth of compassion and understanding amid the cataclysm of

[16] P. 264. [17] P. 119.

suffering . . . the themes, that is to say, that make up the chief concern of *War and Peace.*

Allen Tate's *The Fathers* is another case in point. An extremely well-written, incisive novel, it is concerned with the defects in antebellum Southern society that brought its ruin when war came. It is not really a war novel, nor was it intended to be. Mr. Tate depicts the advent of George Posey, a "morally neutral" person as Walter Sullivan, has it,[18] into the traditional society of northern Virginia. With the coming of the war, the society's ethical code is no longer sufficient to act as a guide for behavior and the prewar Virginia world collapses. In Lacy Buchan, the narrator of *The Fathers,* Mr. Tate created a well-drawn, sensitive character, but he was not interested in taking Lacy beyond the onset of the war. We leave him after the battle of First Manassas, when the fighting in Virginia is only beginning. Lacy does not himself serve as a major protagonist; he is a relatively uncritical narrator, through whose eyes we witness the events of the novel. Nor is there any attempt to show the Army of Northern Virginia itself.

DuBose Heyward's *Peter Ashley* is even less concerned with the embattled Confederacy and its soldiers than Mr. Tate's *The Fathers.* He desires to show the South preparing for secession, not fighting for independence. His theme is the transformation of a doubting Unionist into a loyal Confederate soldier. Southern society becomes so caught up in the fervor for secession that at the onset of hostilities even the most reluctant of secessionists ceases to oppose separation. Peter Ashley is above all a Charlestonian, and once the issue is drawn, his loyalty to his society is such that there could be no question of his not "going with my native state." Mr. Heyward's frame of reference is almost exclusively political; there is none of the curiosity about the underlying social and ethical structure that produced the political attitudes such as marks Mr. Tate's *The Fathers* or Miss Gordon's *None Shall Look Back.*

Though William Faulkner's *The Unvanquished* takes place for the most part during the war and involves considerable fighting, it too is not really a novel about Confederate armies. It is a behind-the-lines story, about an elderly Southern lady and two small chil-

[18] *Ibid.,* p. 115.

dren, one white, the other Negro, who become embroiled in the fighting when their area is overrun by Yankees. A very exciting narrative indeed, it chronicles the breakdown of peaceful ethics and the increasing hold that violence takes on community life, until after the war young Bayard Sartoris dramatically rejects further recourse to killing. The focus is on young Bayard, and we watch him as he experiences the war as a child and finally grows to manhood during the war's aftermath. But the episodic quality of the story—it is not a continuous narrative but a series of stories, originally published separately—prevents Bayard's personality from being developed in depth. Only in the final, Reconstruction episode are we really allowed to look within Bayard's consciousness.

Thus far, *Absalom, Absalom!* is really Faulkner's best war novel. A far more profound book than *The Unvanquished,* there are several brief but memorable war scenes in it. But the Civil War is but one among many developments in the rise and fall of Thomas Sutpen and his grand design over the course of a half century. The war serves mainly to postpone for four years the wrecking of the self-made Mississippi baron's hopes for a plantation dynasty. Yet even in passing, Faulkner masterfully illuminates the Confederate cause and the men who made up its armies. The picture of Charles Bon writing a letter to Judith Sutpen by campfire as Joseph E. Johnston's depleted army trails after Sherman's hosts in North Carolina will be remembered long after most of the lieutenants and colonels of the fictional Confederacy have been forgotten.

The war is also only a phase, albeit the climactic one, of Andrew Lytle's *The Long Night.* Pleasant McIvor is a man seeking revenge against a clan of men who murdered his father. Only after his personal war causes the death of a Confederate comrade does Pleasant renounce his purpose, and then it is in order to leave the army and flee to the hills, where he must live with himself and the knowledge of what he has done. Some of Mr. Lytle's battle moments, notably Shiloh, are skillfully done. In the total purpose of the novel, however, the war and the soldiers are but the culminating incident of a story not essentially concerned with the Confederacy.

There are, of course, many Southern novels primarily focused on the fighting itself. Perhaps the best known is Mary Johnston's *The*

Long Roll and its sequel *Cease Firing.* Miss Johnston's novels have been justly praised for their fidelity to detail, their intimate presentation of Confederate operations both from command and rear rank. But in truth it must be said that this is about all her novels have to commend them to a modern audience; they are fictionalized history, with characters designed primarily to furnish individual plot suspense and thus give body to the historical events of the war. Miss Johnston is desirous of one thing above all: to show how well Southerners fought. As Mr. Lively points out, here is "the true historical novel . . . the gospel according to Sir Walter Scott, in which actual historical personages are always close by on the wings of the fictional stage, and in which recorded fact is used to shape the developing story to the pattern of actual circumstances."[19] The external, historical events completely dominate the fictional elements, and the subplots and characterization are always subordinate to Miss Johnston's central purpose: the telling of "the Southern side of the war."

Fictional characterization and plot suspense are even less important to Evelyn Scott's *The Wave,* even though, paradoxically enough, most of the events described therein are fictional. *The Wave* is a panoramic view of the war, North and South, as it changes the lives of hundreds of persons. It contains numerous episodes, with the characters of each one different. Miss Scott's intent was to take the external, history-book story of the war and translate it into the lives of numerous Americans, of various social castes and positions. The end result is still the historical war, however, and the fictional characters are not of any structural importance. Miss Scott's intention is primarily expository: to present typical Americans caught up in a social revolution, in order to describe the revolution.

We have noted a few of the better Civil War novels written by Southerners. As we have seen, some are chiefly concerned with the impact of the war on the social pattern. The war is not seen in them as an ordeal in itself so much as the catastrophe that destroyed antebellum life. The characters in these novels tend for the most part to be representative of certain Southern traits and attitudes, and in

[19] Pp. 16-17.

their reaction to the events of war the society's own characteristics and values are illustrated.

Other novels view the war only as an episode in a larger story, so that the image of the Confederate soldier and armies is not developed in detail. Still other novels, though concerned primarily with the war, seek primarily to give historical events some human relevance, and the fiction is subordinated to the battle reports.

What is lacking in all these novels, from Mary Johnston to William Faulkner, from August Evans Wilson to Caroline Gordon, is the quality that makes a novel such as *War and Peace* more than just an artistic representation of Russian society during the Napoleonic wars, or than a mere justification of Russian strategy and tactics during the 1812 campaign. And that is, a protagonist, or protagonists, for whom the war becomes the great personal experience of his life, transforming the individual, so that the novelist shows a great character developing in a time of stress . . . a man in whom, as Andrew Lytle has said of Bezukhov, a personal crisis and his country's crisis are so joined and fused that they become one. There is, in short, no Southern counterpart of Pierre Bezukhov, no character who can exemplify and embody the South at war, in whose actions and through whose eyes and mind the Southern cause can be understood. And without such a character, the image of the Confederate soldier and the wartime South is fragmented and incomplete.

To find a Southern character with the qualifications of a Pierre Bezukhov, we must look elsewhere than in novels. We must look to nonfiction. For there is no fictional Confederate soldier one-half so convincing, and so memorable, as some of the real-life Confederates as seen through their diaries, letters, and memoirs. In particular I think of John Hampden Chamberlayne as seen through the letters that comprise the volume entitled *Ham Chamberlayne, Virginian,* from which I quoted earlier. Nor is there a novel about a Southern family undergoing the ordeal of war, deprivation, death, and defeat nearly as vivid or as exciting as the story that unfolds in the letters of a Charleston, South Carolina, family, as published in a volume of their correspondence, *The Mason Smith Family Letters.* Much the same might be said of that moving journal of wartime life in the trans-Mississippi, *Brokenburn: The Diary of Kate Stone.* Such real life narratives as these dwarf the fictional accounts of the embattled South.

Ham Chamberlayne, for example, was a young Richmond lawyer and a promising literary man. He was thus quite articulate, and—in a way that no fictional Southern soldier has yet been allowed to be—extremely reflective and thoughtful. In the paragraph previously quoted from his letters, he speaks of the gigantic stature of General Lee, and the shadow that Lee's personality is likely to cast in future years, which "lengthening through the years behind him will mark a continent with a giant form." It is high Confederate rhetoric, of a sort not unfamiliar to readers of Confederate narratives. But what is quite unfamiliar in Confederate writing is the passage by Ham Chamberlayne that immediately follows:

> Big thing! ! !
>
> Why is it that I can never let myself loose and write on without feeling somehow ashamed? There must be some taste of the ludicrous in high degree of emotion of whatever kind the instant we cease to sympathize with it.[20]

Here Ham Chamberlayne is being completely frank and analytical. He is looking right at himself, thinking out loud, so to speak. We are *inside* his consciousness, and because his mind is a very keen and observant one, we are given a picture of a Confederate soldier unmatched in its depth and sincerity. There is self-perception, awareness of subjective, personal reaction. The young Confederate expresses his awe and admiration for his commanding general, and then shyly balances his rhetorical outburst with another observation that reveals his awareness and honesty in a way that lets us believe instantly in him and trust him entirely. We know, as we somehow never know for sure in fictional Confederates, that he is not merely orating for the effect his words will have, that he is not striking a pose consciously designed to illustrate the characteristics of a society. The result is a remarkable picture of a man. Observe, too, the very next paragraph of that same letter to his sister:

> How great a teacher is this abominable "civil combustion," as Gordon Tacitus has it. "Heaven and earth come together to overwhelm me," said

[20] P. 126.

the Spider when the turks head swept away his dirty web. India saw hundreds of women and children murdered, Lucknow suffered siege, Cawnpore massacre; in Balaklavan trench and Scutari hospital, fever, frost, wound and want slew each his thousands; Italian crops were trampled by Gaul & Hun amidst smoke and death; but we were very comfortable. 'Twas so far off. Now the turks head sweeps some of us. Whereby we will learn how to read history, while we make it for ourselves.[21]

This is the kind of detachment, of lofty vision, that we get in *War and Peace* when Prince Andrew lies wounded under the blue sky or when the captured Bezukhov observes his captors and his fellow Russian prisoners. It is a philosophical passage of unusual depth and perception. We see a sensitive, devoted soldier—and Ham Chamberlayne was a completely sincere Confederate and a brave and skilled artillerist—looking at himself, his region, the war with a disenthralled wisdom, marvelling at what is happening to mortal Virginia men. I do not know any other depiction of the Army of Northern Virginia, its soldiers, and the society from which they came that can come close to it for vividness, integrity, and a high-minded realism. Nor in any Confederate war novel I have read is there a moment such as that in *Ham Chamberlayne, Virginian* when, writing to his mother from the trenches of Petersburg in the gloomy December of 1864, he suddenly interpolates this comment: "But the whirligig of time ever brings round its revenge as Goethe says . . . that man of peace whom to quote now is to bring echoes from a dead past already almost inconceivable."[22] Coming in the middle of a long letter full of news of friends, restrained expressions of grief for the dead, and account of a narrow escape in a raid, and a description of a girl of whom he has become enamored, the understatement of the passage adds to its poignancy. Its effect on the reader is similar to the passage about the returning Confederates previously noted in Cable's *The Cavalier,* but it is all the more moving and pathetic because of what goes before and after it.

Likewise the account of the Mason Smith family's wartime years, as seen in the letter from a mother and her children and friends, is a behind-the-lines portrait of almost tragic dimensions. The letters that the mother wrote from Richmond in 1864 at the bedside of her dying son, wounded at Cold Harbor, have a genuine quality of grief

[21] Pp. 126-27. [22] P. 299.

and loftiness about them that gives dignity and stature to an episode that in most Civil War fiction would have been stylized and sentimental. As we read the *Mason Smith Family Letters* we get a picture of what the war meant to the South such as no single Confederate novel provides.

Both *Ham Chamberlayne, Virginian* and the *Mason Smith Family Letters,* it must be remembered, are correspondence. They are not private meditations. They are written, to be sure, to close friends and intimates with whom relatively few constraints are expected, but they are nevertheless necessarily external and objective. Particularly with Ham Chamberlayne's letters this makes the accomplishment all the more remarkable. For even as frank and as honest as he was, he must necessarily have marshaled his thoughts to formalize them for others. What might a good novelist do with such a character, in similar circumstances? For like Tolstoy with Prince Andrew, he could show us what his fictional character was thinking and feeling, directly, subjectively. The formal constraint required of Ham Chamberlayne even when writing to one as close to him as his sister would not be involved. And Aristotle's dictum about history and poetry holds good for the Civil War, too; the probable impossible more nearly approaches the universal experience. If Ham Chamberlayne could give us what he does, think what would be possible in fiction.

But so far there has been no Ham Chamberlayne in Southern war fiction. There is no character of intelligence and sensibility such as he, who could go through a war, fight well enough to win battlefield promotion and high commendation, maintain his intellectual interests as best possible, compose book reviews from the Petersburg trenches, and all the while see what was happening to him and his fellow soldiers and friends back home as from the outside, with the perception that comes at moments of absolute detachment. He was not a "typical" Confederate, to be sure, but there must have been many others like him. Nor was Prince Andrew a "typical" Russian. It is in the image of men like Ham Chamberlayne that a novelist might fashion a Confederate soldier capable of the insight and intelligence needed to inform a protagonist of a great novel. Anyone of lesser stature and intelligence would not do, just as the story that Tolstoy tells in *War and Peace* would have been impossible without Prince Andrew and Pierre Bezukhov.

It must be emphasized that, among other things, *War and Peace* is a great social novel. It describes a country, a people, and a culture. Its portrait of a Russian society during the Napoleonic wars is masterfully done. But the social portraiture was achieved not by a concentration on social types at the expense of the personal insight and individuality of its chief characters so much as through such insight. If we compare *War and Peace* with Thackeray's *Vanity Fair* we see its superiority at social portrayal. Looking at English society of the early 1800's from outside his characters, Thackeray achieved a superb satire. But Tolstoy showed Russian society through the eyes of a protagonist of complete honesty and perception, and the result is more than just satire. Rather there is a quality of profound understanding and compassion accompanying the critical objectivity.

The moral for Southern writers, I think, is obvious. If they would write of the Civil War with the breadth and penetration of great literature, they must be willing to bring to the Confederacy not merely loyality but also understanding. They must write not in defense but in analysis. The defense will then take care of itself. Tolstoy did not seek to "defend" Napoleonic Russian life, but that was what he achieved. Similarly Southern writers must be willing to see the Civil War South, its soldiers, its noncombatants, for what they were, as individuals, and not as they represent certain preconceived social virtues. They must be willing to open up their regions and its armies to the insights of a Ham Chamberlayne. They must face up to the creation of a protagonist of intellectual depth and vision, through whose eyes the war and the society that fought it can be seen without the condescension that would be needed to force the story into the limited perceptions of a too literal, too restricted intelligence. Anything less will fall short of complete portrayal.

It is precisely here that *Gone with the Wind* fails. It has the requisite qualities of sweep and range, but where Miss Mitchell did not succeed was in her perception of character. Scarlett O'Hara is an interesting lady, and Rhett Butler a fine figure of a man, but neither sees deeply enough into what is happening to provide the perspectives that make *War and Peace* a great work of literature. Only Ashley Wilkes might have furnished the subtlety and depth to be to the embattled South what Bezukhov was for Napoleonic Russia. But Miss Mitchell never dared to venture into Ashley's mind. From first to last, *Gone with the Wind* is Scarlett's story, and therein the limitations of author and story are contained. To unfold a story of the range of *War and Peace,* Miss Mitchell could only provide the moral perceptions of a Becky Sharp, and even there she was the inferior of Thackeray in social discernment and satirical acuteness. She was never able to make Rhett Butler into an individual; he is a type at all times. Ashley Wilkes, whom she intended to be a type, is her only believable male character of any importance. The scenes of besieged and burning Atlanta, Scarlett's struggle for existence back at Tara after the evacuation, the mobilization of the Klan during the Reconstruction, are exceptionally fine action sequences, but they stand by themselves in an otherwise shallow story. Where underlying the events of *War and Peace* there is a profound philosophical and moral foundation, behind the events of *Gone with the Wind* there is nothing. The surface is often rich and glittering, but deeper than that Miss Mitchell could not go.

In his study of Civil War fiction, Robert A. Lively notes that "stories of Northern life are focused on the abilities and the characters of single heroes or heroines, individuals whose society is depicted as the hostile setting for their lonely struggles and ambitions. With a Southern writer, on the other hand, families or whole communities tend to divide the author's attention and stretch his canvas to cover a social rather than a personal scene."[23] The concentration on individuals possible to Northern novelists brought about a book like Stephen Crane's *The Red Badge of Courage,* in which the individual in battle, his subjective reactions, his fears and hopes, are everything. Crane produced an unforgettable picture of youth at war.

But that is all. The story exists in a vacuum; only the informed student can recognize it for a Civil War battle story, probably set in Chancellorsville. *The Red Badge of Courage* is the ultimate achievement in a completely subjective, completely isolated war

[23] P. 147.

narrative, with the protagonist existing without benefit of society, history, reflective thought, abstract idea, or accumulated knowledge.

I doubt that a Southerner could have written a book such as Crane's. Southern novelists, whether writing of the war or of other subjects, have never been able to view man alone, by himself, outside of any society, existing with no sense of past or future, thinking only of the immediate instant. In any Southern war novel the Confederate soldier would have to be a Confederate as well as a soldier, and the war cannot be separated from the region that fought the war. It is not the way of writers like Faulkner, Wolfe, Warren, and others to isolate a man from all that surrounds him and gives perspective to his life and thoughts. For Southern novelists man exists in a society, and they must fit him into it.

What the Southern novelist who would create a great Civil War novel can do is not to forsake his sense of society and history, but add to it the ability of a Crane to see the lonely individual soul as well. He must not let the society obscure the individual; rather he can look at the war and the society through the individual and create an individual capable of realizing the full psychological, social, and above all ethical dimensions of the subject. He can show the Civil War as a tremendous social cataclysm, but one that happened not to waxen images but to men, in a region peopled by individuals who are not stereotyped as social exemplars but released by a social code into their full stature as men. Through the perceptions of such a protagonist, the full tragedy of the Civil War might be captured in fiction.

4

MARY JOHNSTON AND THE HISTORIC IMAGINATION

LAWRENCE G. NELSON

WE ALL have wonderful lives," the heroine says in one of Mary Johnston's novels. "One is rich after this fashion, one after that." This is from *Hagar,* the one book of Miss Johnston's which comes closest perhaps to telling the truth of the inner life of Virginia's foremost historical novelist. It is the only novel of hers that has a contemporary setting;[1] the time is the late nineteenth century and the early twentieth. It is not of course autobiography; it is perhaps a dream of what the author's life might have been. The dreamy young Hagar lives in a world of wonder and reads a bit of everything in her grandfather's library, from mythology to Darwin's *Origin of Species.* She wants to write stories "like Hawthorne, like Poe" and does, despite Colonel Ashendyne's disapproving comment, "It isn't necessary for you to write, and in the Old South, at least, we've always rather deprecated that kind of thing for a woman" (p. 223). In her later life Mary Johnston wrote in her autobiographical notes that she "lived among people who were used to reading books but not to writing them." Hagar quietly goes her own

A LECTURE given for the Institute of Southern Culture at Longwood College, July 26, 1961.

[1] *Sweet Rocket* (1920) has a contemporary setting but it has little or no action and it is a very special kind of novelistic writing; it is a book of discussion and dream.

way, which is the way of a programmatic progressivism and an esoteric mysticism, and becomes an outspoken supporter of the radical causes of the day, political, social, and religious; she outrages her family by active participation in the cause of female suffrage, and in other ways.

Hagar is not a very good novel, though there are good things in it, as in all of Mary Johnston's work. It is an honest book and it is not hysterical, but it is overweighted with doctrine and its parts are not closely fused. The feminist speaks plainly enough: Hagar (and Miss Johnston) want to see woman as "mind undying, self-authoritative and unrelated, the arbiter of her own destiny, the definer of her own powers, with an equal goal and right-of-way" with man (p. 274). Hagar thinks of herself as an "idealist-realist," and so did Mary Johnston. There is exactness of observation in this writing, there are fine terse journalistic notations on contemporary events and personages, there is loving description of natural beauty, and there is the intense glow of unearthly romance that is always present in Mary Johnston's writing about the love of man and woman and the love of man and woman for the widened vision, the Sense of the Whole. Hagar steadfastly refuses to marry the properly conservative Virginia gentleman her family wish her to marry, and in the end finds someone of her own kind, a man who will let her live her own life. Hagar the Outcast clings to her vision and to the promise of the days ahead: she had from the beginning "a strange passion for the future, for all that might become" (p. 264) and "she never lost the child's and the poet's power of coalescence" (p. 196).

In *Hagar* the author's feeling for the future clashes sharply with her feeling for the past, and the resultant discord is not resolved by the continuous talk about the coming unity of science and mysticism, now "fairly within hailing distance of each other" (p. 251). All is one, no doubt, and it may be that in some sense All is in the Self and the Self is in All; I do not intend to pronounce upon the validity of the author's way of the spirit; the crucial problem here for Mary Johnston, as I see it, is how shall the visionary or prophetic imagination work in harmony with the historic imagination in the making of the historical novel?

Mary Johnston was visionary in grain, but she was also a deeply grained Virginian and a clear-eyed realist, superbly fitted by heritage and training to recreate in tragic romance the history of Virginia and of the South. Let us try to understand what she was, what she tried to do, and what she actually did. *Hagar* is only one of her twenty-two novels; it appeared in 1913, when the author was forty-three years old. It was her eighth novel and there were fourteen that came later, of various sorts and of varying degrees of excellence, but all of them marked indelibly by a certain magical or visionary quality of mind and spirit, an intense and fervent romanticism or an intense and fervent romantic transcendentalism or transcendental intuitionism (I'm not sure what to call this extraordinary quality of vision) tempered by a native realism. Like most writers and like most of us ordinary mortals Mary Johnston was a mixture of qualities, idealist and realist, transcendental dreamer and hard student of historical happening, a strong-minded feminist who celebrated the heroic virtues of men, gentle and simple, aristocrat and commoner. She never married and I know of no love affair in which she was involved. She was subject to repeated illnesses but kept a strong mind and a stout heart; she was frail but indomitable.

She was, as she tells us in autobiographical notes preserved in the Johnston Papers at the University of Virginia,[2] a dreamy, self-centered child and girl. She had only a few months of formal education but read voraciously in her father's library, well stocked with historical writings and all the English and American classics in prose and poetry and drama. Her mother's death left her at sixteen the domestic head of a large household, with five younger sisters and brothers. Her hard experience in practical management did not change her essential nature; fact and dream were both alive and real in her.

Poetry was living in her from the beginning, and romance. She liked storytelling and she revealed talent in composition at an early age. When she was about six or seven she was riding past a wood

[2] The Johnston Papers in the Alderman Library at the University of Virginia are a rich and varied collection of letters, diaries, notebooks, manuscripts, pictures, clippings, and the like, all directly related to the life and work of Mary Johnston. I regret that I was able to examine only a very small portion of this extensive collection.

and as she stared dreamily at it these magical words sprang up in her mind, *Therein my love lieth,* and she began to frame faery verses and fantasies. Here began, I imagine, a lifelong romance between the girl Mary Johnston and great creating Nature. In *Miss Delicia Allen,* Miss Johnston's next to the last book, published in 1933, an old great-aunt says, "I have a notion that the mass of things start—or maybe are suddenly recollected, picked up and swung along with—in infancy" (p. 288).

Let us hear her own words about herself.

> In the enormous land of Letters the great region called Idealism was by nature my region. And I was born in the enchanted forest called Romance. It was native to me to begin, to continue, to write Romance. Nowadays it is spiritual romance that I begin, as inexpertly as ever, to try to give body to, but when I began it was the straightforward romance, the romance that isn't ending either, of adventure, of tragic or lyric circumstance, of the love of man and woman.[3]

Here is the plain truth, set down with modesty but with clarity and force. Poetry, and romance, and idealism; and now one more necessary ingredient to make the mixture thick and firm: history. "I cared deeply for poetry and I cared for history. I was born with the historic sense, the historic imagination. The sense of waves, of currents, of direction; the sense of process." And again: "I have what is called the historic imagination. All times are to me my own time,—I have the sense of continuity,—ancestral life is nothing more nor less than the love of the Whole."

This is the historic imagination certainly, and the visionary imagination too; and the question rises, whether one of these kinds of imagination is an imperfect or a perfected form of the other, whether one is a diseased or corrupt form of the other, or whether they are in some way one. I cannot say.

This advanced conservative Southerner also tells us that the "chief intellectual struggle" of her life was "away from dogma in religion." She sought "wider and deeper being for us all" (*The*

[3] This quotation and those in the first, third, and fourth paragraphs following, except for the quotations from novels, are from autobiographical notes in the Johnston Papers. My excerpts were mostly taken from typed transcripts of the author's writing, which is not easy to read; the transcripts are probably not letter-perfect.

Wanderers, p. 382). She could say, with Swedenborg and others, that "God is Total and Divine Man" (*Michael Forth,* p. 17). What is said in *Foes* is undoubtedly her own belief: "I am Christian, where Christ is taken very universally—the higher Self, the mounting Wisdom of us all" (p. 110). Another expression of faith could link this antinomian free-thinker with the more orthodox sort: "Every one is Satan and every one is Christ and every one is that third who moves from Satan into Christ" (*Michael Forth,* p. 339).

There were other things and people wherein Mary Johnston's love deeply lay: Virginia, especially the great Valley of Virginia and the mountains of her native county of Botetourt; the family she took care of; her father, John William Johnston, lawyer, legislator, and railway executive, and the Old Order for which he had fought as captain, later major, of the Botetourt Artillery. "I was born," she wrote, "in an impoverished state of battle-grounds and impassioned memories and a clinging of the heart, as fervent as it was natural, to a dead and gone Social Order."

The "historic imagination" in Mary Johnston, nourished by Scott and Shakespeare and by most of her uninhibited reading, by her natural piety, her devotion to her family heritage, by her native sense of poetry and romance, and by the romantic history of her beloved Virginia, led her inevitably to the writing of those first stories which she called "straightforward romances," "the romance that isn't ending either." The times were right, at the turn of the century, for this way of writing. She pleased hundreds of thousands of readers; with these early novels she scored the most spectacular popular success since *Uncle Tom's Cabin* and before *Gone with the Wind.* She needed money to make up for her father's financial reverses, and she made a great deal of money. She spent a great deal of money on travel; she made repeated trips abroad, with her father and with other members of her family, to England, to the Continent, to the Middle East.

The old enduring straightforward historical romance of adventure and of the bittersweet of love can be and often is a stereotype, a thing of shreds and patches, of technicolor tinsel and trapping; it can be routine cloak-and-sword heroics, mechanized melodrama, blood-and-thunder juvenile. Mary Johnston's writing, especially her early writing, has sometimes been confused with these copies of the real thing, these false Florimels, but it is not of this order, though at times it has shadings of all these. The genuine stuff of serious and responsible art is there: the sense of actual and meaningful history; purposeful action, heroic and ignoble and in between; characters of all sorts, good and bad and mixed, somewhat enlarged but not inhuman, not incredible; sound motivation and structure. This popular writer had basic common sense, restraint, a clear vision of daylight realities. And always there is that clear, high, unique note of authentic earthly and unearthly romance conjoined that gives to the writing of Mary Johnston a sustained magical radiance and resonance, a faery light and sound that plays over sea and land and in the heavens too. She and her writings were even from the beginning as soft as moonlight and as hard as the everlasting rock upon which the moonlight sleeps.

No doubt many readers and critics of today would not be inclined to accept this rather glowing estimate of Mary Johnston's 'prentice pieces. In the middle thirties of this century, at the time of the author's death in 1936, her narrative effects were described as "part tinsel, part silk, part old-fashioned stage-illusion."[4] She wrote, it was said, "rosy-hued, swashbuckling novels, skimming the surface of thought and reveling in action." Romance periodically comes upon evil days and there are always those readers and critics who entertain no very high opinion of the historical novel, whatever be the degree of serious art in it. One must make distinctions, as carefully as one can, between the shoddy and the genuine, and one must make a place for the highhearted tale of love and adventure when it is superior and distinctive. One perceptive critic, Edward Wagenknecht, writing in the *Sewanee Review* in 1936,[5] clearly separated the work of Mary Johnston from the mass of popular lightweight cloak-and-sword romances. These narratives of hers, he said in effect, are highly colored but they are not overcolored; there are

[4] Stanley J. Kunitz and Howard Haycraft, *Twentieth Century Authors* (New York, 1942), s.v. "Mary Johnston," pp. 732f. The quotation at the end of the paragraph is also from this source.

[5] "The World and Mary Johnston," *Sewanee Review*, XLIV (April-June, 1936), 188-206. In the Johnston Papers there is a copy of an earlier version of this article which the author sent to Miss Johnston.

conventionalisms in them but they are conventionalisms deliberately accepted, shaped, and ordered. Another early critical judgment does fine justice to the artistry of the young Mary Johnston and the older Mary Johnston too: "Her facts were sound, her storymaking instincts true, and . . . she did not know how to be uninteresting."

The critic of 1936 was already making a minority report. "Miss Johnston's position in our contemporary literature is somewhat anomalous. Twenty-five years ago her romances of colonial Virginia were selling by the hundreds of thousands. Today she is a neglected writer."[6] This or something like this must still be said today. But I shall say more on this point in a later section of this essay.

Mary Johnston's first romances were *Prisoners of Hope* (1898), *To Have and to Hold* (1900), *Audrey* (1902), and *Sir Mortimer* (1904). They are the work of a dreamy girl who has matured into responsible adult womanhood and seeks fitting embodiment of her dreams. She has worked hard at the historical records of Virginia's early centuries; she knew what happened probably as well as any scholar of the period at the turn of the century; she writes with controlled imagination what might have happened, and as we read we believe that it really did happen.

The language in these prose romances is poetical and Elizabethan, that is, it is fanciful, gay, ardent, vigorous, at times direct and slashing, at times courtly, mannered, euphuistic. Shakespeare is probably her primary inspiration in mood and manner of expression. The narrative has "something of the strength and fragrance of Elizabethan and early Jacobean work," a distinctive quality which Mary Johnston found in the earliest writings out of Virginia and commented on in her little history book, *Pioneers of the Old South,*[7] published in 1918. But the composition and the idiom in these stories are all her own; nobody else would have written in quite this way.

This then is traditional romance with a new Virginia accent. For this is the New World along with the old; these are the heroic beginning times, the founding years of Virginia, when "Red America, black Africa, white Europe" (*Miss Delicia Allen,* p. 301) came together and fought and oppressed each other in a new hemisphere. These are the great days of discovery, wandering, colonization,

[6] *Ibid.,* p. 188. [7] New Haven, p. 101.

battles and besiegements, piracies, massacres, gold hunting, slave hunting; the times of heroic enterprise and frustration, failure, tragedy, and triumph. These are the years "wrought of gold and iron,"[8] the Golden Age and the Iron Age that are also the setting of Sidney's *Arcadia* and Spencer's *Faerie Queene.* For Mary Johnston's romance is the romance of inclusion, not of exclusion; it has strength, inner coherence, form, and a base of historical truth. She is writing of life, "that may now be gold, now iron, but never again dull lead" (*Audrey,* p. 321).

The sense of tragedy is strong even in these early books. This tragic sense was in Mary Johnston from the beginning; it rises out of a patrician, conservative, and traditional vision of life and Mary Johnston was patrician, conservative, and traditional to the core of her being, though with a difference. Her themes arise out of the passions of men in time and history, out of their ambitions, jealousies, rivalries, and the havoc and desolation they cause. The struggle for power is a pervasive theme in all her writings in one form or another. "Who should rule, and who should be ruled?" she asks in her *History* (p. 62). "Here is an extremely old and important question, settled in history only to be unsettled again. Everywhere it rises, dust on Time's road, and is laid only to rise again." The conflicts grow more intense in the later books but they are present vividly enough in the first stories. The writing is impassioned, but the ruling spirit of it is detached and judicial; it is also generous and sympathetic. The author shares the fine feeling of the simple girl Betty in *Prisoners of Hope,* who is sorry for all the oppressed and persecuted, slaves, servants, Indians, Quakers (p. 41). Two of these four romances end happily, after great trial and suffering, *To Have and to Hold* and *Sir Mortimer;* the first book, *Prisoners of Hope,* ends in the separation of the lovers, and *Audrey* ends in sudden but unsurprising tragedy when Audrey is killed when she saves her lover Haward from being killed. Love is a great reconciler, but Love's ways are hard.

These books have substance and realism along with their many colors of romance. *To Have and to Hold,* best seller of 1900, is now a part of our literary heritage, along with *The Three Musketeers,*

[8] *Ibid.,* p. 95; there said of the notable year 1619.

Don Quixote, and the *Arabian Nights.* Stark Young wrote a spontaneous appreciatory postscript in a letter to Mary Johnston in 1936: "I shall never forget the high rapture when I had finished *To Have and to Hold.*"[9] With that I shall leave these writings which are Mary Johnston's initiation into the world of imagination and history, the first chapters in a lifelong Discovery of America and the South.

Problems of caste and conscience that made their first appearance in the early novels are heightened and deepened in *Lewis Rand,* a long, ambitious creation that was years in the making. It appeared in 1908, the year following *The Goddess of Reason,* Mary Johnston's only completed verse drama, a respectable performance that had a modest success on the stage in Boston, Philadelphia, and New York with Julia Marlowe in the leading role. But Mary Johnston's best poetry is in prose, not in blank verse. *Lewis Rand* is a powerful full-length tragedy centered in the rise and fall of a Jeffersonian Democrat, a *Novus Homo* risen from the people and desperately entangled in the coils of his own nature.

The tobacco roller's son, a favored disciple of Jefferson and in double rivalry with the Whig patrician Ludwell Cary, wins both political power and the love of Jacqueline Churchill, allied by blood and breeding with the conservative Cary clan. He is unable to control his vaulting ambitions and gets involved in the Aaron Burr conspiracy in the western lands. Here again is the gold and iron of tragedy and romance fatefully intermingled. It is like Shakespearean tragedy, a remorseless study of man invoking his doom through the deep compulsions of his own nature. The story looks to be a subtle and ingenious following of the tragedies of Macbeth and Othello both. Love and hate and the passion for power play a complicated secret game in the heart of the rising Democrat. He is saved from the abyss of the conspiracy by his magnanimous rival, and by Jefferson too, who now must disown his foster son; Rand in a passion of fury and resentment murders the high-minded Ludwell Cary; Cary's brother Fairfax slowly draws the net of detection around Rand, who moves through a hell of remorse to cleansing confession just before Cary comes to certain knowledge of the identity of the murderer of his brother.

[9] Johnston Papers.

Lewis Rand is one of Mary Johnston's most successful romances; she wrote that it seemed to her the best work she had done but she was "not blindly fond of it."[10] In this book she moves into the heart of Shakespearean tragedy, wherein man's virtues and vices can assume each other's form and hide in each other's secret places, and his purest choices and intentions bring him to disaster. Miss Delicia Allen knew something of this tragic twilight: "Oh, the twining streams of knowledge and of ignorance, and neither running clear, not clear knowledge, not pure ignorance" (p. 229)!

The complex and tragic errors in the historical relation of man and woman now rose to the forefront of Miss Johnston's mind. In 1909, in Richmond, she joined the Equal Suffrage League of Virginia and labored in that cause. She makes her position clear: "While I am a suffragist, I am not simply suffragist; I am feminist rather than suffragist. And while I am feminist, I am not simply feminist; I am humanist rather than feminist."[11] This proud and forthright pronouncement was probably true, in her sense of the meaning of those particular words. She wrote to Thomas Nelson Page in 1910 asking his support of the movement.[12] He replied with a polite no, and then asked her to leave such matters to those who in effect had nothing better to do. This is rather like Turgenev's letter to Tolstoy asking the great novelist of the Russian people to give over his fanatical obsessions about religion and return to his proper field of work, literature.

In this same letter to Page, Mary Johnston spoke of her next book, which was to be about the war; she said that she saw bands of ragged, hungry, heroic Confederates everywhere. For years she saw them and she traced their movements all over Virginia and the South. The work was first planned as three volumes, centering in turn upon the Confederate generals Jackson, Johnston, and Lee; it was in the end published in two volumes, a mighty composition of over 1,100 pages. It seems to me to be her finest creation, her

[10] Notation in diary, Johnston Papers.

[11] Johnston Papers.

[12] Page's letter is preserved in the Johnston Papers. Both letters were edited by John R. Robertson and printed in the *Virginia Magazine of History and Biography*, LXIV (July, 1956), 286-90, under the title, "Two Virginia Novelists on Woman's Suffrage."

magnum opus, and I shall return to it after some necessarily brief comment on the novels that followed.

Mary Johnston held stubbornly to the beliefs that overwhelmed the novel *Hagar* (1913), but her art is finer in the next three books. *The Witch* (1914) and *The Fortunes of Garin* (1915) are superior tales of high adventure, the one set in King James's witch-hunting England of the early seventeenth century and in the New World also for a time, the other in the golden dawn of courtly love in twelfth-century France. *The Wanderers* (1917) is a unique Book of Love, or Book of Woman; it is a series of short narratives portraying the changing relations of man and woman in history from the early days of man to the French Revolution. These are all masterly inventions and of great interest; they are highly colored labors of love and of the historic imagination, though it seems to me that Miss Johnston had no very clear understanding of classical Protestantism. I suppose it was not to be expected that she would approve the theology of Luther or of Calvin.

In these three books the visionary or prophetic imagination is finely fused with the "historic imagination"; at least there is no very obvious trace of dissonance. The next three books, Miss Johnston's postwar writings, are another matter. The great world conflict probably had something to do with the loss of harmony and balance in these fictions, and illness also very likely made its contribution to the disastrous imbalance.

Foes (1918) returns to the theme of the conquest of hate by a love that is aware of Identity and Oneness; the story is a "straightforward romance" of the Jacobite uprising in England of 1745, despite the overcharge of mysticism toward the end. *Michael Forth* (1919) is a full-blown "spiritual romance" from the start. It is another ambitious version of the Quest of the "I" or the beyond-man or superman in a pleasant authentic Virginia setting of home and university in the beginning; when the pilgrims go to Africa the story is lost and drowned in continuous waves of transcendental apperceptions or recollections or intimations of Identity and Oneness on the part of almost everybody in the party. The book is an amazing mixture of narrative and preachment, direct and indirect, and it shows some residual skill in the management of the mixture. The family home in Virginia sings its old ballad from beginning to end (pp. 32, 359). The home-town pastor, befuddled by esoteric talk of planes and states of being and degrees of awareness, breaks out vigorously, "I hate all the new-fangled lingo!" and the narrator Michael laughs gently and agrees that "language was yet Boeotian" (p. 360).

Sweet Rocket (1920) has a magical charm in the sweetness and radiance of its setting, but there is no story at all, the whole pleasant band of kindred spirits devoting themselves wholeheartedly to intensification of perception, higher vibration, superconsciousness, and the like. Poetry yields to prophecy, and the visionary imagination has clearly driven the historic imagination off the field.

A critic in the *Bookman* of 1922[13] wrote pleasantly and tolerantly of the "mystical welter" and "metaphysical maze" in these three doctrinal books but thought that the author had found her story again in *Silver Cross* and in *1492* without sacrificing the "spiritual implications." I agree. These two books both appeared in 1922. The first is a small but enchanting creation, the adventures of a monk and a courtesan in the quest of love and the spiritual realities behind the shows of organized religion; the time is the early sixteenth century. The other returns to the New World at its very beginning, and is a superb novel of aspiration and discovery and the golden and the iron side of exploration and settlement. The narrator, a Spanish Jew, faithfully records the epic tale of glory and shame and begins to make discoveries within himself. The historic imagination comes into its own again in this detailed account of the whole achievement of the great admiral, Christopher Columbus.

Mary Johnston writes best about "pilgrims, adventurers, explorers, poets—all the race of romance" (*Michael Forth,* p. 329), but much depends upon just what they are looking for and where and how. She needed, I think, the substance of actual historical event for ballast and balance; she needed this solid earth and time and space, and she has all that in her best historical fictions. I think she was now fully aware of the perils of doctrinaire writing, of an art that loses its integral meaning in peripheral preachment. Whether her characteristic message was authentic and valuable New Thought

[13] Unsigned article, "The Literary Spotlight, X: Mary Johnston," *Bookman,* LV (July, 1922), 491-95.

or an old and illusory Gnosticism, it is not my business to say; it seems to me to be an odd and sometimes an oddly attractive mixture of the old and the new.

Mary Johnston lived in the present as much as any of us and was a capable manager of her own affairs; according to all reports she was interested in people and in their affairs too; she was not a recluse, though no doubt she had her reticences and withdrawals. The present, though, was not the right material for her art; she had a passion for the past and a passion for the future. Her passion for the past was not sentimental archaism; she knew that we make our present out of our past. She wanted to know the whole story and its meaning, and her way of knowing was to write historical novels, history filled out and made real by the historic and dramatic imagination. And she had a passion for the future which impelled her to write visionary and prophetic romances of the spirit, for she was convinced that a great change, a vast increase in spiritual awareness, was coming into our life as one individual man and woman after another gained "unitary consciousness," and she wanted to picture the premonitory and preparatory forms of the new awareness in her historical fictions.

The stories she writes are real stories and yet they are also meant to be true histories, that is historically plausible initiations into what she assumed to be intellectual and spiritual freedom ("all sense grown one and lifted into emotion grown music, and thought changed to light"—*Miss Delicia Allen,* p. 306), men and women learning to know themselves and each other. This evolutionistic view of human experience ("the savage receding, the man beckoning, the after man watching from afar"—*Lewis Rand,* p. 24) drew her from regionalism to a sort of universalism; but she instinctively kept coming back to her region and its history, drawing strength and authenticity from native wells of fact and endeavor. She sometimes got lost in the present and in the a-historical future; she never got lost in the past, certainly not in the past of her native region.

After the books of 1922 there followed four excellent tales of the New World and one visionary piece set in no known world. *Croatan* (1923), *The Great Valley* (1926), and *Hunting Shirt* (1931) are all three extraordinarily fine stories of the Virginia western frontier and life with the Indians. *Croatan* is the story of Raleigh's lost colony, living with friendly Indians, and especially of the happy settlement of a love affair in which three young men, English, Indian, and Spanish, are in love with the girl Virginia Dare, who for a time serves as prophetess for another tribe who call her Dawn-of-the-High-Day. *The Great Valley* is a more complex and even better narrative of the separation of a couple caused by an Indian raid and their final happy reunion after the wife has lived with the Indians more or less happily and has borne a child to the chief who has married her. The inner spiritual action is as important as the outer, and both actions are handled with a fine restrained imagination. *Hunting Shirt* is an American *Foes,* with an Appalachian frontier setting, a simpler and more believable version of the pursuit for revenge, and a mysterious change of hate to love and brotherhood between the white man and the red man he had been stalking. Intertwined in this story is an exquisite idyl in the romance of Hunting Shirt with a white girl brought up by Indians. There is homely realism in these stories of the frontier and there is the eldritch beauty of unearthly romance that we have come to expect in the writing of Mary Johnston.

The Slave Ship (1924) is a raw, powerful narrative of the slave trade in the eighteenth century. A young Byronic Jacobite, shipped to the colonies after Culloden, escapes to the horrors of a slaver captained by a pious cousin; he is hardened to the ugly business, but slowly the change comes, aided by Quaker reform movements, and he arrives at the transcendental vision of God as the Greater Self and so is strong enough to return to his original servitude and endure it. The action in this novel is authentic, and the abundance of transcendental talk has dramatic value.

The hero sees slaves everywhere in the Great Ship of Slaves that is Society. "The slave both cannot and must free himself, and there is your paradox. . . To find in the dark, without fingers, a catch or spring that may or may not be there—there being everywhere" (p. 243)! The answer to the existentialist *angst,* the agony of separate existence, is the One that is all selves; and the answer leads to another agonized question: "God knows how we can be One Thing that hates and hurts itself so, and can't give messages to itself from itself . . . one tragic, pitiful, insane Thing" (p. 248)! "These seas and these islands have a terrible history. Well, that is man" (p. 184)! This virile book is probably meant to shock and then bring healing to the wound it gives.

The Exile (1927) is another visionary piece somewhat like *Sweet Rocket* except that there is a little more action in this story, and the time is presumably in the future. The characters and their talk have charm and distinction; the action seems to be of no great consequence. The book, though, remains in the mind rather like a piece of music, perhaps because of the spellbound atmosphere of the island.

Mary Johnston's last two books, *Miss Delicia Allen* (1933) and *Drury Randall* (1934), move back into familiar territory, western Virginia around the time of the war. The war itself seems not to be the central action in either book, especially not in the second one, in which the protagonist hates the war, goes the way of a conscientious objector and a liberal journalist, a later and more mature Hagar. He too hunts the game of Self, "the stag of ten," and learns to endure the tragedy of the loss by drowning of his wife and children. The mood of reconciliation dominates these two books; one might suppose that they were deliberately contrived to heal and cover over some of the old breaches between the author and her native region; but this is only a conjecture. One is reminded at times of the last plays of Shakespeare, centering on family reunion after separation.

Miss Delicia Allen seems to me to be the better book, a richer and wiser invention, but here too some of the action is not easy to explain. There is more Virginia history and tradition in this book than in *Drury Randall.* Her grandfather takes the young Delicia to see the last Indians go from the South: "1619 to 1844, and year by year the Indians falling westward and Africa coming to stand in the land, like the corn and the tobacco and the cotton and the rice" (p. 18). The life of the plantation and the close relation of master and slave are vividly pictured in this book, also details of family and family connections in the region and in England. Delicia gives up her English lover, a poet who is already married, and in the end turns to her old childhood playmate, finding a home in him, in Virginia, and in the world too.

Perhaps Miss Johnston was beginning to accept the present and the modern world. But she didn't quite know what to do with it. Nor did it know what to do with her; it seemed simply to move away from her, uninterested in her high achievement, which cannot be denied but can be forgotten. She began to lose her vast reading audience in the years immediately after the First World War and apparently nothing she did after that was sufficiently attractive to get back her following. Perhaps it was her bizarre metaphysics that alienated the reading public. The critics found her difficult to handle, her transcendentalism intractable.

The writer of the 1922 *Bookman* piece is an honorable exception; he treats her with respect and speaks some fine truths about her.

> She is a pacifist, but perfectly ready to describe a battle up to the hilt; her description will shirk nothing but will be free from such hopeless embitterment as Barbusse's. She is a mystic bent upon the expressive embodiment of what eye hath not seen and ear hath not heard until she saw and heard it; but she is absolutely without the proselyting zeal and spirit. She is a tolerant dissenter from many men's thoughts and ideals; yet to know her is to respect her work, however much you dislike it . . . and to honor her purpose and admire her courage in a difficult adherence.[14]

Other readers and critics of the thirties and thereafter were unwilling to make her acquaintance and to learn to know her work. Again there is an honorable exception; and there may be others that I have not come upon. Edward Wagenknecht in the 1936 *Sewanee Review* article surveys Miss Johnston's whole body of work with fine discernment. His judgments are mostly favorable; he chiefly stresses the futuristic transcendentalism of the later novels and sees in the characters "allotropes" of "the New Man, the New Woman that the age is even now in process of developing."[15] This is certainly one legitimate way of reading the romances of Mary Johnston.

But most people seemed not to read her at all. She became increasingly neglected, ignored, and misunderstood. Devotees of a tendentious new realism began to scale down her achievement, to diminish or dismiss it as old-fashioned romanticism. Most of the standard histories of American literature and studies of the American novel in the last three decades either say nothing very much to

[14] *Ibid.*, p. 495. [15] Wagenknecht, p. 191.

the purpose about her work or set it alongside the novels of John Esten Cooke, Thomas Nelson Page, Maurice Thompson, and Winston Churchill in the "Southern succession" that is called a "line of filiation that connects Cooper with the rebirth of historical romance near the end of the century."[16] A critical comment on her books at the time of her death is probably representative of the most favorable opinion of that day; the notice centers on "the rich concentration of evocative detail and magically compelling historic atmosphere" in Mary Johnston's writing and says that she is, "however minor, in the authentic tradition of the great Sir Walter."[17]

There has never been a collected edition of the novels of Mary Johnston, and today all her books are out of print except for the little history, *Pioneers of the Old South,* and *To Have and to Hold* in cloth and paperback. This is not a matter for surprise; *habent sua fata libelli,* superior books even must yield to their destiny. But I can't help wondering if this is the right destiny for a productive and distinguished writer who is "probably the most powerful of the

[16] Robert E. Spiller and others, *Literary History of the United States* (New York, 1948), I, 610. Here are a few other representative judgments:

Alexander Cowie in *The Rise of the American Novel* (New York, 1951), p. 472, says that "Thomas Nelson Page and Mary Johnston are approximately in the same line as Cooke."

A. H. Quinn in his *American Fiction* (New York, 1936), pp. 501-4, discusses the work of Mary Johnston in a chapter, XXII, on "The Romance of History and Politics"; he calls her "the most consistently productive of the historical novelists," admits her skill in the recreation of atmosphere, says that her characters "speak in that stilted artificial language which is the chief blemish of the minor writers of the historical romance."

Edward Wagenknecht prints a shorter version of his *Sewanee Review* article of 1936 in his book, *Cavalcade of the American Novel* (New York, 1952), under the title, "Allotropes and Mary Johnston," in Chapter X ("Some Southern Novelists of the 'Nineties and After"), pp. 197-203. The book is inscribed "In Memory of Mary Johnston American Novelist" and has a quotation from *Michael Forth* on the dedicatory page.

Harlan Hatcher in *Creating the Modern American Novel* (New York, 1935), p. 18, in a comparison of Stephen Crane and Mary Johnston says that Crane "eschews the romantic attitude toward the Civil War so dear to the Mary Johnstons"; on p. 19 are some critical strictures on the Gettysburg chapter in *Cease Firing.*

Maxwell Geismar, *Rebels and Ancestors: The American Novel, 1890-1915* (Boston, 1953), p. 385, speaks of F. Marion Crawford, Charles Major, and Mary Johnston as "nostalgic or forgotten names now"; on page 44 he seems to accuse Crawford and Johnston of a "sort of literary deception or charlatanry."

[17] Kunitz and Haycraft, pp. 732f.

entire American school of historical romancers"[18] and who is, despite her obvious flaws, her limited range of characterization, her overuse of favorite themes and structural patterns of development, her insistent perverse intrusive metaphysics, perhaps the most distinctive and valuable American historical novelist after Cooper and Simms.

Temperamental faults and deficiencies in men and in authors are inalienably conjoined with their highest capabilities in their finest and most characteristic work. In Mary Johnston's novels of the War between the States, *The Long Roll* (1911) and *Cease Firing* (1912), all the "forms of imagination" that I have fancied were the author's —the lyrical, the prophetic, the visionary, the epical, the dramatic, and the historic—are for once rightly bound together in an intense and continued unity of creative effort to produce the work I have called her masterpiece. To speak a little proudly, Blake and Milton here touch hands and join forces, and Swedenborg and his aides retire from the field of battle, though still overlooking the conflict from afar.

The *Bookman* critic of 1922 said that Mary Johnston's Civil War novels "did not lessen her huge and loyal following." *Time* said in 1936 in a brief notice of the death of the author that they were "dear to the hearts of all ex-Confederates," and it may be that they have been read by a goodly number of "common readers" continuously up to this present. At any rate they have lived on in old home libraries, especially in the South, and in secondhand bookshops; and they have usually held their high place in serious literary history, especially of the last ten or twelve years.[19] But their enduring value

[18] Francis Butler Simkins, *A History of the South* (New York, 1953), p. 438.

[19] Quinn, pp. 503-4, writes favorably of these books: "there is a reality in the atmosphere, a sense of tragic struggle against odds, which is very appealing"; but he finds the action clogged and the fictional characters submerged by the wealth of military material.

Ernest E. Leisy in *The American Historical Novel* (Norman, Okla., 1950), p. 17, says they are "old style" "in many respects"; on p. 165 he sees in them "a real achievement in following the record and in understanding the struggle"; here also he finds that "the wealth of historical detail clogs the action of the story."

Sheldon Van Auken in his article on the Southern historical novel in the *Journal of Southern History*, XIV (May, 1948), 169f., writes of these novels of

I think has not been rightly asserted or demonstrated. For this, in my opinion, is Mary Johnston's finest achievement; this is the book (the two volumes may be taken as one work) she had to write, the one she worked at the hardest and at the height of her energies of mind and will. It is right that she essayed and brought to completion this large fiction and history of the Confederacy; she was the one person who wanted and was able to tell the whole story in definitive fictional-historical form from the Beginning to the End.

This prose epic of the Confederacy[20] is Mary Johnston's best history and her finest fiction, the consummate expression of her love of her state and her region and her family and family heritage. This is the nearest thing we have in American literature to *War and Peace*. But there was no peacetime in the new nation of the South; it was born in war and came to an end in war. The very names given to the two volumes are military: the drum rolls that meant action and the cessation of hostilities. The books are inscribed to veteran warriors, Mary Johnston's father and her cousin. Both volumes are dedicated "To the Memory of John William Johnston, Major of Artillery, C. S. A. and of Joseph Eggleston Johnston, General, C. S. A." Most of the significant military campaigns of the war are recreated in detail, not only in Virginia but all over the South.

This book is Mary Johnston's finest piece of poetry, a massive epical romance in prose, an extended ode or elegy for the dead Confederacy, a monumental work of the historic imagination. It is a highly organized mixture of history and romance and tragedy and comedy, and pastoral and folk tale and fable and legend; it is a rite of oblation endlessly repeated; it is probably the completest and the most authentic embodiment of the Southern Myth. It may not be a great novel, but it is a strange and strangely attractive and unique piece of work, very much like the strange attractive unique

Mary Johnston: "Perhaps no southern war novel so accurate historically and so detailed was published between *Cease Firing* and Clifford Dowdey's *Bugles Blow No More* (1937)."

Robert A. Lively in *Fiction Fights the Civil War* (Chapel Hill, 1957), p. 59, says too that Mary Johnston's two books and Clifford Dowdey's *Bugles* are notable for their accuracy but that the reality of their characters is destroyed by the burden of historical detail.

[20] John Calvin Metcalf, *American Literature* (Richmond, 1914), p. 342: "These works form a sort of prose epic of that mighty struggle."

nation that was a-borning for four years and never really got to live, the gallant, absurd, proud, foolish, bookish, chivalric, ignorant, sentimental, nostalgic, pastoral, artless Doric Dixieland, with its love of rhetoric, its devotion to family, and its obsessive addiction to tradition and sentiment, piety and violence.

I don't know whether this Southland ever existed or not, but it lives in these books, in this loving, detailed, imaginative reconstruction of the time and the region. This writing has all the mixed qualities, the closely allied faults and virtues, of the author and of the order of life she is writing about; it is a rare compound of history and literature, of actuality and aspiration. There seems to me to be in the book and in its author and in the region as recreated in the book a fine, precarious unity of being, wrought by simplicity, an ingrained Greco-Roman idealism, and a passionate loyalty to the person, to Nature, and to the old ways. An unsympathetic reader might think there is too much history in the book, too much military detail; he might say, as some critics have said, that the story and the characters are submerged under the weight of documentation. Or he might say that the speech of the lovers and other leading characters is conventional or "literary," of an old-fashioned or antique order of sensibility.

I think I can understand this criticism but I would say in return that it is not rightly centered on the special quality and purpose of the book. But I am a partisan reader and critic. There are those who say that they got most of their knowledge of English (and Scottish) history out of the novels of Scott and Shakespeare's English history plays, and there are no doubt many readers of Tolstoy who prefer the *War and Peace* version of the Napoleonic campaigns of 1805 and thereafter to exact documented history. I suppose I got most of my not very extensive knowledge of the Confederacy out of these very books and the somewhat similar but lesser writings of John Esten Cooke, Thomas Nelson Page, Sidney Lanier, and others, and I shall have to add the name of Thomas Dixon, Jr., and, for the other side, a few lives of generals and some not very impressive books by Edward Payson Roe.

Mary Johnston is of course partisan too. She writes, "My idea is to state the case for the South at once and definitively and then through all the remaining chapters to leave alone all bitterness, all recrimination, all abstract rights and wrongs."[21] She does not hold entirely to this purpose but she does tell the truth as she knew the truth, without rancor and without fear. Hers was a book of war and war was abhorrent to this frail, sensitive, spiritual woman. But she was determined to write the story, chiefly for her father as she says, and she carried it through to the end.

The whole view of war is in these books, as it is likely to be in all superior epical or historical poetry or fiction—*War and Peace, Henry V,* the *Iliad.* War is a great beast, it is reversion to savagery, it is barbaric and elemental force and cruelty, it is stupid and absurd, it is "a hard necessity and a savage pastime," and yet it seems also to be a glorious adventure, a high cause, with nobility in it and chivalry and goodness and love. It is a "great and deep Cup of Trembling! . . . It's universal destruction," Margaret Cleave tells her children near the beginning of the story (*LR,* p. 23); near the end the author quotes good authority on this point: " 'War is Hell,' said Sherman, and is qualified to know whereof he speaks" (*CF,* p. 407).

Most of the characters know they live in a world of puzzling contradictions. An anonymous soldier says of war, "It ain't exactly Christian, and it's so damned avoidable" (*CF,* p. 42). Another, "seeing that men have always warred and I reckon are always going to war," proposes a macabre *reductio ad absurdum,* imagining the earth a smooth round battlefield, "just a nice, smooth, black, eternal plain—with maybe one wide river to carry the blood away" (*CF,* p. 408). Margaret Cleave, again, tells the truth in a sort of poetry: "Oh, the world, the world that it is! Oh, the divided heart of it, the twisted soul, the bitter and the sweet and the dark and the light" (*CF,* pp. 213f.). This is the ruling or constitutive metaphor and the tragic theme at the heart of this book and of all Mary Johnston's books, the idea of spiritual division or dismemberment, "a unity that tears its own flesh" (*CF,* p. 289), the civil war that is always going on everywhere, in the relation of man and man, of man and woman, in individual man, in society, in nature, in nations, and in the universe. The centered figure spreads its tentacles of meaning every-

[21] Diary notes, Johnston Papers.

where in the book, the hard question echoes and reechoes in all reaches of the story and there are all sorts of tentative answers and none of them clear or definitive.

This is a great traditional theme, this question that has no positive answer, for the question is rooted in the tragic existence of humankind, from which arises the tragic vision of things as they are and as they will be. In this book there can be no solution in a turn to esoteric metaphysics, though there is some talk now and then of a better way; and this talk also has thematic significance. Two of the leading characters agree near the end that this is not the way to settle it: "It is not, and it never was, and it never will be. And that despite the glamour and the cry of 'Necessity!' . . . the necessity is to find a more heroic way" (*CF*, pp. 448f.).

"Twenty years ago," the pro-Johnston critic wrote in 1936, "in her Civil War novels, Miss Johnston anticipated all that is valid in the realistic war novel of today."[22] I agree with this judgment and think it probably still holds good today, twenty-five years later, with some qualification. Mary Johnston was determined to tell the whole story, but she does not forget that she is telling, or remembering, a traditional story; she is living in and creating an old world that arose out of a still older one and inherited a discipline of tradition that sets limits which she must not overpass.

All forms of human life are in these books and all forms of love and hate, except, I should say, the perverse and the obscene. There is a traditional epic wholeness and comprehensiveness in this writing and also a traditional epic wholesomeness, if I may be permitted to use that old-fashioned word. Mary Johnston's novel is not a modern love story or a family chronicle set in the past times, against the background of one or other of the crucial military engagements of the war. It is the whole story of the war and the people, and I believe it is told in the right way. The detailed narrative of military maneuvers, battles and besiegements, raids, forays, scouting missions, and the like are as much a part of the big story as the personal loves and hates and tragedies and triumphs of the named characters and the choral voices of the anonymous body of soldiers.

[22] Wagenknecht, *Sewanee Review*, p. 202.

Everybody has his day and his say, the political and military leaders, the generals and statesmen, all classes in society from the classically educated patricians down to the simple untutored mountain people, some of them rascally and no-count, women of all degrees and temperaments, scholars, slaves, children. They are all separate persons but they are all conscious of regional unity. In the first chapter of *The Long Roll* the Botetourt Resolutions of December, 1860, are passed by "the general voice of the county," and then we meet the county people separately and learn to know them as persons—the lawyer, the university student and the country schoolmaster who couldn't go to the university, the miller, the tollgate keeper, the V.M.I. cadet, and so on. We follow the fortunes of the home county people through the course of the war, the combatants and the stay-at-homes, but these actions are ingeniously intertwined with the larger regional actions over the whole South.

The narrative centers continuously and variably on the fortunes of the Botetourt Cleaves and the Albemarle Carys and their wide-ranging connections; they are all in one way or another representative of the characteristic manhood and womanhood of the South. They play leading roles in the great drama of the war because they are "our best people" and "in Virginia, at least, everybody, sooner or later, follows the best people" (*LR,* p. 13). This is a people's war and tribal loyalties are strong. "Dreadful as was this war, it had as a by-product the lessening of caste. Men came together and worked together as men, not as conventions" (*CF,* p. 49).

Everybody has a share in the action, from the great generals down to the shiftless Steven Dagg, perennial deserter, who has a touch of Spenser's Braggadocio in him and something of Homer's Thersites and Plautus' *miles gloriosus.* For all the characters are in a sense figures out of older times; they are completely themselves and real, but they are poetic creations who echo and repeat actions and themes out of the whole range of English literature and the Biblical and classical tradition in which it is centered. "No better men in Homer," says Fauquier Cary in the first scene of the story, naming more than a dozen U.S. Army men from all over the Union serving in the Southwest. Not all the generals in the story are as able as Jackson and Joseph E. Johnston, as glamorous as Stuart and

Ashby, as grand as Lee; but they all earn a place in the story, little or large, triumphant or tragic, as time and chance may decree.

For all is one, one large epic action that from the very start encompasses the stresses and urgencies, the clarity and exaltation of tragic poetry. It is as if the whole writing were the voice of the South itself, telling its own story through the characters and all their actions, finding voices to express its inmost aspirations, its high exalted dreams, its glooms and despairs, its revulsions and fears, its secret meaning.

Critical analysis of a long panoramic war novel like this is not a simple matter. It is a "form" of fiction and it is a "form" of history; the two things grow into one another and the fusion is a third thing for which there is no good name except the word "epic" that I have been overusing. Yet it is like Shakespearean drama in that it can reconcile all opposites by inclusion. In the greatest historical novels "history as well as the novel is carried beyond itself, and raised to a higher power."[23] It becomes poetry, "a great word that holds all other words" (Mary Johnston said this of freedom in *The Wanderers,* p. 367). Such a novel as this deals with large tribal and racial destinies and at the same time makes history "a kind of extension of our personal experience."[24] *War and Peace* is the accepted exemplar, the archetype of the historical novel, and it is history and fiction and historical theory all in one. It is the triumphant illustration and vindication of its own thesis. So too in a lesser way is this picture of the embattled Confederacy, risen out of division and slowly moving to dismemberment and doom.

The "high Verity"[25] of the historic and dramatic imagination

[23] H. Butterfield, *The Historical Novel* (Cambridge, 1924), pp. 3, 87. This little book, so much better I think than any other writing on the subject, was done by the Master of Peterhouse and Vice-Chancellor of Cambridge University when he was a young fellow of his college. Inevitably it reminds one of the authoritative and seminal judgments of G. M. Trevelyan on the union of poetry and history: "Truth is the criterion of historical study; but its impelling motive is poetic. Its poetry consists in its being true. There we find the synthesis of the scientific and literary views of history" (Introduction to Complete Edition of the *Illustrated English Social History* [London, 1954], I, xiii; see also the earlier essay "History and Fiction," in *Living Age,* CCCXIII [June, 1922], 565-73).

[24] *Ibid.,* p. 96.

[25] "None has ever come to conclusions with Imagination, nor seen where its high Verity begins or ends" (*Michael Forth,* p. 80).

illuminates the emotional and spiritual meanings in the factual record, makes the past, as we say, "come alive" and tell its own story in the world of art, the world of persons that is both made and found by the superior historical novel or romance. History and fiction give and take from each other; they cannot do without each other, though the relation is variable and not clearly determined; there is also a mutual mistrust and suspicion. They can be happily allied but they are separate disciplines too and each must preserve its own integrity of purpose. The right fusion of history and fiction is the problem of the individual novelist, and there is no solution of the problem that will escape calumny and criticism on either side.

Tolstoy's history and theory of history in *War and Peace* are both matters of controversy; so too are most or all of the crucial actions and issues in history, and to complete the circle so too are the relative excellencies of the historical novels in our past and present. A recent analyst of the Civil War novel presents his own selection of the fifteen "best Civil War novels" and then a listing of thirty "other representative Civil War novels," admitting at once that his "conclusions are at crucial points frankly subjective."[26] He places *The Long Roll* in the second list.

Mary Johnston's realistic book of tribal war and ethnic passion (*LR*, p. 604) echoes everywhere old prose and poetry and old modes of Decorum.[27] The intermingled stories of love and war have their moments of crisis and their pauses, silences, and relaxations. There is fine artistry throughout in the disposition of light and shade, the innumerable contrasts in tone and coloring from the severest epic to the smallest anecdote. Illustration would be interesting but tedious; most of the incidents and episodes are "immemorial" (*LR*, p. 133), known in song and story, yet they are unique, fresh, and alive in this new-created world. The structure is panoramic and

[26] Lively, p. 13.

[27] Apart from Shakespeare, Homer, the Bible, Milton, Spenser, and Scott, there are references or allusions to Bunyan, Plutarch, Pope, Swift, the Butler of *Hudibras*, Byron, Shelley, Poe, Aesop, etc., etc. There is a comment on the recent work of Darwin (*L.R.*, p. 299). Greek and Roman history and mythology are everywhere present; English and Continental history too. Song, as in the Shakespearean drama, is a pervasive functional element in the composition: ballad, spiritual, catch, chant, love songs and war songs of past and present. There are a number of "Tolstoyan" symbolic or prophetic dreams and visions.

symphonic, with complex contrapuntal effects throughout, most of them simple and obvious enough once they are perceived, some of them so subtle as to be felt rather than understood. Every episode, every sentence almost, is keyed to the theme of Division. All the tensions and antinomies of man here find repeated expression in this true American drama of love and hate in their innumerable forms, acting out, as near the end in the Petersburg lines, "a thousand weaknesses and again a thousand heroisms" (*CF*, p. 446).

It is the Tale of Troy all over again, in another world of epic with the necessary epical auxiliaries of romance, legend, superstition, and mythology. The young Cleaves in the beginning are debating "which was the greatest, Achilles or Hector." "Tell her it was Hector, and let's go to supper!" Will says to the older brother Richard. "She'll believe you" (*LR*, pp. 21f.). Both are great but it is Hector who defends the beleaguered fortress of the South and soon sees that a day will come when Troy-Richmond must fall; and he is slowly beaten to his knees and bleeds to death. The sensitive flowerlike Miriam, who reads Malory and the *Faerie Queene* and the like and thinks that "everybody really belongs in a book" (*LR*, p. 32), cannot endure the loss of her brother Will and the stresses of the war; her mind and body break and she is like the pretty lady Ophelia as she talks distractedly "of books, of Hector and Achilles and people in the 'Morte d'Arthur' " just before her death (*CF*, p. 361).

"The glamour is at the beginning," says General Cary at the end (*CF*, p. 449). That is not quite right; the world of epic and romance is beglamoured from beginning to end, but we know what he means. We hear it again in the words of Margaret Cleave (a kind of Hecuba-Cassandra character and perhaps the spiritual center of the whole writing) near the end, "All is turned to iron and clay and blood and tears" (*CF*, p. 361). Miss Lucy, aunt to the three beautiful Cary girls, dreams of the "golden, tranquil world" of her girlhood, the world of Mr. Jefferson and Mr. Madison, and thinks, "I have lived out of a gold world into an iron one" (*CF*, pp. 110f.). The women, "the best soldiers" according to General Johnston, know best the desolation of war, yet the wild-rose mountain girl Christianna, after her experience of Richmond in the Seven Days, can still see the ragged soldiers of the Confederacy arrayed in the splendor of the Shakespearian lines she learned from "a book of reading pieces at school": "All furnished, all in arms, all plumed . . . Glittering in golden coats like images" (*LR*, pp. 583f.).

The first volume centers on Stonewall Jackson, "Fool Tom Jackson" in the beginning, rising to his name and fame; it ends with his death and funeral. The second volume rises to the heights of Gettysburg, and then comes the downward movement after the double disaster of the failure of the Southern invasion of the North (a sally out of the beleaguered fortress) and the fall of Vicksburg, not Troy but "one of the small Asian towns" around Troy (*CF*, p. 164). Signs and portents of the end begin to appear, as in *Julius Caesar* and *Antony and Cleopatra* and all over the world's literature: an eclipse of the moon ("Didn't I tell you . . . that that thar moon was the Confederacy and that that thar thing stealing across it was the End?") (*CF*, pp. 245, 251), shooting stars (*CF*, p. 393), ghosts rising (*CF*, pp. 422f.). Night comes down over the Confederacy (*CF*, p. 414).

The battle pieces throughout are authentic; the best of them are, I think I must say, terrific, as good as anything in Homer or Tolstoy. Here I think Mary Johnston was helped considerably by the actual wartime experience of her father. She covers all the crucial campaigns of the war with unrelenting fervor and fidelity. And Gettysburg: where "Earth and heaven were shaking with the clangour of two shields" and in the sky "there might be imagined, suspended there, a huge balance—here the besiegers, here the fortress's best and bravest" "and at the head the leader most trusted, most idolized" (*CF*, pp. 169, 168).

The love story of Edward Cary, "an Orpheus afoot" (*LR*, p. 175), and Désirée Gaillard is set in the falling movement of the second volume; it is an exquisite idyl of wartime love, doomed from the start. They love at first sight, are separated, come together and are married, know radiant happiness for a time, are thrown apart in a general retreat, are killed by Sherman's marauders, and die together, lying "side by side, like wreathed figures on a tomb" (*CF*, p. 439). In the one story we are meant to read the hundreds and thousands of others, the young lovers everywhere who are cut down by the scythes of war, "poor sacrifices of our enmity," as old Capulet says at the end of the play.

The other love story is cleared of its complications when Richard Cleave and Maury Stafford, rivals for the love of Judith Cary, are cleansed by war's suffering and their own and come to reconciliation and amity, at the very end of the second volume. This complex antagonism rays out its force and meaning in many directions and touches a good many significant issues and lives. This little civil war finally comes to an end.

And the book comes to an end, but the questions do not. An unnamed soldier tells us "that thar don't nothing end. Ef a thing has been, it Is" (*CF,* p. 251). Where has all the blood gone, is the question on an earlier page (*CF,* p. 245)—to the earth and the sea or to the Confederacy? The countrywoman Sairy, wife of the crippled tollgate keeper, knows something about defeat and victory too. "If we don't beat one way we will another! I ain't a-worryin' about that. Nothing's ever teetotally beaten, not even eggs when you make cake. It's an awful safe universe" (*CF,* p. 362). And old Cousin William, a seventy-year-old fire-eater, will not admit defeat either; just before the end of the story, in late February of 1865, he still hopes for aid from England or France; an armchair strategist, he has it all worked out that Lee and Johnston will combine forces and crush the invaders. He has a simple, old-fashioned trust in "the spirit of the men and women of the South. We've got the unconquerable and imperishable! We've got the spiritual might!" (*CF,* p. 443). But Richard Cleave shakes his head.

Mary Johnston's story ends in early April of 1865. There is no account of the years of reconstruction and what followed. Only in the talk of Cousin William is there a mention of "the years when Achilles drew the body of Hector around Troy" (*Michael Forth,* p. 33). "Do you think they will let it rest there, sir! . . . For ten years to come they will make us drink the water of bitterness and eat the bread of humiliation! *Virginia!* And that second war will be worse than the first!" (*CF,* p. 443).

The Unity that rends itself is not so easy a matter, nor is the change from hate to love. Love is a great reconciler but Love's ways are hard. The prophetic imagination is at work in this book but so too is the historical and dramatic imagination. Mary Johnston is writing the true history of the Confederacy and an account of reconstruction and reconciliation would be out of key in that history. There is fine restraint and reticence here and something that a modern critic might wish to call ambivalence; there could be other names for it, like natural piety. Tolstoy has something like it at the end of *War and Peace;* Milton has something like it near the end of *Paradise Lost,* when the Archangel Michael stops his history of man at the Reformation, the great division in the Christian Church: "so shall the world go on" until the end. The talk of the Southern generals about knowing mountainous country might be relevant here. You *can* know it, one says; "it's a matter of learning, like everything else." "But there's precious few of mankind with any talent for learning!" says another (*CF,* p. 225). The ways of learning are not easy either, whatever be the lesson to be learned. "What shall we say who have knowledge/Carried to the heart?"[28]

The contemporary analyst of Civil War fiction says, "Reconciliation of the sections did not prevent subsequent popular success by such unreconstructed rebels as Mary Johnston, Stark Young, or Margaret Mitchell. The achievements of these latter writers were not dependent, either, on the suffocation of northern principles in the cloying fragrance of magnolia blossoms."[29] One more quotation here from the same source: "As for the question of who won the literary war, North or South, we must answer that the issue is still joined. It will remain joined so long as Southerners hold to their southernism and Northerners treasure their achievement."[30]

There is no doctrinaire "naturalism" in this work, and no pretentious romanticism. There are all kinds of realism in it, as I have tried to show in the preceding pages. The whole thing is a remarkable feat of the historic imagination, and what I have called the visionary imagination is mostly held in harmonious abeyance. Although Mary Johnston expressed contempt for the theology of *Paradise Lost,* this work of hers is closer to Milton's poem than it is to the Prophetic Books of Blake; but there is something of Blake in it too.

Johnston's work ends like Milton's. In the poem the Archangel

[28] Allen Tate, "Ode to the Confederate Dead."
[29] Lively, p. 70. [30] *Ibid.,* p. 68.

Michael explains the meaning of what has happened to Adam and Eve and they leave Paradise on a long journey. The country schoolmaster in the novel, telling the "Controversialist" what he thinks, talks of both sides being right and both being wrong, and of a shield that has two sides, both precious metal, one silver and one gold, but most travelers didn't take the trouble to walk around the shield. "So it is, I reckon, in most wars—this one not excepted! Of course, being in, we've done good fighting—" (*CF,* p. 457). This is April, 1865. Lee's ragged band slowly draws "its wounded length westward," from Richmond to Amelia Court House and to Farmville and toward Appomattox. "On moved the Army of Northern Virginia. . . . On and on down a long, long vista."

"The complete artist, neither romanticist nor realist, dramatizes the ethical conflict in its own terms, without imposing special views upon it. He strives to reveal it, to 'realize' it in a full-bodied fiction that implies in every part that whole of which it is a symbolic rather than a merely pictorial or argued representation."[31] Mr. Donald Davidson, whose writing this is, says that *So Red the Rose* is an art work of this kind. I have ventured to purloin the quoted sentences from Mr. Davidson's magisterial Introduction to Stark Young's novel because I believe that Mary Johnston's novel is also, in its own degree, an art work of this kind. But I cannot say any more than I have already said here.

Mary Johnston's two-volume novel is a little like Shakespeare's Henry plays, which are about rebellion and war and other things, a little like *Romeo and Juliet,* which is about love and a family feud, and like *Julius Caesar,* which is centered in civil war in ancient Rome. But it is like nothing else really, though as I have suggested it is crowded with memories of traditional realms of epic and romance in Western literature. If this work is her *Julius Caesar,* she did not go on to *Hamlet* and the plays that followed *Hamlet.* She found no other subject comparable to that one which compelled her to write *The Long Roll* and *Cease Firing.* There was only one Confederacy. She wrote a series of notable historical romances but, I

[31] Stark Young, *So Red the Rose* (Modern Standard Authors ed.; New York, 1953). The quotation is from p. vii of the Introduction, by Donald Davidson.

think, no other great or near-great novel. These later books are good or have good things in them; they are all interesting, they have charm, personality, and distinction; there is enchantment in them; but they do not have, it seems to me, the massive historical-fictional realism of these earlier writings, the tragic romance of Jefferson's Virginia, *Lewis Rand,* and the Story of the War between the States.

Through all these years there went on in Mary Johnston the intense conflict, never completely resolved, that is reflected in her writing: a kind of civil war between the countrywoman and the cosmopolite, the woman and the feminist, the Virginian and the Universalist. She thought she knew where she was going, and maybe she did; she believed that there was something deep in us that knows where it is walking (*The Slave Ship,* p. 312). She believed in the immaterial conquest of time and space by a hard discipline of spiritual refinement, and she gave all of herself to this dream or vision of human perfectibility. She knew the fearful value and the fearful cost of living; she never forgot that there was a fire in us that we must feed with ourselves (*The Wanderers,* p. 234). The tragic vision was constant in her, and its necessary traditional coloring of romance. She had faith in the wisdom of the Whole, however she interpreted that ineffable Oneness, and she believed that "in the main all things work together, and in the end is honey" (*1492,* p. 193).[32]

What of her work will survive, I cannot say; a good deal of it, I should like to think, especially the romances of Virginia and the New World. She wrote finely, sometimes greatly, about great adventures in our American past; and "we do have a heroic past" and "a usable past, too."[33] She has been a neglected writer since before her death in 1936, and it seems not likely that she will now regain her former high place among the American novelists. But who can say?

It would not matter to her; Mary Johnston went her own way and asked for nothing. The county friend who wrote of her after her

[32] Recurrent in Mary Johnston's diaries is the traditional piece of folk wisdom that occurs in one form or another to all of us in our moments of humorous resignation: what will it matter, or what difference will it make, in a hundred years?

[33] Leisy, p. 4.

death called her a great woman; maybe she was. "Beauty and character, courage, gallantry, simplicity—these were the things she prizd wherever she found them," he said.[34] To many readers and critics she has seemed to be behind the times; her eulogist in the Valley said that she was a century ahead of most of us. But she was one of us, and deeply interested, and implicated, in our fallen condition; probably that is why, to recall a fine old critical statement of the thirties, already quoted in this writing, she didn't know how to be uninteresting. She had a wonderful life; she was wrought of gold and iron and some exotic alloys; she was a distinctive and authentic thaumaturge in the world of old romance.

Of Mary Johnston and of all her writing I would say, finally, what she herself said about the indestructible young-old mother of one of her latest heroes: "Showing without the wear and tear of life . . . but within immortally young, forever romantic, forever musical" (*Drury Randall,* p. 55).

[34] The obituary, by Arthur Goodrich, is in printed form and in manuscript in the Johnston Papers.

5

ELLEN GLASGOW AND THE SOUTHERN LITERARY TRADITION

C. Hugh Holman

"I saw in her . . . Virginia and the entire South, unaware of the changes about them, clinging, with passionate fidelity, to the ceremonial forms of tradition," Ellen Glasgow said of one of her characters,[1] and the statement defines in broad terms the principal subject matter of her twenty volumes of fiction. For it was always of Virginia and Virginians that she wrote, and even when her novels were laid elsewhere, they dealt with expatriated Virginians. And it was the Southern tradition as it adjusts itself to a changing social and economic world and as it shapes characters and organizes life which she made her theme. The bulk of her work is "a social history of Virginia from the decade before the Confederacy" to the late 1930's.[2] Her historical novels are a social history of "the retreat of an agrarian culture before the conquests of an industrial revolution,

A Lecture given for the Institute of Southern Culture at Longwood College, July 10, 1957.

---

1 Ellen Glasgow, *A Common Measure* (New York, 1943), p. 27. Hereinafter designated by *CM*. The character was Mrs. Blake in *The Deliverance.*

2 *CM,* 3. Miss Glasgow's assertion may be a statement made in retrospect and she may not have had as firm an intention to write this social history throughout her career as she remembered herself as having. See Daniel W. Patterson, "Ellen Glasgow's Plan for a Social History of Virginia," *Modern Fiction Studies,* V (Winter, 1960), 353-60.

and the slow and steady rise of the lower middle class."[3] In her novels of the city and in her ironic comedies of manners, she described and analyzed what she called a "tone of manners [which] rang hollow [because] the foundations of the old aristocratic order . . . had never safely settled back on their corner-stone of tradition."[4]

From her first effort in 1897 until the conscientious rewriting of the galley proofs of *In This Our Life* in 1941, while Death stood with his poised emphatic period, Ellen Glasgow consistently supplied what were to her the South's greatest needs, "blood and irony." "Blood," as she explained ". . . because Southern culture had strained too far away from its roots in the earth; . . . irony . . . [as] the safest antidote to sentimental decay."[5] She could look back, in 1943, and feel that her novels were a unity, almost an entity, and that in the last one she "was assembling, in a single figurative pattern, all the varied yet closely related themes of [her] earlier and . . . later books."[6] Francis B. Simkims has called Miss Glasgow a "transmitter of what [she] saw, smelled, felt, and imagined . . . [one of the] expounders of the truth about Virginia."[7] There is no need to insist upon the point, even with the literary critics, for Elizabeth Monroe was speaking for a vast majority of them when she said, "Miss Glasgow's whole art has been oriented by the culture to which she was born—she has criticized it but has made her art out of its systems of tradition."[8]

Yet it is generally believed that Miss Glasgow, although she made Southern *social* tradition her subject, was outside—and indeed, opposed to—the *literary* tradition of the South. She has been used repeatedly as a whip with which to chastise us for our traditional literary sins, and she herself believed that she was outside the literary traditions of her region. She asserted that, Poe excepted, there was no serious tradition of art in the South. She believed that the South was a region where "a congenial hedonism had estab-

[3] *CM*, 75. [4] *CM*, 238, 237. [5] *CM*, 28. [6] *CM*, 263.

[7] "The Education That Doesn't Educate: The Persistence of Virginia Folkways," *Virginia in History and Tradition: Institute of Southern Culture Lectures at Longwood College, 1957*, ed. by R. C. Simonini, Jr. (Farmville, Va., 1958), p. 14.

[8] *The Novel and Society* (Chapel Hill, 1941), p. 140.

lished . . . a confederacy of the spirit," where "pride, complacency . . . , self-satisfaction, a blind contentment with things as they are, and a deaf aversion from things as they might be . . . stifle both the truth of literature and the truth of life," where "generous manners exacted that the artist should be more gregarious than solitary," and where katharsis was more readily found in action than in art.[9] She felt that she had consciously broken with the Southern tradition in letters, and asserted: "I had resolved to write of the South not sentimentally, as a conquered province, but truthfully, as part of a larger world. I had resolved to portray not Southern 'types' alone, but whole human beings, and to touch, or at least feel for, the universal chords beneath regional variations of character. Because I distrusted, with reason, the entire Southern scene in fiction, and, especially, the prevailing nostalgic note in which it was commemorated, I had tried, in youth, the long distant view and the unknown approach to my subject."[10]

Beginning in this way, with Darwin and Henry George in her mind and with the ideals of critical realism before her, she went alone and in revolt. The principal Southern novelists then were Thomas Nelson Page, "Charles Egbert Craddock," James Lane Allen, George Washington Cable, and John Esten Cooke. She was truly a rebel against their methods, attitudes, and assumptions. By the late twenties the movement generally known as the "Southern Renascence" was underway. Allen Tate, Caroline Gordon, William Faulkner, Thomas Wolfe, John Crowe Ransom—what Miss Glasgow called "an impressive group of Southern writers [who] recoiled from the uniform concrete surface of an industrialized South"[11]—were producing a new literature of revolt. Miss Glasgow was then writing her incisive and superlatively urbane comedies of manners and her somber, quiet tragedies of the country. People by then had stopped asking her to write like Thomas Nelson Page or James Lane Allen, and even her "hopeful publisher" had ceased urging her "to do an optimistic novel of the far West."[12] But the popular writing of Southerners, a writing then achieving international attention and national notoriety, was descriptive of Gothic horrors, heat, and intolerable violence or was weaving elaborately obscure intellectual

[9] *CM,* 135-37. [10] *CM,* 152-53. [11] *CM,* 147. [12] *CM,* 177.

webs that linked grace and distinction with cruelty and astringency. Although there was certainly artistic gain in being asked to write like William Faulkner or Allen Tate rather than like Page or James Lane Allen, the sense of alienation was quite the same. She had apparently fallen between two stools, and, although she occupied the floor with peculiar grace, yet she was, she believed, "still obstinately facing the wrong way."[13] Much about modern writing shocked her: it seemed to her lacking in style, in conscious art—"the voice of the amateur," she said with some dismay, "is the voice of authority." Much modern writing seemed to her the product of "pompous illiteracy, escaped from some Freudian cage," and she deplored the anti-intellectualism of "the cult of the hairy ape and the 'mucker.'"[14] Clearly she felt that she was outside the main currents of Southern writing, both before and during her time.

Comparatively few have challenged her thus placing herself outside the Southern literary tradition. The compendium *Southern Renascence,* which examines the literature of the modern South, contains an essay by John Edward Hardy, who argues that she was really a "sentimentalist" after all, and a sentimentalist with no aesthetic sense, no sense of form, and an unfortunate fondness for "ideals."[15] At the opposite extreme, Barbara Giles, in an article in *Mainstream,* the Communist literary journal, has praised Miss Glasgow's work and felt that only her sense of despairing fatalism removed it from the "great tradition," a tradition in this case certainly different from that of Southerners, old or new.[16]

It is this belief that she is a "sport" in the Southern literary scene which calls forth this essay; for, although Miss Glasgow can do handsomely without the Southern literary tradition, it does not fare very well when it is so defined that she is excluded. For the exclusion from the Southern literary tradition of a gifted and accomplished writer who made the accurate representation of the

[13] *CM,* 177.

[14] *The Woman Within* (New York, 1954), pp. 267-69. Hereinafter designated by *WW.*

[15] Ed. by Louis D. Rubin, Jr., and Robert D. Jacobs (Baltimore, 1953), pp. 236-50.

[16] "Character and Fate: The Novels of Ellen Glasgow," *Mainstream,* IX (September, 1956), 20-31.

South one of her major objectives is so incongruous that it invites an examination of what that concept of tradition is and whence it came.

One may fruitfully ask whether there are other writers who, like Ellen Glasgow, are outside this Southern literary tradition. The first obvious one is Edgar Allan Poe, whose right to inclusion in the tradition has been challenged on two grounds. The first is that Poe was not actually a Southerner, despite the fact that he was educated from babyhood on in Richmond and England and attended Mr. Jefferson's university, that he began his professional literary career in Baltimore and Richmond, and that he was so thoroughly Southern in manner, attitude, and prejudice that at least one moderately friendly critic has called him a "professional Southerner."[17] The second objection is that Poe elected to write about a landscape of the soul rather than a geography of Southern regions. Two fallacies are to be found here: the first is the biographical fallacy, which holds that to be a part of a tradition one must be physically of it not only in the germinal but in the total portion of his career. The second is the Platonic fallacy, to use John Crowe Ransom's term, a fallacy which holds that the most significant things about art are its subject matter and its utility and that form is excrescence, craftsmanship suspect, and "it is not meters but a meter-making argument that makes a poem." Hence a Southerner by accident not even of birth but merely of adoption, Poe is excluded, and those who would reinstate him in the Southern literary tradition, men like Arthur Hobson Quinn and Hervey Allen, are likely to catalogue the Southern qualities in his physical landscapes and to locate his settings in the hills around Charlottesville or among the sand dunes on Sullivan's Island, as though Poe to be Southern must become a local colorist.

A group of modern writers who inherited many of Poe's ideas about art, the *Fugitive*-Agrarians, is also excluded from this tradition. They share with Poe the misfortune of often selecting non-Southern subject matters, in their case European and seventeenth-century subjects. When the members of the group were young and *Fugitive* poets, they declared themselves in revolt against that

[17] N. Bryllion Fagin, *The Histrionic Mr. Poe* (Baltimore, 1949).

same elegiac sentimentalism that called forth Ellen Glasgow's protest. As "New Critics," they are open to the attack of all Platonists—conscious and otherwise—who would insist that art justify itself by being useful as something other than art, for theirs is an Aristotelian concern with art as form and craft.

Thomas Wolfe, with his wild rhetoric and his impassioned evocation of place and mood, has also been generally excluded from this tradition. Because he left the South and because he centered his dramas in the inner emotional life of man, he has been considered a Southerner only by accident of birth, despite the detailed accuracy and love with which he described his land, its legends and its people.

Also excluded is William Faulkner, who has compounded a vast legendary history of a mythical kingdom of the soul, setting its action in the Mississippi in which he lives, who has been one of the most constant and ambitious experimenters with form in the modern novel, who has borrowed techniques from Irish novelists, French novelists, American expatriate novelists, and formulated them into his own peculiar idiom of language and form. This man, who certainly qualifies by birth, life, and subject matter, was generally excluded from the Southern tradition in the thirties because he was erroneously hailed as a social radical attacking the South and its ways, a violent critic of the tradition. In recent times, indigenous Southern materials have been sought for in his works in an attempt to reclaim him, but his apocalyptic horrors seem to have needed the canonization of a Swedish committee before his Southern excellence was seen. Generally, the Southern elements described as traditional in him are those of the Southern folk and frontier-humor tradition—the tradition of Augustus Baldwin Longstreet and George Washington Harris.

In 1956 at a symposium on "Agrarianism as a Theme in Southern Literature,"[18] Professor Willard Thorp, a remarkably well-informed man on things Southern, raised the question of the new writers like Flannery O'Connor and William Styron, who seemed to him to be working in a different tradition. His question is the same one that

[18] Louis D. Rubin, Jr., and others, "Agrarianism as a Theme in Southern Literature," *Georgia Review,* XI (Summer, 1957), 145-64.

has been raised provocatively or irritatingly about every new Southern talent since Poe. Its assumptions, although Professor Thorp is too kindly to intend them in this tone, are the same as those of John T. Westbrook, who recently wrote a not very fond farewell to Southern regionalism in which he said, "The happy truth is that the South has lost its 'regional integrity.' . . . An old South, already too minutely autopsied in prose and poetry, should be left to rest in peace, forever dead and (let us fervently hope) forever done with."[19] I believe William Styron to be the most promising of our young writers and his *Lie Down in Darkness* to be a distinguished but uneven earnest of that promise, so that I prefer not peaceably to see him placed outside the limits of the Southern literary tradition. It is certainly true that Southern writing is undergoing a serious change in its subject matter and its methods and is becoming increasingly less distinctively regional, as the South shifts from a small-town, agrarian culture to an urban, industrial culture. Yet the qualities which have been present in much of the writing of the region in this century seem to be maintaining a noticeable continuity in this pattern of change.

What, in fact, shall we say of a so-called Southern literary tradition which excludes the best writers of the South? What should we say of a critic-historian who defined the English Renaissance tradition so that it excluded Spenser, Shakespeare, Donne, and Milton? Shall we accept a Southern literary tradition which omits Poe, Glasgow, Tate, Warren, Ransom, Faulkner, and Styron, and which assures us that our literature—or at least that part distinctively ours—is lacking in artistic seriousness, critical severity, aesthetic control, and moral earnestness, and that it suffers from excessive rhetoric and a deplorable sentimentality?

The acceptance of such a tradition as the dominant one in Southern letters, with the attendant assumption that our best writers are "sports" or geographical accidents, is the reflection from the outside of an unmerited contempt for Southern culture and the indication from within of a painful inferiority complex. It is as though our critics had decided that nothing good can come out of

[19] "Twilight of Southern Regionalism," *Southwest Review*, XLIII (Summer, 1957), 234.

the South and that all variations to this law shall be called "sports"; and as though we, too, had accepted the "law" and were determined to renounce any variants from it as non-Southern. Actually the Southern view of life and letters is fairly consistent—sufficiently so for us to say that there is *a* Southern literary tradition—an agglomeration of characteristics no one of which is necessarily Southern in itself but some combination of which has more frequently occurred in the Southern states than elsewhere in our country.

Miss Glasgow put her finger on the difficulty in her own case when she said, "A contemporary critic, whose sun rose in the Middle West, and is now slowly westering in New York, has politely assigned my first books to 'the Southern school of local colour.' . . . On the contrary, my first immature novels were conceived and written in an impassioned revolt, not only from the school of local colour, but from the current Victorian tradition in letters, and, more especially, from the sentimental elegiac tone this tradition had assumed in Virginia."[20] The Southern tradition from which she was turning was a mixture of the local color school and the plantation tradition, an indigestible fusion of the "I swan" school and the moonlight and magnolias tradition.

Miss Glasgow talks much of her revolt against this "evasive idealism" and "elegiac sentimentality." And, indeed, it was such books—she contemptuously called them "little vessels of experience"[21]—that dominated Southern literature after the Civil War. This fiction, which was enormously popular, served two practical ends: it capitalized upon the Northern interest in the people and customs of the late Confederacy and, by exploiting the idiosyncrasies of Southern types and racial strains in the backwoods, the mountains, and the multiracial groups of Louisiana, provided a marketable literary product for the Southern writer in the only munificent market available to him, the North. In the hands of its best practitioners—"Charles Egbert Craddock" and George Washington Cable—it developed into a very real but minor art form. The same impulse was partially present in the plantation tradition, a tradition that was principally born of the act of looking

[20] *CM,* 49. [21] *WW,* 97-98.

back to glory in the period after the Civil War.[22] But an additional and more powerful motive behind the plantation tradition was the justification of the old and unhappily fallen order. Thomas Nelson Page was the describer and defender of a past world of which he said that it "partook of the philosophical tone of the Grecian, of the dominant spirit of the Roman, and of the guardfulness of individual rights of the Saxon civilization. And over all brooded a softness and beauty, the joint product of Chivalry and Christianity."[23] It was thus, as Ellen Glasgow saw, that "the spirit of adventure had disintegrated into an evasive idealism, a philosophy of heroic defeat."[24] Because the Southern writer for half a century usually wrote within one or the other of these sentimental traditions, he always wrote of the South "as if it were a fabulous country."[25]

These traditions Ellen Glasgow eschewed. "It was not," she asserted, "that I wished to come back to the picturesque or the provincial. On the contrary, I had learned that there are many facets of human nature and that the aspect we call the regional is only the universal surveyed from a shifted angle of vision."[26] So it was, too, with Poe, Wolfe, Faulkner, and the others in their differing ways. They did not belong in the local color–plantation school; hence they were declared not to be Southern.

But there are other ways of using regional materials than those of exploiting the eccentricities of the region for the amusement of the outsider. One strand of Southern regionalism—the strand in which the writer as outsider comments, usually humorously and always condescendingly, upon the strange antics of the natives—is peculiar to the antebellum frontier writing of men like Longstreet, Baldwin, and George Washington Harris, and it finds frequent employment in Gilmore Simms's border romances. Another strand uses the region as a basis for apocalyptic myth, making its history a vast drama of the soul, as Faulkner and Warren do. Another, and that used by Miss Glasgow, uses the region because it is artistically

[22] See Francis Pendleton Gaines, *The Southern Plantation: A Study in the Development and the Accuracy of a Tradition* (New York, 1924).

[23] *The Old South: Essays Social and Political* (New York, 1927), p. 5.

[24] *CM*, 155. [25] *CM*, 195. [26] *CM*, 153.

available and forms a satisfactory means of talking about universals in social patterns and terms. It is this latter strand of regionalism that was in Marjorie Kinnan Rawling's mind when she said, "Ellen Glasgow stands alone in our generation as the creator of the only unmistakable regional literature of the South."[27] And it is this sense of the continuum of the social context of regions as a means of talking about universals that Allen Tate had in mind when he defined regionalism as "that consciousness or that habit of men in a given locality which influences them to certain patterns of thought and conduct handed to them by their ancestors. Regionalism is thus limited in space but not in time. When the regional man . . . assumes that the present moment is unique, he becomes the provincial man. He cuts himself off from the past, and without benefit of the fund of traditional wisdom approaches the simplest problems of life as if nobody had ever heard of them before."[28] Mr. Tate, who believes that there is a group of Southern traditionalist novelists and that Ellen Glasgow and William Faulkner are prominently among them, defines a "traditionalist" as a "writer who takes the South as he knows it today or can find out about it in the past, and who sees it as a region with special characteristics, but otherwise offering as an imaginative subject the plight of human beings as it has been and will doubtless continue to be, here and in other parts of the world."[29]

This definition describes Miss Glasgow's work admirably and places her solidly in a Southern literary tradition. Unfortunately, Mr. Tate's own position in that tradition is under question by the very people who question Miss Glasgow's; and, furthermore, his is a definition based upon the use of a subject matter. I believe that we can find sounder grounds for admitting Miss Glasgow and the others to the Southern literary tradition. I should like to describe certain characteristics of Miss Glasgow's work, using in the main her own comments on it, and indicate the pervasiveness of these characteristics among writers in the South, with the idea

[27] "Regional Literature of the South," *College English,* I (February, 1940), 386.

[28] "The New Provincialism," *The Man of Letters in the Modern World* (New York, 1955), p. 325.

[29] P. 330.

that a cluster of many of these characteristics does define, quite loosely, I admit, a significant tradition in Southern letters.

In the first place, evil is a reality to Miss Glasgow and to the characters in her novels. She opens her autobiography, *The Woman Within,* with a description of her "earliest remembered sensation." As an infant, staring, "as contented and as mindless as an amoeba," at the windowpane, she saw "a face without a body staring in at [her], a vacant face, round, pallid, grotesque, malevolent. Terror . . . stabbed [her] into consciousness." No one else saw it, but she saw this "bloated mask of evil" staring down at her, she asserted, "once, and forever."[30] So, too, evil has a palpable existence for her characters, as when "an evil odour tainted the air and the sunlight" for Jenny Blair in *The Sheltered Life,*[31] or when old General Archbald sensed man's hunger for war and knew that "what the world needed . . . was the lost emblem of evil."[32] In Poe this darkly nighmarish evil casts a lurid shadow over all life. In Faulkner it is a potent and gigantic force. To the Fugitive-Agrarians the denial of its existence produces Ransom's *God without Thunder,* the impotent deity of the modern world. In Styron it creeps with skin-crawling pervasiveness. This sense of the blackness at the center of life is certainly not uniquely Southern, but it is a portion of the Southern vision of experience to a greater extent than it is of that of any other region in America, despite the fact of Hawthorne and Melville.

This sense of evil in Miss Glasgow is coupled with an awareness of man's imperfectibility and his inadequacy. The world for her is not and probably will never be civilized.[33] One of her spokesmen characters said, "The truth is, however much we disguise it, that a Red Indian lurks in every man we call civilized. There is cruelty in the last one of us, even if it has turned inward."[34] Wherever we turn it is the same: man is hopelessly oppressed. "People who have tradition are oppressed by tradition," she said, "and people who are without it are oppressed by the lack of it—or by whatever else they have put in its place."[35] She could never recall a time

[30] *WW,* 3-5. [31] Garden City, N.Y., 1933, p. 312.
[32] *Ibid.,* p. 373. [33] *CM,* 38-39.
[34] *Sheltered Life,* p. 252. The character is General Archbald.
[35] *Ibid.,* p. 295.

when "the pattern of society, as well as the scheme of things in general, had not seemed to [her] false and even malignant."[36] And she declared, "For as long as the human race remains virtually, and perhaps essentially, barbarian, all the social orders invented by man will be merely the mirrors of his favourite imperfections."[37]

She struck here a note that has resounded in Southern writer after Southern writer, one that is, in fact, absent only in the sentimentalists of the last third of the nineteenth century. For Gilmore Simms man was eternally imperfectible; and the paradox of his need to work for social improvement and the hopelessness of his ultimately achieving it is repeatedly struck in the multitudinous pages of this much misunderstood man. The blackness at the core, the darkness in man's being is the great theme of Poe's stories and his poems. Mallarmé sensed this quality in Poe when he likened him to "*Calme bloc ici-bas chu d'un désastre obscur*"—"a calm block fallen down here from some dark disaster."[38] Only a New England transcendentalist who denied the existence of evil as a portion of reality could have called Poe, as Emerson did, "a jingle man." The extent to which Faulkner's writing has employed this sense of man's capacity for evil—one is almost tempted in Faulkner's case to use the theological term "total depravity"—for a long time obscured the greatness of his work to an American audience secure in its faith in progress and perfectibility. And certainly this dualism is present in the *Fugitive*-Agrarians, who have made a mythic Manichaean drama of modern America, a tragedy in which Good, symbolically represented by the Agrarian way, is betrayed and destroyed by Evil, symbolically represented by the Industrial way. In Wolfe, too, a great struggle goes on within his characters in such terms as these. And Styron, because his melodramatic actions are also rooted in a scene of man's imperfectibilitarian nature, has been called a mere imitator of Faulkner's chambers of horrors.

But to Ellen Glasgow and her characters not only is evil a reality and man as prone to evil as the sparks fly upward, but these

[36] *WW*, 42. [37] *CM*, 144.

[38] "Le Tombeau d'Edgar Poe," I. 11, in Stéphane Mallarmé, *Poems*, with translations by Roger Fry (New York, 1951), p. 108-9.

attitudes do not result in the nihilism of Edwin Arlington Robinson's despairing scientist, who believes that we are

> . . . no greater than the noise we make
> Along one blind atomic pilgrimage
> Whereon by crass chance billeted we go
> Because our brains and bones and cartilage
> Will have it so.[39]

Rather they result in a tragic sense of life. In its simplest form, this quality in Miss Glasgow's thought and work found expression in her defense of Asa Timberlake in *In This Our Life:* Readers, she protested, read him "by material standards alone" and forget "that character is an end in itself." [40] Of Dorinda Oakley, in *Barren Ground,* she said, "She exists wherever a human being has learned to live without joy, wherever the spirit of fortitude has triumphed over the sense of futility."[41] And she summed up the doctrine of the novel as being that "one may learn to live, one may even learn to live gallantly, without delight."[42] A confirmed pessimist, confident that the happy end, either in fiction or philosophy, was false,[43] she was always writing in some form or other the kind of book which she described *Vein of Iron* as being, a "drama of mortal conflict with fate."[44] Defeat was inevitable, but in the "conflict of human beings with human nature, of civilization with biology . . . tragedy lies, not in defeat, but in surrender."[45] A Greek sense of fate hangs over her world, and nobility is the function not of actions or of effective alterations in the world but of the spiritual qualities called forth by the world's hostility. She wrote feelingly of "the cold, implacable inhumanity of the universe."[46] It is little wonder that she and Thomas Hardy found much to admire in each other's works.

In this respect Miss Glasgow is peculiarly Southern. As Richard M. Weaver has said, "perhaps the most important of all [his virtues] is the Southerner's discipline in tragedy." Belief in tragedy is essentially un-American, but it is very Southern.[47] C. Vann

[39] "The Man against the Sky," *Collected Poems* (New York: Macmillan, 1916), ll. 216-20.

[40] *CM,* 253. [41] New York, 1933, p. viii. [42] *CM,* 155.

[43] *CM,* 118. [44] *CM,* 175. [45] *CM,* 250. [46] *WW,* 168.

[47] "Aspects of Southern Philosophy," *Southern Renascence,* p. 30.

Woodward describes the situation well: "The inescapable facts of history were that the South had repeatedly met with frustration and failure. It had learned what it was to be faced with economic, social, and political problems that refused to yield to all the ingenuity, patience, and intelligence that a people could bring to bear upon them. It had learned to accommodate itself to conditions that it swore it would never accept and it had learned the taste left in the mouth by the swallowing of one's own words."[48] Almost every major writer of the Southern states, except for those committed to the plantation tradition, the local color school, or the fiction of sociological documentation, has seen life in such patterns. Indeed, the extensive use of Southern history by serious Southern novelists has been as a tragic fable of man's lot in a hostile world, and few are the Southerners who have felt themselves for long the darlings of a special providence. From Poe's damnation to Faulkner's myth of the reduplicating tragic history of Yoknapatawpha County, to Wolfe's half lugubrious "Lost O Lost and by the wind grieved," to the ambiguous calamity of Warren's Willie Stark and the dark destruction of Styron's Peyton Loftis, Southern writers and their characters have known what it is like to surrender their best hopes to the worst disasters, then pick up the pieces with stoic fortitude, and begin to make another dream that though lesser is equally doomed.

For Miss Glasgow, who sought situations in which "fate had been imprisoned in a single luminous drop of experience,"[49] such situations were usually found in the familial relationships in a changing social world. She did not seek to re-enact the Manichaean drama of the Agrarians, and yet from her earliest to her last novel she was concerned with the conflict between the world within which the "aristocratic tradition" had held sway and the newer world of science and industry.[50] Although she documented in her historical novels the triumph of the industrial world over the aristocratic tradition and applauded from time to time the exten-

[48] "The Irony of Southern History," *Journal of Southern History,* XIX (February, 1953), 5. This essay is in C. Vann Woodward, *The Burden of Southern History* (Baton Rouge, 1960), pp. 167-91.

[49] *Sheltered Life,* p. 155. [50] *CM,* 13.

sion of humanity and justice which resulted from it, she ultimately stood with the Agrarians, though neither she nor they would have admitted it. For her the symbolization was beauty *versus* ugliness. In the finest of her novels, *The Sheltered Life,* science and industry clearly mean the coming of ugliness symbolized by the aristocrats living on in the decaying grandeur of Washington Street and ultimately being driven out by the stench from the chemical factory near the river.[51] To smells, she added noise. "So much of modern life," she observed, "was merely talking against noise."[52] She viewed John Fincastle, in *Vein of Iron,* as the symbol of the "fate of the philosopher in an era of science, of the scholar in a world of mechanical inventions."[53] She spoke contemptuously of the economic system that "fostered our industries, and brought forth our vast American fortunes and a mushroom plutocracy."[54] But, like Poe, whose enthusiasm for science she had shared as a young lady, she came to ask of science:

> How should he love thee? or how deem thee wise,
> Who wouldst not leave him in his wandering
> To seek for treasure in the jewelled skies,
> Albeit he soared with an undaunted wing? [55]

And she pitted herself against science and its material meaninglessness. She said,

> Science, the promised savior, may become in the end, the destroyer of man—and of the awkward pattern Western man has agreed to call civilization. It is a civilization built on science, that has discarded philosophy. Yet fewer scientists and more philosophers, less knowledge and more wisdom, might, whether we are saved or lost, at least make us worth saving. And it has always been a vital question in the human mind whether it is better to be saved unworthy, or to be lost but worth the saving. That has been man's eternal choice.[56]

Certainly Miss Glasgow might have been thinking of the "Twelve Southerners" who issued the Agrarian manifesto as *I'll Take My Stand*[57] when she wrote, "One may share the generous wish that all mankind should inherit the world's beauty, without consenting

[51] Pp. 5-6. [52] *Ibid.*, p. 179. [53] *CM,* 171. [54] *CM,* 255.
[55] Edgar Allan Poe, "Sonnet—To Science," 11. 5-8.
[56] *WW,* 280. [57] New York, 1930.

to destroy that beauty because it is beyond the reach and the taste alike of the vast majority."[58]

She recognized that for the present world much of the beauty of the traditional past had vanished, and she would have applauded Allen Tate's backward look at the Agrarian movement, in which he said, "The Old South perpetuated many of the virtues of [a unified Christendom] but to try to 'revive' the Old South, and to build a wall around it, would be a kind of idolatry; it would prefer the accident to the substance."[59] I have said elsewhere of this Agrarian myth, "Its value is not in its correspondence to actuality but in its ability to give expression to the sense of truth inherent in a people at a particular time."[60] With this idea Miss Glasgow was in complete agreement, for she said:

> The Old South . . . has vanished from the world of fact to reappear in the permanent realm of fable. . . . What we are in danger of forgetting is that few possessions are more precious than a fable that can no longer be compared with a fact. The race that inherits a heroic legend must have accumulated an inexhaustible resource of joy, beauty, love, laughter, and tragic passion. To discard this rich inheritance . . . is, for the Southern novelist, pure folly.[61]

Elizabeth Monroe described this attitude well when she said, "[Miss Glasgow] is interested in introspection as it defines a code which has lost its meaning without losing its hold on the imagination."[62] Clearly Ellen Glasgow was at home with the broad pattern of Southern Agrarianism from Thomas Jefferson's *Notes on the State of Virginia* and John Taylor of Caroline's *Arator* essays to *I'll Take My Stand* and Faulkner's "The Bear" and *Sanctuary,* that symbolic horror story of modern life.

She shares, too, with the other Southern writers a deep-rooted sense of the past. To the confident believer in progress, the past is an imperfect niche upon which the present mounts to a more glorious future. If man is, as Whitman thought him, "an acme of things accomplish'd, and . . . an encloser of things to be," the past

[58] *WW,* 277.

[59] "The Agrarians Today," *Shenandoah,* III (Summer, 1952), 29.

[60] "Agrarianism: The Utility of Myth," *Georgia Review,* XI (Summer, 1957), 164.

[61] *CM,* 142-43. [62] *Novel and Society,* p. 150.

is of less interest to him than his body through which he gains identity.[63] If man can perfect himself and his society and evil can be eradicated by human efforts, then, as James Russell Lowell said,

> Time makes ancient good uncouth;
> . . . we ourselves must Pilgrims be, . . .
> Nor attempt the Future's portal with the Past's blood-rusted key.[64]

But if one holds the older tragic view of man and life, then history is not something over which we rise triumphant but a record of what we are and of what limits we operate within. The Southern writer seems almost incapable of thinking except in terms of the past and the present and their interplay. Simms in the days of the great sectional conflict used the past as a means of understanding the present. Faulkner sought in the past the narrative frame for his vast legend of man in his universe. Robert Penn Warren has repeatedly turned backward for theme and subject. Thomas Wolfe, at the time of his death, was projecting a historical novel. Ellen Glasgow said, "In my blood there were remote inheritances from the past three hundred years in Virginia; and when I recorded events that occurred before I was born, I seemed to be writing things that I had actually known."[65] Where the usual historical novelist "works up" his period, Miss Glasgow's method was quite different: "What I needed and what I had worked to attain," she said, "was a distillation of the past, not the dry bones and the decaying framework of history."[66]

As Louis D. Rubin, Jr., has pointed out, "The interplay of past and present, of the historical and the contemporaneous, causes all the modern Southern writers to be unusually sensitive to the nature and workings of time."[67] This awareness lies behind Allen Tate's definition of regionalism as the timeless local character of people and places. It lies behind Thomas Wolfe's elaborate preoccupation with time as quantity in fiction. It lies behind William

[63] "Song of Myself," 1. 1148, and "Crossing Brooklyn Ferry," 11. 63-64.
[64] "The Present Crisis," 11. 86, 88, 90.
[65] *CM*, 67. [66] *CM*, 170.
[67] "The Historical Image of Modern Southern Writing," *Journal of Southern History*, XXII (May, 1956), 161. This essay appears in *South: Modern Southern Literature in Its Cultural Setting*, ed. by Louis D. Rubin, Jr., and Robert D. Jacobs (Garden City, N.Y., 1961), pp. 29-47.

Faulkner's complex dislocations of time sequence in his many narratives. It helps to explain the inverted structure of action in William Styron's *Lie Down in Darkness.* It is the center of the action in Tate's "Ode to the Confederate Dead." It is the basis of Robert Penn Warren's elaborate formal tour de force *World Enough and Time.*

Ellen Glasgow shares this intense concern with the nature and meaning of time. For example, she said of *The Sheltered Life,* "I have treated the past and the present as co-existent in time, and time itself as a subjective medium."[68] Repeatedly the time patterns of her novels are elaborate structural devices, as well as the record of the flow of events. "The sense of time is more difficult to achieve [than a sense of space]," she asserted, "and since it cannot be forced, it remains, I think, the most important problem that confronts the writer of fiction."[69] She had high praise for Virginia Woolf, and her most distinguished single piece of writing, "The Deep Past" section of *The Sheltered Life,* appears to be modeled on Mrs. Woolf's famous time experiment, "Times Passes" in *To the Lighthouse.*[70] She prefaced the section of *A Certain Measure* which deals with the novels of the city with the statement: "What was time itself but the bloom, the sheath enfolding experience? Within time, and within time alone, there was life."[71]

Almost equally acute, although less noteworthy, is her use of place as a dimension in her novels. The sense of place is sharply present everywhere. One may with justice say, as W. H. Frohock does, of James T. Farrell's documentary novels of Chicago that they might have taken place anywhere,[72] but no one would ever say of a novel by Thomas Wolfe or William Faulkner or Gilmore Simms or John Pendleton Kennedy that place is not itself an essential portion of the subject matter of the piece. Even James Branch Cabell's mythic kingdom has an emphatic history and a definite geography both of terrain and of spirit. For Ellen Glasgow the sense of place is powerful: "The fibers of my personality are interwoven, I feel, with some indestructible element of the place; and this element is superior to time and chance, as well as to the

[68] *CM,* 183. [69] *CM,* 159. [70] *WW,* 277; CM, 116. [71] P. 188.
[72] *The Novel of Violence in America* (Dallas, 1950), 75-76.

material substance of brick and mortar."[73] And she declared, "My social history had sprung from a special soil, and it could grow and flower, naturally, in no other air."[74] In *The Deliverance*, according to her own testimony, she attempted to "depict the land as a living personality, and to portray its characteristics in the central figures."[75] She sought to find "an elusive spirit or poetry of place, which speaks, not of the present, but of the deeper life that was lived . . . in the past."[76] And she said of *Barren Ground* and *The Sheltered Life*, "The scene, apart from the human figures, possessed an added dimension, a universal rhythm deeper and more fluid than any material texture. Beneath the lights and shadows there is the brooding spirit of place."[77]

But beyond these matters of belief and attitude which Miss Glasgow shares with the best Southern writers is her sense of the importance of form and technique, of craftsmanship and artistry, a sense common to the best Southern writing. In attempting to define the "Southern essence" in Poe, she wrote of "the formalism of his tone, the classical element in his poetry and in many of his stories, the drift toward rhetoric, the aloof and elusive intensity."[78] She might have added his Aristotelian attitude toward art as an end in itself. At the very beginning of her career, she perceived clearly "that the assembling of material, the arrangement of masses, may have greater effect than the material itself."[79] She was keenly aware of the importance of technique. She declared, "I wanted not an inspiration . . . I wanted an art. I wanted a firm foundation; I wanted a steady control over my ideas and my material. What I understood more and more was that I needed a philosophy of fiction, I needed a technique of working."[80] Throughout *A Certain Measure* Miss Glasgow discussed the technical problems of her fiction, problems of point of view, of style, of narrative structure, of arrangement. Essay after essay is a particularized statement on the art of fiction, and the volume is the almost disinterested and certainly detached but magnificently informed comment of an artist on the artistic problems of her best work.

[73] *WW*, 26. [74] *WW*, 195. [75] *CM*, 31. [76] *CM*, 85.
[77] *Barren Ground*, p. viii. [78] *CM*, 132-33. [79] *CM*, 16.
[80] *WW*, 123.

As such it ranks very high in that limited field where the supreme excellence is generally recognized to be Henry James's prefaces.

She has emphatically declared,

> Only as a form of art has fiction ever concerned me . . . the minute we begin deliberately to break up, divide, and construct a pattern, we have dropped back among the physical unities. And though the physical unities may not lie at the heart of the matter, it is essential that a novelist should have command, not only of his material, but of its proper manipulation. Brushwork may not be the highest end of art, but it remains the solitary means by which an artist may arrive at the highest end. It is unfashionable nowadays, it is even considered a little absurd, to regard a work of fiction as a form of art. . . . [But] from my unimportant point of view, only a form of art appears in a certain measure to be worthy of the dedicated service for forty years.[81]

Here, in her urbane and almost diffident way, Miss Glasgow has asserted that art is a transcendent value in itself, that it is, as Allen Tate delights to assert, "a unique form of knowledge," and that art for art's sake is not trivial but basic.

Her attitude is very much like that of American's first major practical critic and first major theorizer on aesthetic problems and literary techniques, Edgar Allan Poe. The rejection of this attitude has led the bulk of American critics and historians to dismiss Poe's criticism, and particularly his "Philosophy of Composition," as mechanical and lacking in seriousness, whereas the French saw in these things elements that were so startlingly new that Baudelaire and Mallarmé founded a school upon them. The same Aristotelian method, with its insistence upon the analytical examination of individual works, underlies the New Criticism and finds its finest expression in the critical writings of John Crowe Ransom, who is self-consciously "inorganic" and anti-Platonic, Allen Tate, Robert Penn Warren, and Cleanth Brooks. It is at least a contributing factor to Faulkner's being the most persistently experimental of American novelists, to Warren's penchant for structural experiments, and to the formal concerns that have been present with the best Southern writers. From Hugh Swinton Legaré's classic standards to Gilmore Simms's many structural examinations of novels—his essay on Cooper is still one of the finest pieces of analytical

[81] *CM,* 104, 184-85.

criticism of fiction made in America in the nineteenth century—to the New Critics, Southern criticism has seen its technical problems as problems of overwhelming interest. In this respect, as in the others, Ellen Glasgow was centrally in the best Southern literary tradition.

All these characteristics of Miss Glasgow's art set it apart from the bulk of American writing in the nineteenth century and from much of the best writing in the twentieth that is not Southern. Yet these characteristics are held, as I believe I have demonstrated, in common with many other Southern writers, if we look beyond the local color school and the plantation tradition. These characteristics are: a sense of evil, a pessimism about man's potential, a tragic sense of life, a deep-rooted sense of the interplay of past and present, a peculiar sensitivity to time as a complex element in narrative art, a sense of place as a dramatic dimension, and a thoroughgoing belief in the intrinsic value of art as an end in itself, with an attendant Aristotelian concern with forms and techniques. It is true that these are the characterristics, too, of much of the best European art; but, as C. Vann Woodward has pointed out, the South has attitudes and has undergone experiences "shared by nearly all the peoples of Europe and Asia" and understandable to them, whereas most Europeans are baffled and dismayed by the American "national faith in unlimited progress, in the efficacy of material means, in the importance of mass and speed, the worship of success, and the unquestioning belief in the invincibility of American arms." [82]

The South has a tradition that is neither elegiac nor sentimental, a tradition that has been held with philosophical seriousness by many good writers and has been given artistic expression through proudly self-conscious craftsmanship and criticism. Poe, Ellen Glasgow, Faulkner, the *Fugitive*-Agrarians, Styron—these writers are Southern; for they run counter to the stream of writing in most other sections of the nation but they have a common home in the tradition of Southern literary art.

[82] *Journal of Southern History,* XIX, 4-5.

6

JAMES BRANCH CABELL AND SOUTHERN ROMANTICISM

DOROTHY B. SCHLEGEL

IN ORDER to understand the extent to which James Branch Cabell was both influenced and repelled by Southern Romanticism, it is necessary, at the outset, to define the temper and direction of this movement in its relationship to that occurring simultaneously in the world at large.

The ideational complex of the word *Romanticism* carries with it not only one implication, but many, as is admirably set forth by A. O. Lovejoy in his book entitled *Essays in the History of Ideas*.[1] According to Lovejoy, Romanticism may, on the one hand, indicate a return to nature and to primitivism, as was the case with such English poets as Joseph Warton, Wordsworth, Keats, and Shelley. On the other hand, it may concern itself with the faraway and the long ago. The German Goethe and the American Edgar Allan Poe were both fascinated by such romantic manifestations as the luxuriance of Gothic architecture, the mystery of early Celtic tales, or the horrors of the Inquisition. French Romanticists, such as Rousseau and Alfred de Musset, were chiefly preoccupied with exploring the terrain of a still more hidden and secret universe—

A LECTURE given for the Institute of Southern Culture at Longwood College, April 18, 1958.

[1] Baltimore, 1948, pp. 228-53.

that of the inner soul of man. Goethe and Novalis concentrated on one particular aspect of man's inner nature, the struggle of the individual to attain the unattainable, and thereby to make of himself a kind of minor deity in the everyday world.

If an attempt be made to discover the common denominator in all of these various manifestations of Romanticism, one might not go far wrong were he to say that in each case the romantic artist has been concerned with the exploration of the *remote* in time or in space. The Romanticist has been from his genesis a world traveler, or a *mundivagant,* as Cabell would say. He has been wont to journey either far back or far forward in time; he has traveled to great distances horizontally upon the surface of the earth or vertically between Heaven and Hell; or he has sought to dig to the very roots of nature, human or otherwise, to uncover the secrets of hidden, barely accessible universes.

The Southern Romanticist has been willing to adopt only two aspects of the romantic complex of ideas. In a sense, he has been willing to travel vertically in space, as is manifested by his general acceptance of the Christian Heaven and Hell. He will not, however, seek in the skies above the Platonic ideal of the philosophers. Secondly, he has traveled back in time—first, to the Middle Ages and, more recently, to the eighteenth century. From the Middle Ages he has, according to Cabell, gleaned three concepts: his conviction that he is God's vicar upon earth, whose duty it is to right the wrongs that exist; his belief that he must defend his own honor at all costs; and his concept of *domnei,* or woman worship, which with Cabell, as with poets from the time of Homer, carries with it the implication of the pursuit of the ideal incarnated in the body of a beautiful woman.[2]

The chivalric aspect of Southern Romanticism has provided the richest nourishment to the genius of the *younger* James Branch Cabell. The tendency of the Southerner to see himself as a knight in shining armor riding forth to fight for a cause which he believes to be right has provided Cabell's multivolumed *Biography of the Life of Manuel* with many a crusader, who is set upon doing what he believes to be his duty, at no matter

[2] James Branch Cabell, *Chivalry* (New York, 1926), pp. 2-3.

what expense to himself, or to anyone else either, as the *older* Cabell adds ironically in a later volume.[3] The chivalric thread in Southern Romanticism has enabled Cabell to create, also, his never-never land of Poictesme, that region so much like Virginia and yet so different from it, wherein the artist may move at will and breathe freely without fear of recrimination from his readers.

More recently, instead of returning to the Age of Chivalry, the Southern mind has preferred, after the events of the nineteenth century, to go back only so far as its own Golden Age, the eighteenth century, the Age of Classicism, that age when men had assumed the gallant attitude toward life which enabled them, as Cabell writes, "to accept the pleasures of life leisurely and its inconveniences with a shrug."[4] Paradoxically, then, for romantic reasons, the South has tended to adopt in its daily life the tastes and standards of Neoclassicism.

This reversion to the more immediate past, coinciding, as it did, with Victorianism, has led the aristocratic Southerner to place renewed emphasis, at least outwardly, upon measure and good taste, both in *décor* and in conduct. In spite of a thin film of Gothic architecture, which spread over the face of the South at the turn of the century, the Southerner still held dear to his heart and continues to cherish the white columns of Monticello and of the University of Virginia. The South still prefers today the forthrightness and simple dignity of the great, four-square rooms of its colonial mansions along the James to the erratic little nooks and eccentric crannies of Gothic interiors. In behavior, as in architecture, the South has continued to insist upon restraint and outward conformity in human relationships. Erratic behavior it deems, as it always has, "tacky." Conversation, it feels, should not lead to altercation and to romantic turbulence. The Southerner must therefore restrict carefully his words to small talk—to comments upon the weather and to inquiries as to health, for these are matters about which no one is apt to become greatly disturbed. The Southerner avoids sedulously controversial and personal matters, thereby rendering taboo the exploration of the inner recesses

[3] *Let Me Lie* (New York, 1947), p. 285.
[4] *Preface to the Past* (New York, 1936), p. 158.

of the individual—of that area which the French romantics term succinctly the *moi.* The Southerner consistently refuses to embrace this personal aspect of Romanticism. Nor does he have much sympathy with the type of "itchy-footed" romantic, who hankers after distant corners of the earth. The average Southerner is quite content to remain under his own blue skies surrounded by his own warm friends. He wishes to maintain the even tenor of his own life in his own milieu.

This classical frame of mind, which insists upon restraint and decorum rather than a restless Bohemianism, has produced in the South a life which possesses much beauty, harmony, and proportion. The South has long seemed to the Southerner and to many a crass invading Northman to be the last outpost of charm and security in a world covered by the smoke of nineteenth- and twentieth-century industrialism. The Southerners have maintained for themselves even in the face of tragedy a satisfactory and a satisfying manner of living, which has enormous appeal to the majority. They have made of life itself an art.

This second reversion to the past, to the more immediate past, in this case, on the part of the Southerners has contributed likewise to the genius of Cabell. First, on the negative side, it has furnished him with the impetus to rebel violently against the ways of the South which attempt to confine in a strait jacket the non-conforming artistic temperament. On the positive side, it has provided him with the inspiration for his tales contained in the book specifically entitled *Gallantry,* which deals with life in the seventeenth and eighteenth centuries. It has given also a *modus vivendi* to many of his middle-aged characters, in his books other than *Gallantry,* and to his younger protagonists when they have lost their chivalric illusions, for the chivalric attitude seems, in the main, to be that of youth—of a young man or of a young nation—whereas the gallant attitude is that of the coming of age of an individual or of a people.

There is, in addition, a third attitude toward life, isolated and labeled by Cabell, an attitude which Cabell seems to feel is peculiar to romantic artists, among whom he invariably classifies himself. This attitude, termed by Cabell the *poetic* attitude, causes the artist, who rebels against the imperfections and the unnecessary strictures of the world about him, to create from the raw material of everyday life a far better world than that which he has ever known.[5] If one applies Cabell's criterion to the South, one must conclude, however, that the South, in its turn, shares with the romantic artist the poetic attitude, for the Southerner likewise attempts to create in his own mind a far more beautiful world than that which surrounds him. The South then, by virtue of its very chivalry and its gallantry, is itself poetic.

Although Cabell and the South were alike in that they had both adopted the chivalric and gallant attitudes to some extent and that they both desired to create the worlds they wanted from the raw materials of the life about them, yet they differed so significantly that their respective outlooks seem, at first glance, to have little in common. In the first place, they were unlike in that they worked in different media. The South worked in life; Cabell worked in words. They differed, too, in that the chivalric South would not admit that it might be wrong, whereas Cabell always considered all human beliefs, including his own, suspect and something of a luxury. His mouthpiece, Charteris, in *Preface to the Past* expresses Cabell's opinion as to human fallibility when he says,

> All human ideas are probably incorrect about everything. It is certain we have no way of checking off the correctness of any human ideas. All human ideas . . . should be valued only as the playthings with which one purchases diversion. One plays with them during the night season of a not-yet-ended Walburga's Eve, which is called 'living,'—and during which almost anything is rather more than likely to happen.[6]

Lastly, they differed in the types of Romanticism which they elected to make their own. The conservative, agrarian South has been willing to travel back in time only to the Ages of Chivalry and of Gallantry; in space it has journeyed only to the Christian Heaven and Hell. In contrast, Cabell's mind has ranged through all of time and all of space—through all myths and all history. In this process, he has become a mental vagabond upon the surface of the earth, a sort of François Villon, who is bound to differ violently from his more provincial neighbors. He came to look

[5] *Ibid.*, p. 15. [6] P. 17.

upon himself as a Wandering Jew among men, one who had lived, as it were, through the ages. In fact, time and time again in his romances, taking a cue from this favorite myth of his, he refers to himself as a Peripatetic Episcopalian. He is a modern-day Faust, who will be content with no pat explanation of the universe. To this wanderer through all of time and all of space, the temporal, the finite, the particular tend to take on a cosmic insignificance in the total scheme of affairs. The insistence of his neighbors upon their fixed little notions of life seems ludicrous to this rebellious cosmopolite in a world "where almost anything is rather more than likely to happen."

Cabell's immense erudition and his sophistication had the effect of alienating him from his associates. When he detected what he considered to be flaws in the point of view of his neighbors, he could not refrain from telling them so. They, in their turn, naturally tended to look askance at the individual who disturbed their equanimity and came to resent bitterly his criticism. In *Faust* Goethe expressed skillfully the tension which has always existed between society and its critics when he wrote: "Die wenigen die was davon erkannt, . . . hat man von je gekreuzigt und verbrannt." [7]

As Cabell grew older and suffered the inevitable disillusionments of maturity, among which might be reckoned the shattering condemnation of *Jurgen* in the 1920's, he seems to have perfected a technique which had been practiced widely by such eighteenth-century critics of society as Montesquieu, the author of the *Lettres Persanes*. He developed more and more their habit of looking at himself and at his own people with the cold, impersonal eyes of a traveler from a far country. As a result of his observations, this stranger from Parnassus grew ever more rebellious against the fixed mores of his fellow Southerners, and he came to feel that the Southern chivalric attitude toward life, involving as it does a strictly fundamentalist religious position, tends to create in the minds of the individuals who have subscribed to it a deplorable priggishness and intolerance. He complained bitterly of these traits as he saw them manifested in his own people. In *Let Me Lie* (1947) he wrote of the average Virginian: "No power can shake

[7] Boston, 1954, p. 186.

. . . [his] belief in his own eternal rightness," and likewise "no power in nature can upset the faith of a Virginian of the old school as to the myths among which he was reared, and of which he needs to be worthy."[8] His irritation at Virginians' implicit belief in what he considers to be their false illusions is even more clearly set forth in *Special Delivery,* when he writes,

> Of beauty and of chivalry and of gray legions they spoke, and of a fallen civilization such as the world will not ever see again, and, for that matter, never did see; of a first permanent settlement, and of a Mother of Presidents, and of a republic's cradle, and of Stars and Bars, and of yet many other bygones, long ago at one with dead Troy and Atlantis.[9]

In this passage Cabell undoubtedly had in mind the fact that Virginians insisted upon the truth of the Pocahontas story, even after historians had rejected most of the details surrounding it; that they believed in the first-white-settlement-in-America legend, in the teeth of the indisputable fact that Saint Augustine had been founded some forty-two years before Jamestown; and that they claimed Virginia Dare, the so-called "first" white child born in America as their own, when actually some eight or ten boys—the Spaniards didn't bother to count the girls—had been born in Florida, before Virginia Dare had been born in Virginia, actually on Roanoke Island, which is now not part of Virginia anyway, but of North Carolina.[10]

Cabell felt, too, that there was no hope that Virginia would ever abandon its myths, for, he complained, "Virginians did not read." Since they did not "honor any writer," no one felt inspired to write. "There were [therefore] no written words to outline . . . [the] babblings" of their "demagogues," who spoke only "big words . . . in . . . praise [of Virginia], and in the praise of all her customs." Imitating Jeremiah, Cabell wrote, partly in resentment of the neglect accorded to his own words, "With all these never-idle talkers Virginia had played the wanton in a little corner, in the plashed mire of her stagnant backwaters, saying, speak to me of my pre-eminence! And all they had spoken to the desire of Virginia, very egregiously."[11]

[8] Pp. 284-85. [9] New York, 1933, p. 52.
[10] *Let Me Lie,* pp. 45-76. [11] *Special Delivery,* p. 52.

Because Cabell criticized the South, he must not, however, be thought hostile to it. Emotionally he loved his country and his state and his city and his family, but intellectually he saw their shortcomings. Like Dante, who bitterly reproached the city of Florence, which he loved above all other places on the face of the earth, so Cabell chastised Richmond, Virginia, and the South. On the other hand, one may be quite sure that Cabell himself would be the first to spring to the defense of his homeland should any stranger seek to malign it. And always it must be remembered that regardless of what Cabell has said about the South in his attempts to improve it, he has always elected to live his life in Virginia, for he feels, along with his fellow Southerners, that he is far better off at home than he would be anywhere else, and he writes frequently with the deepest affection of Virginia—especially of the Northern Neck, which he seems to consider a last haven of refuge, a Garden of Eden, in a world gone mad.

If Cabell had limited himself only to a carping criticism of the ways of the South, he and his work would have amounted to nothing. But this was not the case.

From Cabell's rebellion against the world about him were born his speculations as to the springs of all human behavior. He then proceeded to universalize his ideals to the extent that he created an impressive philosophy. His best and most complete expression of his outlook on life is contained in his *Biography of the Life of Manuel,* that long allegory of the struggles of the human race from the thirteenth-century redeemer who pulled himself up from the mire by his own bootstraps to the Virginians of Cabell's own lifetime.

Because of Cabell's dismay at the average Southerner's unwillingness to face what Cabell deemed to be the truth, and perhaps because of a similar inability which he must, at times, have detected in himself, he studied the phenomenon of human illusions in general. From this he came to the realization that mankind as a whole is loath to face reality. Man, it seems, must live by his dreams. He will not and cannot accept things as they are. Man dreams either of the past, when he believes that life has been better, or of the future, when he hopes that it will be better. If he dreams of the past, he takes refuge in ancestor worship and joins the D.A.R., the U.D.C., and the Society for the Preservation of Virginia Antiquities. If he dreams of the future, he envisages some hereafter of shimmering light and rainbow colors, wherein Grandfather Satan will punish the sins of the wicked. If the dreamer is really striving for justice, he believes that the sins of the dreamer himself will be punished as well. Because of his pride, then, he must, perforce, dream of a hell in which the flames will be very high and very hot indeed to punish adequately his own beautiful crimes. And so out of the cocoon of his own cranium man spins the beautiful fabric of his own dreams. He creates what he thinks "ought to be" rather than "what is."

And why is it that people from time immemorial have refused to face the truth? Cabell attributes this human propensity, which is probably due in reality to man's fears and to his insecurity, to man's dullness and his vanity. Man's dullness will not permit him to understand that he is simply a little midge clinging to the surface of a vast sphere, which is whirling madly through space.[12] Consequently, his vanity makes him insist that he, as an individual, should be accorded special attention by someone—if not by his immediate associates in this life, at least by a deity in the life to come.[13]

And life to most human beings, Cabell included, is, at times, eminently unsatisfactory. The routine of life itself divested of its niceties—its candles, its lace tablecloths, its silver tea sets—is ghastly. Birth is bloody and cruel; death is corruption. The human being in his progress through life is hideously and irremediably alone. Even a man's own mate fails completely to understand his dreams, ambitions, and ideals. A man's wife will not read his books but chatters fatuously about the amount of money the books would bring in were he to make certain changes in them. A man and his wife talk *at* each other rather than *with* each other. If there is often no real understanding between a man and his wife, there is infinitely less between man and the rest of the world.

Cabell presents a pathetic little picture of man's utter incomprehensibility to his fellows in the Harrowby-Kennaston episode near the close of *The Cream of the Jest*. There Cabell presents us with

[12] *Beyond Life* (London, n.d.), p. 280. [13] *Ibid.*, p. 278.

two men, Dick Harrowby and Felix Kennaston, who, in many ways, have much in common. Both are Richmonders who have inherited sizable fortunes; both travel in the same social circles; both have dabbled much in the occult. On one occasion, for one brief golden moment, Dick Harrowby finds that his callers, the Kennastons, and his own wife seem miraculously disposed to listen briefly to his talk of his hobby, that exploration of the hidden, the occult, which had much in common with Felix Kennaston's own interests. Yet Harrowby's pleasure at being accorded a moment's attention is short lived, for it is quenched first by Kennaston's rather flippant treatment of Harrowby's subject and then by Mrs. Harrowby's remark to the effect that if they allowed Dick to start on his hobbies, he would bore them all to death. She proposed, as women are wont to do, that they all have a drink.

The reader can sense Harrowby's frustration at the interruption, his eagerness to resume the subject, which is absorbing to him, at least, and should have been to Kennaston; and his bitter disappointment when Cabell wrote laconically of Harrowby's thoughts: "And we obeyed her, and—somehow—got to talking of the recent thunderstorms, and getting in our hay, and kindred topics." This lack of anything remotely resembling comprehension and sympathy among human beings is emphasized when Cabell has Mrs. Harrowby, so soon as the Kennastons have left, remark cattily about the guests to whom she has just been so cordial that she wonders how Mrs. Kennaston could keep on rouging and powdering at her age, and why Kennaston never had anything in particular to say for himself. "Do you suppose it is because he has a swelled head over his little old book, or is he just naturally stupid?"[14] she asks, with the Philistine's uneasy distrust of the aesthetic intelligence.

There were these four people, probably as well qualified as any in the world to understand each other. Their interests and environment were almost identical. For a brief moment, it seemed that there might have been some point of contact established among them, and yet all four had floated past each other and had failed to communicate anything whatsoever to each other. They could have, they perhaps should have, but they didn't. In *Beyond Life* Cabell

[14] New York, n.d., pp. 216-20.

states still more clearly the incomprehensibility of man to man when he writes, "For each of us is babbling in the night, and has no way to make his fellows understand just what he would be at. It may be there is some supernal audience which sees and hears with perfect comprehension. Yes, such of course may be the case. But in that event I shudder to think of how we must provoke and bore that audience."[15]

As a result of the desolation of this life, man seeks refuge in his dreams. In *The Cream of the Jest* Felix Kennaston, clutching his Sigel of Scoteia, junkets back and forth between Lichfield (Richmond) and Poictesme in search of the ideal. He leaves this terrestrial soil and his talking-scolding wife, who, nevertheless, would lay down her life for him and goes off to that never-never land where all is as it should be, where at last are perfect justice and beauty. In Poictesme, he catches fitful glimpses of the ideal, the girl of his dreams, la belle Etarre, but Cabell, like a true romanticist, whose dominant trait is rebelliousness, cannot allow even his own dreams to remain undisturbed. Like Don Quixote, who destroyed at a blow the painfully contrived cardboard visor to his helmet, and like Heine, who bitterly burst every romantic bubble that he had ever created, so Cabell rebelled even against his own dreams. Suppose his dreams were to come true? Would he be content? Would man be satisfied with what he had, if he had what he wanted? The answer to that question Cabell provides in *Jurgen*.

In *Jurgen* the Romanticist is vouchsafed a prolonged residence in Poictesme. And what does he find there? His beautiful maidens are for the most part a dreadful disappointment to him. Dorothy la Désirée, on the very heels of her assertions of love for the young Jurgen, meets Heitman Michael, the man whom she eventually marries. Guinevere, the beautiful bride of King Arthur, whom people praise for her freshness and for her chastity has neither one nor the other, as Jurgen has good reason to know from personal experience. Anaïtis, the Cabellian representation of the fertility goddess of the Ancients, is a little oppressive in her ardor—so much so, in fact, that Jurgen is quite relieved when he becomes a solar myth, descends to Hades for six months, and so rids himself of her

[15] P. 300.

attractive, but insistent, presence. In Hell Jurgen has the rather doubtful privilege of marrying one of the most attractive, but dangerous, of females, the vampire Florimel, who is vacationing in the nether regions. Although he admires her beauty, yet her sharp little white teeth do serve constantly to remind him of her vocation, and even with this seductive creature, life degenerates into its usual tedium. They visit the "in-laws" and spend evenings with the Asmodeuses, where the gentlemen talk politics, much to the boredom of pretty little Florimel.

Through all of Jurgen's journeyings through the various dream worlds, he can have and can be just what he wants. Because it suits his fancy, he becomes successively Jurgen, the Duke of Logreus; Prince Jurgen of Cocaigne; King Jurgen of Eubonia; Jurgen, the Emperor of Noumaria; Pope John the Twentieth; and, finally, when, as a solar myth, he is forced to ascend into Heaven, he sits on the throne of God himself. But never is he completely satisfied, and even on the very throne of God he feels a gnawing discontent, for always a shadow had attended him, "a shadow that renders all things not quite satisfactory, not wholly to be trusted, not to be met with frankness."[16] Cabell presents the common plight of man most effectively when he describes Jurgen's communion with his own soul, as he sat splendidly enthroned in Heaven.

> "And what will you do now?" says Jurgen aloud. "Oh, fretful little Jurgen, you that have complained because you had not your desire, you are omnipotent over Earth and all the affairs of men. What now is your desire?" And sitting thus terribly enthroned, the heart of Jurgen was as lead within him, and he felt old and very tired. "For I do not know. Oh, nothing can help me, for I do not know what thing it is that I desire! And this book and this sceptre and this throne avail me nothing at all, and nothing can ever avail me: for I am Jurgen who seeks he knows not what."[17]

As even Heaven itself fails then to satisfy this fastidious visitor from Earth, Jurgen, the knight-errant, shrugs his shoulders, thereby indicating his transition from the chivalric to the gallant attitude towards life, and asks one of the four archangels who are in attendance upon him, "the quickest way out of Heaven," for he wishes to return to the more congenial illusions of Earth. Although he has

[16] New York, 1934, p. 317. [17] Pp. 305-6.

admired and envied much that he has seen in Heaven, he feels that he cannot really believe in what he has seen. And certainly there is little satisfaction to be derived from the vague, empty beauty of Heaven. Instead he is beset with a great longing for that comfortable, prosaic life of his on Earth. And so he returns of his own volition to the everyday world and to his own wife, Dame Lisa, who nagged frightfully, but who still was as comfortable as an old shoe. His residence in the lands beyond common sense had stripped him of all his illusions. Heaven was no more satisfactory than Earth. This ideal destination of man was scarcely worth the struggle of attaining it.

Jurgen's chivalric ideal of women, too, had vanished into thin air along with his dreams of Heaven. He who had once worshiped all women for their "sacred, sweet, intimidating beauty" now "began to suspect that women, also, are akin to their parents; and are no wiser, and no more subtle, and no more immaculate, than the father who begot them."[18]

Jurgen has then finished his quest of the ideal with faith in nothing, "not even in his own deductions."[19] He felt like "a rudderless boat that goes from wave to wave."[20] He knew nothing and he had nothing, for "man possesses nothing certainly save a brief loan of his own body."[21] When Cabell demolishes Jurgen's illusions, he destroys symbolically at the same time the illusions of a trinity composed of the poet Cabell, of the South, and of the entire human race.

Along with Jurgen's skepticism concerning the traditional concepts of Heaven and Hell went, however, a profound regret that he could not retain the simple, innocent faith of his childhood. Cabell may well be considered as presenting his own point of view when he has Jurgen say regretfully to Jurgen's grandmother's God in Heaven:

> God of my grandmother, I cannot quite believe in You, and Your doings as they are recorded I find incoherent and a little droll. . . . God of my grandmother, I cannot quite believe in You, yet I am not as those who would come peering at You reasonably. I, Jurgen, see You only through a mist of tears. For You were loved by those whom I loved greatly very long ago; and when I look at You it is Your worshippers and the dear believers of old that I remember. And it seems to me that dates and

[18] Pp. 336-37. [19] P. 338. [20] P. 339. [21] P. 340.

manuscripts and the opinions of learned persons are very trifling things beside what I remember, and what I envy![22]

In spite of the criticism which *Jurgen* has received, partially on the grounds of its religious disrespect, these words are not flippant. They are rather the words of a man who has paid religion the supreme compliment of thinking long and deeply about it.

Cabell's religion, in fact, bears a close affinity to that of the so-called skeptics of the eighteenth century. It resembles closely the philosophy evolved by such writers as Toland, Diderot, and D'Holbach. Cabell seems to be impelled by much the same urge as was Diderot, when the latter called out, "Elargissez Dieu. Voyez-le partout où il est, ou dites qu'il n'existe point."[23] Diderot came to feel that matter in motion, which is constantly forming new combinations, is God. Cabell has something of the same idea, although he uses different terms to express his concept. His matter in motion is symbolized by a stupid, deathless Russian, one Koschei, the demiurge, who creates things as they are, even Jurgen's grandmother's heaven. This demiurge in the human species becomes the spirit of romance, which leads man to reach ever toward the stars, to dream himself ever upward. The spirit of romance is thus the creative principle, which on the physical plane creates oncoming life. Viewed in this light Cabell's so-called erotic imagery, which was greatly condemned by the twenties, has a legitimate place in his books, for the sexual impulse is but the demiurge working in man, who is ever creating, ever producing new life, which will in turn work to bring about a heaven on earth. On the spiritual plane, the demiurge is the artistic impulse in man, which enables him to create art—to bring into being something which had not existed before. Man, and especially the artist, becomes perhaps God through this creative activity, for Cabell holds something of the idea that Goethe set forth in his little poem entitled "Prometheus": the artist because of his creativity rivals God. Man in the cosmos of both Goethe and of Cabell is perhaps his own Prometheus.

Manuel, the hero of Cabell's great *Biography*, becomes therefore

[22] P. 304.

[23] J. Assézat and Maurice Tourneux, eds., *Pensées philosophiques*, in *Oeuvres complètes de Diderot* (Paris, 1876), I, 138.

a most significant character, for he is the great progenitor of that race of human beings whom Cabell traces through many centuries and through many countries in order to show man's gradual evolution from the cave man. Yet, throughout time, Cabell himself admits rather regretfully, Manuel and his descendants, Jurgen included, remain one and all "pretty much the same in most times and stations" and "come by varying roads" to "pretty much the same end."[24] The name *Manuel* is suggestive, nevertheless, of what might be wishful thinking on the part of both Cabell and of humanity as a whole. *Manuel* is probably a compound of the English word *man* and the Latin-French diminutive *el*, meaning "little." *Manuel* thus becomes "little man." The connotation of this name is heightened by its relationship to the Hebrew word *Emmanuel*, meaning "God is with us." It seems quite obvious, therefore, that Cabell meant the name *Manuel* to suggest that God, or the creative principle, is indwelling in the body of man himself. While Manuel is primarily a man of action, yet even this father of Cabell's brain children has some faint glimmer of light, which does impel him to try to make something of himself. The real man of ideas is, however, Jurgen, who had deluded himself into believing that he had seen Manuel, the incarnation of the redeemer, ride off into the west on his great silver stallion, much as Lee had ridden off on Traveler. Jurgen, who has thus caught a vision of the ideal, becomes the prototype of the knightly crusader, the young adventurer, who eventually learns, however, to shrug his shoulders, when his illusions prove to be vain. He does not die like Don Quixote, but he elects simply to return to real life and to live on with his earthly ideals, which he bequeaths to his progeny.

Cabell's somewhat pessimistic view of the essential nature of man is brilliantly stated in one masterly paragraph in *Preface to the Past.*

> Fundamentally [he writes] my protagonist does not change, in any one of my books; but remains, instead, under all temporal garbs and all surface strains, very much the same blundering male ape, reft of his tail and grown rusty at climbing, forever aspiring but forever cautious, forever hungering for companionship and for comprehension and for sympathy, and yet, none the less, retaining forever inviolate that frigid and pale and hard small core of selfishness which . . . [was] the heart of

[24] *Preface to the Past*, p. 30.

Manuel. . . . Yes: I am afraid that, at bottom, under every permissible human grace and large human gesture, and under each of my three human attitudes, that obscure heart trouble has been perpetuated in every one of the descendants of Manuel as ineradicably as it yet endures in all the descendants of Adam.[25]

Since romance or faith is man's only hope of salvation, Koschei and romance then become synonymous terms. Man, ostensibly the underdog though actually the vehicle of romance, thus becomes in Cabell's cosmology the Cinderella of a vast cosmic fairy tale. And man's greatest literary creation on Earth, the Holy Bible, is, then, by extension, the greatest romance of all. "It is past doubt," says Cabell, "the boldest and the most splendid example of romance contrived by human ingenuity."[26] It is one vast Cinderella story, which sets forth, after "the disregard and contumely accorded [to God] from the Genesis of humanity," his "ultimate very public triumph celebrated amid the unimaginable pomp and fanfare of the vision seen from Patmos."[27] Christianity, too, Cabell regards as the Cinderella legend set forth in more impressive terms.[28] He believes that if the accounts recorded in the Bible "really happened—if one great Author did in point of fact shape the tale thus, employing men and women in the place of printed words—it very overwhelmingly proves that our world is swayed by a romancer of incalculable skill and imagination."[29]

And so to show his "confidence in this Author's literary abilities," Cabell in *The Cream of the Jest* has his protagonist, Felix Kennaston, who one cannot help believing is Cabell himself, be "presently confirmed" at his little neighborhood church, "to the delight of his wife and the approbation of his neighbors." Furthermore, Cabell reports that his hero was undeniably pleased and flattered when not long afterward he was elected to the vestry of the church to replace one William T. Vartrey (of the Lichfield Iron Works) who had not long before been "gathered to his grandfathers."[30]

Felix Kennaston therefore joined the Episcopal church to honor the Author of the Universe and at the same time to pay homage to Mother Sereda, the high priestess of conformity. Like Job, Kennaston seems to have been silenced by powerful arguments as to the great-

[25] Pp. 236-37. [26] *Beyond Life*, p. 139. [27] *Ibid.*, p. 136.
[28] *Ibid.* [29] *Ibid.*, p. 139. [30] P. 167.

ness and glory of God. And yet the reader finds that he is not completely convinced by all of this surface docility.

In *Beyond Life* Cabell confirms our suspicions that Kennaston had joined the church primarily to be doing what was expected of him rather than from any strong religious conviction, when the author once again borrows the eighteenth-century technique of looking upon a human convention with the cold eyes of a visitor from another planet. Cabell describes his attendance at a church service in this fashion:

> Or put it [he writes] that I am expected to evince my religious faith. I must set about this by putting on my best raiment,—for . . . like children, we needs must "dress up" for everything we "play at,"—and by going into a building, of which the roof is indecorously adorned with a tall phallic symbol, and by remaining there an hour and a half. There too we perform a drill, of standing, sitting and kneeling, and we read and sing archaic observations from little books. Sometimes the formulae we repeat are not unastounding, as when we gravely desiderate the privilege of dipping our feet in the blood of our enemies, or even request that our adversaries be forthwith carried alive into hell. An honest gentleman, whose conduct upon weekdays I cordially revere, emerges from the vestry, in what to the unsophisticated might appear to be a collocation of the fragments of a black bathrobe and of a nightgown; and after forbidding us to worship stone images (which really does seem rather a superfluous exhortation) announces that the Neighborhood League will meet on Monday evening, and devotes some twenty minutes to revising one or another well-meant utterance of Christ into conformity with more modern ideas. The plates are passed, into which we put money, to pay for the heating, lighting and general upkeep of the building, and the living expenses of the clergyman and the janitor. Now all this is likewise more or less harmless, yet, sanely viewed, it is difficult to connect in any way with religion.[31]

To Cabell a sane view of religion is rather the recognition of the Spirit of Romance as the First Cause and a veneration for this creative drive. Although later in his life, in *Special Delivery*, he does give evidence of feeling a need for a more personal God,[32] through most of his writings his godhead seems to be something much akin to the Spirit of Affirmation of Goethe and to the Everlasting Yea of Carlyle. He usually refers to the creative principle as the Author of the Universe, for like such eighteenth-century deists as Shaftesbury, he must create God in his own image. As men have done from

[31] P. 202. [32] P. 234.

the beginning of time, he worships that which he most admires. But to his Author of the Universe he refuses to attribute omnipotence, for he feels that this world is much too imperfect to be the creation of an all-powerful deity. John Charteris in *Beyond Life* expresses Cabell's conception of the creative principle at work in man and in nature in these lines:

> I prefer to take it that we are components of an unfinished world, and that we are but as seething atoms which ferment toward its making, if merely because man as he now exists can hardly be the finished product of any Creator whom one could very heartily revere. We are being made into something quite unpredictable, I imagine: and through the purging and the smelting, we are sustained by an instinctive knowledge that we are being made into something better. For this we know, quite incommunicably, and yet as surely as we know that we will to have it thus.
>
> And it is this will that stirs in us to have the creatures of earth and the affairs of earth, not as they are, but "as they ought to be," which we call romance. But when we note how visibly it sways all life we perceive that we are talking about God.[33]

If the South has its dreams and its illusions, it is not unique in this respect, for, as has been seen, it shares this characteristic with the whole human race. Man must have his dreams in order to exist at all. Even though man's dreams may have no basis whatsoever in reality, yet through wishing and through striving to fulfill his wishes man creates what he wants. Because he does not want what he then has, he ever dreams himself upward, and so he himself becomes Goethe's "living stairway," which leads him to Heaven.

The chivalry and the gallantry of the South thus provided Cabell with the raw materials for his poesy. Although Cabell had drunk deep of such continental authors as Goethe and Cervantes, yet Southern Romanticism furnished him with the initial dynamics governing his philosophy of life and of art. To the South, Cabell owed a great debt of gratitude. The South, in its turn, and Virginia, in particular, should not forget to pay homage to this great stylist, for, as he wrote of himself on the title page of *Smire,*

> He . . . [was truly] of that small band, standing out as isolated figures far separated down the ages, who have the gift of speech; and who are not workers in this or that, nor ploughmen nor carpenters nor followers for gain of any craft; but who serve the Muses, and the leader of their choir, the God of the Silver Bow.[34]

[33] P. 312. [34] Garden City, N.Y., 1937.

7

FAULKNER AND THE SOUTH

JAMES B. MERIWETHER

LET ME begin by saying that I am painfully aware of the wideness of the scope of my topic. It is one that cries out for a broader and deeper treatment than this occasion permits— it would, indeed, make a valuable and appropriate subject for an entire book, one which could illuminate almost every aspect of Faulkner's life, most of which has been spent in the South; and of his work, most of which has its setting in the South. Such a book is badly needed, for there are errors and misunderstanding about both his life and work which are numerous and serious, which have wide currency, and which ultimately depend upon lack of knowledge of the facts of Faulkner's Southern background and the Southern setting of his fiction.

Such a book would need to explore the causes and trace the effects of Faulkner's decision, in the mid-1920's, to settle down in Oxford, Mississippi, and make it the center and focus of his life and writings, for no major American writer has identified himself more closely with his community or made more important use of it in his work. It would need to discuss such general topics as language and dialect, for which Faulkner has so fine an ear, and humor, which plays so fundamental a role in his fiction, and which has its basis in

A LECTURE given for the Institute of Southern Culture at Longwood College, April 21, 1961.

the Southern oral tall tale and the literary tradition of backwoods or frontier humor with which we are most familiar in the works of Mark Twain. Such a book would need to follow, in Faulkner's thought and in his fiction, the progress of his attitude toward and knowledge of the Southern past and the Southern present; it would need to investigate the question of how much he knows about other parts of the South than his own; it should compare Faulkner's rare early pronouncements on the Southern racial problem with his frequent and widely publicized recent ones and would attempt to determine how much real inconsistency there is in them (very little, I would say), how much authorial irony, and how much reportorial misunderstanding and misinterpretation. It might well deal with the vexed problem of literary influences: what Southern writers does Faulkner read, and how does he read them? What effects on Faulkner's life and work, this study might ask, have been produced by the professionally anti-Southern attitude of the more extreme left-wing American press, which has almost uniformly been bitterly hostile to him? And what of Faulkner's reaction to the equally bitter, if not so influential, condemnation of the extreme Southern right?

Such a book has not been written, and it may be that it could not be written now. Further, I think that it should not be written now; there is the question of the propriety of such an examination of a living writer, and Faulkner has made it clear that he considers biographical investigation of him for the most part as an invasion of his privacy. He once told a friend, as they passed by the window of a bookshop and saw displayed a copy of the collected letters of Thomas Wolfe, that he hoped they wouldn't pick his bones like that when he was gone.[1] As individuals we must respect that attitude, even if as scholars, students, and admirers of Faulkner's works we feel an urgent need to know more of the circumstances of the creation of those works.[2]

[1] The friend was the late Saxe Commins, Faulkner's editor, who gave me the story April 1, 1957. I understood that the episode had just happened, and Commins had been with Faulkner in New York earlier that day.

[2] Faulkner's well-known views on privacy obviously reinforce the very natural difficulty that an author who is a literary pioneer might have in recog-

But if lack of space prevents consideration here of some aspects of the topic, and if others should be avoided because they infringe too closely upon Faulkner's privacy as an individual, it is still possible now to come to grips with some of this subject's most interesting features. If many of our conclusions must at present be tentative, we can nevertheless make our decisions on the basis of a considerable body of evidence—not only upon Faulkner's published writings, but also upon his increasingly numerous public utterances, and upon his silences too.

Let us begin at an appropriate point for a literary study, with a manuscript—or rather, in this case, with the typescript of Faulkner's novel *Absalom, Absalom!* In its opening chapter appears a description of the protagonist, Thomas Sutpen, whose background is that of a poor white in the West Virginia mountains, but who appears abruptly with a gang of slaves in the north Mississippi territory of the 1830's, hacks a plantation out of the wilderness, and takes as his wife Ellen Coldfield, the daughter of a small merchant in the raw little frontier community of Jefferson. According to Ellen's sister Rosa, who narrates this part of the story, Sutpen married for respectability; what he wanted was "Ellen's and our father's names on a wedding license . . . that people could look at and read just as he would have wanted our father's . . . signature on a note of hand because our father knew who his father was."[3] When Faulkner sent the typescript of the novel to his publisher, his editor wanted to delete the passage, and wrote in the margin of the page, "Knowing Sutpen's father wouldn't have encouraged anyone to sign a note." To which Faulkner replied, in another marginal comment, "It would in the South. If they had known who his father was, more than Compson and Coldfield would have appeared to get him out of

---

nizing how biographies, collections of letters, and scholarly monographs may assist the process of rendering his work more acceptable to a wider audience. Faulkner's attitude toward the world of scholarship and criticism might be described as at best a patient tolerance based on good manners, and his impatience with arid pedantry and irresponsibly impressionistic criticism has generally been well controlled. (His attitude toward the world of journalism has, for good reason and with good effect, on occasion been less temperate.)

[3] New York, 1936, p. 16.

jail. *Leave as is.*"[4] (Faulkner emphasized the last three words by underlining them.)

This is an illuminating exchange; the book by Faulkner with its strongly and individually Southern setting; the confusion and unbelief of the Northern editor; the author's explanation, brief and to the point; and the concluding warning, *Leave as is.* Our sympathies are with Faulkner, of course; one doesn't have to be familiar with the background of this novel to believe in it. The community of Jefferson needs no marginal gloss to explain its ways to the sympathetic reader. And yet a word must be said for the editor too. He speaks for many puzzled outsiders to whom the ways of the South are strange and in need of explanation.

To judge by the evidence of published Faulkner criticism, many Northerners have failed to give his works the sympathetic reading they might have afforded, say, the equally alien fiction of a French or Irish writer. The reasons for the failure are basically nonliterary ones. Sectional prejudice, unfortunately, is still strong among us today, in North and South alike, a fact that we can regret but cannot overlook. And for most of his career Faulkner has with commendable and professional determination refused to provide for the puzzled or unsympathetic reader the sort of marginal gloss he supplied that editor in *Absalom, Absalom!,* though his recent public discussions of his work, chiefly at the University of Virginia, represent a substantial, if at times deceptive, departure from former practice.

If sectional prejudice has hurt the reception of Faulkner's books in the North, should we then look South for the more sympathetic, hence superior, audience for his fiction? It would be nice to think so, and potentially, at any rate, the Southerner should be the better reader. The Mississippi novelist Shelby Foote, reviewing a Faulkner book for his hometown newspaper, deplored the fact that Faulkner's reputation for obscurity had frightened off possible readers—"This is regrettable," said Foote, "particularly here in Mississippi, for no readers have a better chance for enjoyment than we have. Speaking

[4] P. 13 of a typescript version of *Absalom, Absalom!* in Faulkner's own collection of his papers. Reproduced as Fig. 14 in James B. Meriwether, *The Literary Career of William Faulkner* (Princeton University Library, 1961).

Mr. Faulkner's idiom, we catch overtones . . . no outlander would suspect. He writes for us."[5] Yet by and large it is still true today, as it has always been, that the South is the worst book market in the nation; though Southerners write books, they don't read them. Is it really worse to be a Northerner reading Faulkner unsympathetically than it is to be a Southerner not reading him at all?

Perhaps, on the whole—certainly in the early years of his career—the greatest degree of justice has been accorded Faulkner abroad; not in England, where after considerable interest in his first few books, the prevailing makers of literary opinion decided against Faulkner through lack of sympathy with his stylistic and structural innovations and where, on the whole, too much anti-Southern sentiment from across the Atlantic has been echoed—not in England, but on the Continent, and particularly in France, where the more extreme Northern interpretation of a barbarous and culturally negligible South was not likely to win acceptance because of the strong suspicion that all Americans are uncivilized. As the French writer Marcel Aymé put it, explaining "What French Readers Find in William Faulkner's Fiction," one charm he has for them is that

> Faulkner belongs to a Southern family and his characters are Southerners. It is odd that the French, brought up to admire the great revolutionary heroes of French history, besides having all read *Uncle Tom's Cabin* in their childhood, should be prejudiced by nature in favor of the Southerners against the Northerners.
>
> It may be . . . that they see in the War of Secession and the crushing of the South the prefiguration of an imminent war and another northern invasion, against which they must stand alone, despite the treaties. One thing is certain. William Faulkner's attachment to his province and his pride as a Southerner do not leave the French untouched. Perhaps the most important element in shaping his genius (which a Frenchman can understand better than an American from Boston) is his love for the misfortunes of his own part of his country.[6]

The problem of sectional, or national, prejudice in literary criticism is always with us, and a strong argument can always be made for ignoring rather than attempting to answer it. Experience goes to show that the problem is inherently insoluble, and little service

[5] Review of *Knight's Gambit* in the Greenville, Miss., *Delta Democrat-Times,* November 13, 1949, p. 18.

[6] *New York Times Book Review,* December 17, 1950, p. 4.

is done an author by that familiar figure, the shrilly defensive critic who belabors obvious ignorance and prejudice. Yet in Faulkner's case there is good reason to call attention to the problem, though its solution can be safely left to time, for Faulkner criticism must be accounted still in its infancy, to judge by the scope and violence of current disagreement concerning the most basic interpretation of his works. And when so many routes remain to be pioneered in this field, it is worth while to erect what warning signs and guideposts our present experience has proved useful, though they might be superfluous when the period of exploration is over and a relatively settled critical era has begun.

The history of the critical reception of an author's works is basic and vital not only to the literary student, but also, no matter how many times he tells us that he is indifferent to criticism, to the author too. It is well known that Faulkner's books did not afford him a living—that is, the means to live while he wrote more books—until late in his career, although at least his books were published. No one, whether author, agent, editor, or publisher, knows just what the relation between a book's critical notices and its reading, buying public will be. A book can receive very good, very bad, or indifferent reviews and sell well or badly with nearly equal facility, it seems. But that in the long run, if possibly not in the short, there is a real connection between criticism and sales cannot be doubted, and when we contemplate today the critical reception and the sales of Faulkner's novels in America during the first half or three-quarters of his career, we cannot help but feel rueful and apologetic about our literary situation, and cannot but admire the firmness and dedication with which he nevertheless pursued his way.

But in what ways was this situation affected by the fact that Faulkner was a Southerner, writing novels with Southern settings? We begin with the fact that most of Faulkner's novels have been published in a period when the critical climate of opinion in this country was predominantly hostile to them, and it is difficult to examine the body of American Faulkner criticism without going on to conclude that Faulkner's Southernness was at the bottom of much of its hostility. A great part of the most influential criticism of his books in the 1930's, for example, was Marxist. Any writer, Northern or Southern, in this period who avoided the matter of politics and dealt with the importance of the individual, not of society, could hardly expect a sympathetic reading from these critics, but the Southern writer probably came in for the greater share of leftist obloquy. Southern scenes, characters, and themes were regarded as inherently reactionary, and were treated accordingly by the critics, unless the writer—Caldwell is an example—used them in the exposition of a Marxist social message.

Edmund Wilson, reviewing the status of American criticism, leftist and rightist, in 1937, summed up the problem with the leftist critics clearly. We have been suffering in America for a long time, he noted, from a Marxist criticism which has become increasingly irresponsible in literary matters. He quoted a well-known leftist critic who had stated that

> *Culture herself* demands that we put the right social values ahead of the right literary values; and whenever we encounter people who want to keep art dustproof, who bewail the collapse of "aesthetic values," it is our duty to ascertain just how far their indignation is a screen for reactionary and unsocial thinking. . . . It is less important that the search for truth should survive than that the cancers of society should be cut out. . . .

There are a number of things to be said against such a position—Faulkner would probably say, if he bothered to comment on it, that it is more important that the search for truth should survive, because different people might have different definitions of cancer—but Wilson summed up the case admirably when he concluded that

> One has to make up one's mind in what capacity one is going to function. And from the moment one is not trying to function as an organizer or an active politician (and agitational literature is politics), one must work in good faith in one's own field. . . . You may say, This is no time for art or science: the enemy is at the gate! But in that case you should be at the gate: in the Spanish International Brigade, for example, rather than engaged in literary work. There is no sense in pursuing a literary career under the impression that one is operating a bombing-plane.[7]

[7] Edmund Wilson, "American Critics, Left and Right," in *The Shores of Light: A Literary Chronicle of the Twenties and Thirties* (New York, 1952), pp. 640-61. The critic was Louis Kronenberger, who had written originally in *Partisan Review;* the quotations cited here are from pp. 648 and 650 of Wilson's article. It is interesting that the rightist critic whom Wilson singled out for discussion in this article, Bernard De Voto, achieved a consistency equal to that of Kronenberger in attacking Faulkner's books which he reviewed, in-

But Wilson's conclusions did not prevent this same critic, the following year, from bombing vigorously Faulkner's next book, *The Unvanquished.* And it is significant that the attack took the form of a regional indictment to which the book was sometimes only incidental. "The twisted heritage which the Confederate South bestowed upon its descendants is something few of them have renounced," our critic's review begins. "It has got into their blood, and all that their weakened minds can do is resort to a rather vague, rueful, and inadequate irony. . . . The South languishes in race infantilism." (Two years later, reviewing *The Hamlet,* the same critic took the same approach. "Mr. Faulkner's forte, like that of the South he inhabits, is decay . . . absolutely nothing inhibits him from exploring the most polluted streams and malarial swamps of the subhuman spirit," he informed his readers, noting gloomily that "we are all aware of the things that go on in the South.") Since *The Unvanquished* is basically an affirmative, even optimistic book, the critic attacked not only Faulkner's material but his attitude toward it. "We are told," he stated, "that novelists should deal with the material they know best. But not forever, surely; and not if that material is a swamp, slowly, voraciously sucking the novelist in." And he concluded that Faulkner's subject matter had in the end defeated him; that in *The Unvanquished* he had done no more than "brightly varnish rotten timber."[8]

What might at first sight appear to be no more than another manifestation of sectional ignorance or prejudice, it is clear from the case of this critic, has its theoretical basis in the belief, which has not been confined to Marxists, that the end justifies the means, a belief that has produced bad fiction and bad criticism with equal consistency. In this country much Faulkner criticism has suffered

---

cluding *The Unvanquished.* And it is ironic that after taking Kronenberger to task for his leftist deficiencies as a literary critic, Wilson should ten years later fall into the same trap in reviewing *Intruder in the Dust.* Though he had much to say in praise of the novel, Wilson entitled his review "William Faulkner's Reply to the Civil-Rights Program" and committed the cardinal critical error of assuming that the views of Gavin Stevens were those of Faulkner (*New Yorker,* October 23, 1948, pp. 120-22, 125-27).

[8] Louis Kronenberger, review of *The Unvanquished* in *Nation,* February 19, 1938, pp. 212, 214. His review of *The Hamlet* appeared in *Nation,* April 13, 1940, pp. 481-82.

from the qualities demonstrated by this review of *The Unvanquished,* qualities which we can join in deploring and in striving to avoid. At the same time, we must be careful, in avoiding the path of Marx through the realms of literature, likewise to shun the way of Senator McCarthy; it is possible to criticize both Faulkner and the South without joining in a sinister Communist conspiracy. But surely, whatever our opinion of their proposed solutions may be, we can pay a full measure of tribute to the concern with economic problems, to the social and political idealism and dedication of our Marxist critics of the 1930's, and yet begrudge them the price they exacted from us in terms of damage to the aesthetic integrity of American culture and regret their still pervasive influence upon our literary situation even today.

That influence, for example, may still affect, in one way or another, present judgments of *The Unvanquished* which owe a literary or critical debt to that novel's early Marxist reviewers even though the current critic may share none of the reviewers' political or economic theories. Let us examine, for instance, one chapter of this episodic novel as an example of the way in which the Southern qualities of Faulkner's writing can make it difficult for some critics to give it a sympathetic reading. This chapter, entitled "Skirmish at Sartoris," takes place in the spring of 1865, and it begins with a description of two things: a wedding and the attempt of Colonel John Sartoris, after his return from fighting Sherman, to rebuild his home, which had been looted and burned by Yankee soldiers.

It soon appears that thanks to the war Colonel Sartoris has more to restore than his home. Carpetbaggers have come to Jefferson, "the two Burdens from Missouri, with a patent from Washington to organise the niggers into Republicans," and there is to be an election, with the carpetbagger candidate for marshal of Jefferson a totally illiterate ex-coachman, Cassius Q. Benbow.

The narrator of *The Unvanquished* is Bayard Sartoris, the colonel's son, who in this chapter is a boy of fifteen. It should be noted that there is a good deal of humor in this novel, despite the serious events of war and reconstruction with which it deals, and much of the humor achieves its final effect because of the youth and innocence of the narrator; like Huckleberry Finn, Bayard gives a straightforward account of events, and the reader is tickled by the simultaneous realization of the real significance of what is going on and of the fact that much of this significance is lost on the narrator.

An example is the report that Ringo, the colored boy who is Bayard's playmate, companion, and body servant, brings back when he first encounters the Burdens.

> Then one day Ringo slipped off and went to town and came back and he looked at me with his eyes rolling a little.
>
> "Do you know what I ain't?" he said.
>
> "What?" I said.
>
> "I ain't a nigger any more. I done been abolished."[9]

Ringo explains to Bayard about the attempts of the carpetbaggers to organize the Negro voters and the determination of the white men of the locality to prevent them.

> "Naw, suh," he said. "This war ain't over. Hit just started good. Used to be when you seed a Yankee you knowed him because he never had nothing but a gun or a mule halter or a handful of hen feathers. Now you don't even know him and stid of the gun he got a clutch of this stuff in one hand [showing Bayard a new scrip dollar drawn on "the United States Resident Treasurer"] and a clutch of nigger voting tickets in the yuther. [229]

The easy, conventional humor of the dialogue and the fact that Bayard makes no comment at all upon Ringo's news can make it easy for the reader to overlook the potential danger in the situation.

Further reason not to take things seriously appears in the lightly, almost farcically handled plot element which consists of the attempts to force Colonel Sartoris to marry Drusilla Hawk, a romantically, even melodramatically drawn figure whose father and fiancé had been killed during the war, and who had then fought, in man's clothes, against the Yankees in the troop of cavalry irregulars commanded by Sartoris. Her mother, with powerful support from all the respectable ladies of Jefferson, is convinced that her relationship with Sartoris could not have been an innocent one. To Drusilla's question, "Can't you understand that in the troop I was just another

[9] New York, 1938, p. 228. Subsequent references to this book are made by page numbers in the text.

man and not much of one at that," her mother snaps: "You wish to tell me that you, a young woman, associated with him, a still young man, day and night for a year, running about the country with no guard nor check of any sort upon—Do you take me for a complete fool?" (233) The point here of course is that Mrs. Hawks *is* a complete fool; in peacetime her analysis of the situation might have been the correct one, her suspicions justified, but she is unable to realize that the war and its killings had in effect unsexed her daughter, had produced results and a situation to which her conventional and practical beliefs are no longer a reliable guide. So Mrs. Hawks manages to bully her daughter and Colonel Sartoris into marrying—this a little surprisingly, for Sartoris is hardly a man to be bullied, and we wonder at his acquiescence.

These two elements in the plot—wedding and election—combine when they are both scheduled for the same day. Bayard gives a cursory and unanalytical account of events: how his father tells the Burdens that "Cash Benbow would never be elected marshal in Jefferson," how all the white men in the locality converge on Jefferson with pistols in their pockets, and how the Burdens kept "their nigger voters camped in a cotton gin on the edge of town under guard" (234). On election day, as Bayard tells it, "when we came into the square we saw the crowd of niggers kind of huddled beyond the hotel door with six or eight strange white men herding them" (236). Inside the hotel the two Burdens, equipped with ballot box and pistol, are preparing to hold the election. Sartoris, likewise armed, enters the hotel alone; after they fire at him he shoots and kills both. Emerging from the hotel he addresses the crowd:

> "Does any man here want a word with me about this?" he said. But you could not hear anything, not even moving. The herd of niggers stood like they had when I first saw them, with the Northern white men herding them together. Father put his hat on . . . and helped [Drusilla] . . . onto her horse and handed the ballot box up to her. Then he looked around again, at all of them. "This election will be held out at my home," he said. . . . "Does any man here object?" [238]

No objection is made; the Northern white men and their captive voters appear no more on the scene, and out at Sartoris the election is conducted without further disturbance. "Let all who want the

Honorable Cassius Q. Benbow to be Marshal of Jefferson write Yes on his ballot; opposed, No," says Colonel Sartoris, and Wyatt, one of his ex-cavalrymen, adds helpfully, "And I'll do the writing and save some more time." He writes them out and the other men drop them in the ballot box. "You needn't bother to count them," concludes Wyatt. "They all voted No." The story ends with Colonel Sartoris and Drusilla left behind to get married at last and the men riding away uttering the rebel yell.

> It came back high and thin and ragged and fierce, like when the Yankees used to hear it out of the smoke and the galloping:
> "Yaaaaay, Drusilla!" they hollered. "Yaaaaaay, John Sartoris! Yaaaaaaay!" [241-42]

And that is all. The author gives us no interpretation, draws no conclusions; no character emerges to sum it all up or give its meaning. We hear no more of the dead Burdens or the defeated candidate for marshal or the herd of Negro voters.

Now let us look at what has been done with this story by the critics. Little has been written about *The Unvanquished,* partly because on the whole it is certainly one of Faulkner's lesser works, and even less has been done with "Skirmish at Sartoris," which is artistically the weakest part of the book. I do not quarrel with this neglect; I must agree, in fact, with a critic who calls it an "unexceptional" piece of writing, "Its characterizations . . . conventional, its situations ordinary, and its conclusions hackneyed." I agree, however, only with the qualification that like most of Faulkner's lesser work, even at its weakest it is worthy of some respect; even when the characters are puppets and the plot is of an ordinary magazine-fiction conventionality, the powerful impress of Faulkner's mind is often present, and we cannot dismiss it until we have tested it with the same searching reading we give his major fiction.

An interesting critical reaction to this story, one based on a failure to accord it such a reading and revealing much about the critic's attitude toward the South, is as follows:

> The marriage is interrupted to enable John Sartoris to drive away carpetbaggers and prevent Negroes from voting. After allowing, in true gallant fashion, two male Burdens . . . to shoot at him first, Sartoris kills them. Sartoris, of course, disenfranchises the Negro—but this is not considered

even briefly. . . . Perhaps there is a strong case to be made for disenfranchisement at that point in southern history. If there is, Faulkner passed up an opportunity to dramatize it. Sartoris seems a cardboard "hero," moving inside a stereotyped, thoughtless action.[10]

Note that the critic is making two points here: first that the story is artistically inferior—cardboard hero, stereotyped action—and second that behind a poor story is poor thinking. Faulkner didn't consider, the critic says, even briefly, the implications of the historical fact of Negro disenfranchisement in writing the story. And his clear implication is that the two failures are connected, perhaps the same: poor historical thinking, ergo poor writing.

Let me postpone for a moment consideration of the reason the critic is advancing here to explain the artistic failure of the story—that Faulkner is ignoring the implications of Negro disenfranchisement here. Instead let us look beyond—or in front of—the historical fact to the fictional action of Sartoris in shooting the Burdens. This is clearly meant to be, and for most readers I think it is, the moral crux of the story. The killing, we are perhaps at first inclined to feel, puts Sartoris in the wrong, entirely in the wrong. And if, within the fictional framework of the story, this is indeed so, if Sartoris is so definitely in the wrong here, then we can say, we ought to say, that it is a major artistic fault that he gets away with it, that Faulkner allows the yelling approval of the ex-cavalry troop at the end of the story to be the only comment on the action and creates a verbal atmosphere of approbation, or at least of toleration, for the violent death of the Burdens.

But this is obviously much too naïve a reading of the story. Let us examine again the context of the shooting. To begin with, Sartoris is certainly established from the opening of the story as a sympathetic character; he is peaceably rebuilding his house, and since its burning had served no military end, the Yankees are as clearly established as villains. Then the carpetbaggers appear, and Faulkner goes to some pains to demonstrate how natural it is to equate them with the looters and burners of wartime: their candidate for office is obviously unfit; they herd the bewildered Negroes like sheep and

[10] William Van O'Connor, *The Tangled Fire of William Faulkner* (Minneapolis, 1954), pp. 101-2.

use bribery (scrip dollars) and force (keeping them under armed guard) to determine their vote.

In the actual shooting, Faulkner is again careful to put Sartoris in as favorable a light as he can, or nearly so. Instead of having it occur on the square, in the open where his supporters could back him up, Faulkner sends Sartoris alone into the hotel, where the Burdens have him two to one. Further, he has the carpetbaggers fire first at Sartoris; since they do so, we might say that Sartoris killed in self-defense.

If this were all there were to the situation as Faulkner sets it up, it would make of "Skirmish at Sartoris" a very simple story, though an unflawed one as far as fictional technique is concerned. It would make the yelling horsemen the true commentators upon the action. And we would have pure Thomas Nelson Page. Given such a reading, no wonder the critic looks behind the fiction for a failure in Faulkner's thinking to explain matters.

But this reading is really hardly less naïve than it would be to see the killing of the Burdens as simple murder. At every point, Faulkner has set up his action to provide a commentary upon Sartoris that prevents the reader from making a simple judgment of his actions. The Burdens have a group of armed Northern whites coercing the Negroes, but on the other side is a group, a larger group, of armed ex-cavalrymen. The Burdens, themselves armed, have the ballot box with them inside the hotel, away from the open square, but after getting his hands on it Sartoris takes the ballot box several miles away to *his* house for the election. The Burdens shoot first—but isn't it clear, really, that Sartoris went into the hotel to shoot them? Didn't he really *force* them to take that first shot at him? Sartoris showed great courage here, but courage is not the same as innocence.

There is little excuse to be sentimental about the failure of the Negroes to vote in this election; the Burdens offered them only the mockery of a franchise. But look again at what Faulkner shows as the alternative: the little touch of having Wyatt write out those ballots at Sartoris adds more than comedy to the scene. Faulkner could have as easily shown all the men voting the same way, but each man filling out his own ballot, if he had merely wanted to show the whites united in their determination to resist carpetbagger domination. And we must remember one more thing about that vote cast at Sartoris. The anticarpetbag group put up no candidate of their own to oppose the illiterate ex-coachman. They simply voted no—no to the election of an obviously incompetent candidate, it is true, but also no to the election of any Negro, just as the killing of the Burdens had represented in one way the only means the Southern people had to prevent a corrupt election, but also represented their refusal to accept Negro voters.

At this point we might recall the other action of the story, that part which concerns Mrs. Hawks's effort to force Sartoris to marry Drusilla. At first sight it is puzzling that a man of determination and force should meekly succumb to a demand based upon a false premise. But surely his reaction to this demand is meant to enlighten us about his reaction to the other situation he faces, where he might likewise be said to accept unquestioningly the dictates of a conventional prewar social system without regard for the fact of a change produced by war. Or perhaps the illumination Faulkner means to provide by juxtaposing the two actions lies in the comparison implied between Mrs. Hawks in the one action and Sartoris in the other—both are strong wills unthinkingly attempting to prevent a change that the war has produced in the course of events.

In sum, though the action here is simple, and both action and emotions involved are so ordinary that we are tempted to call them hackneyed, we find on a little examination that the meaning of the story is by no means simple. Faulkner has obviously taken some pains to prevent his story from pointing out a simple moral. On the whole we can safely assume that the Burdens were clearly in the wrong in the beginning to attempt by force and bribery to elect an incompetent candidate; that Colonel Sartoris was clearly right in attempting to prevent this, and that we must have our doubts about his killing them and about the kind of election that Sartoris favored.

If there is, then, a certain carefully worked out ambiguity to the question of right and wrong here, does it mean that the ending, with the galloping horses and the rebel yells, is supposed to have an ironic effect? I suppose that the point could be debated; the level of writing is not distinguished, the reminder of melodrama in the choice of words and action is insistent. But in defense of this quality we must admit that it is appropriate to the narrator; Bayard accepts his father's point of view and actions unquestioningly, as he should, considering his age and the circumstances of his life for the preceding four years. But we have an even stronger hint that Faulkner intends some irony here. Immediately after shooting the Burdens and dispatching the ballot box to Sartoris, the Colonel stops to make bond in town before following the men to vote. When Wyatt objects, Sartoris replies, "Don't you see we are working for peace through law and order?" (239)—a remark not only unmistakably ironic, but even pathetic, for he obviously believes it himself, and it is hard to withhold our sympathy for him at the moment when he has just risked his life and dominated an excited mob by the force of his character.

All this is not to say that "Skirmish at Sartoris" is good fiction; the characterization remains conventional, the situations remain ordinary. It is not a distinguished story, but it is one which may not be dismissed before seeing that its meaning is not simple and that the action has been constructed with some care.

Let us return to our critic. We have now qualified, to some extent but only to some extent, his charge of poor writing, by showing how carefully its theme has been worked out; and his charge of poor thinking has likewise in one sense been answered. It was careless reading that led him to say that Faulkner didn't consider in the story the disenfranchisement of the Negro; Faulkner on the contrary has meticulously set the act of disenfranchisement into a context where a mixture of rights and wrongs must be considered. We may suppose the critic to have been so concerned with the question of Negro voting rights that he failed to note the other elements in the story, and both the carelessness of the reading and the overly-nice concern for the civil rights of the Burdens' herded voters are borne out by this critic's flat statement that "the Burdens certainly are not carpetbaggers," which would seem to overlook Faulkner's equally flat description of them as "those two carpet baggers." [11]

Nevertheless, we have done less than justice to the critic if we do not come to grips with the underlying assumption of his criticism of

[11] *Ibid.*, p. xi; *The Unvanquished*, pp. 256-57.

the story: that muddled or wrong-headed thinking on Faulkner's part concerning the material of his story is in some way responsible for its lack of artistic distinction. This is a charge that has been raised more than once, and at more than one Faulkner book; it is difficult to answer, but we owe it to Faulkner and to ourselves to try.

To begin with, I might try to support our critic's argument by noting a somewhat shaky grasp of the facts of history apparent in this story. Historically speaking, Sartoris did *not* disenfranchise the Negroes that spring of 1865; he could not, because this was a whole year before the passage of the Fourteenth Amendment, and two before the Reconstruction Acts which enabled Negroes to vote for the first time in Mississippi in the autumn elections of 1867. This mistake in date is irrelevant to the fiction, of course, just as the striking clocks in *Julius Caesar* should not lessen the effectiveness of the play for any audience not gone mad with pedantry. The question here is whether or not his ignorance of the dates of Reconstruction indicates a lack of interest, perhaps even a lack of strong feeling, in Faulkner on the subject, which might in turn be responsible for a less than adequate treatment of that subject in his fiction. If his heart doesn't lie with the Southern victims of Yankee injustice in Reconstruction, it might be asked, then is he much concerned with Southern injustice to the Negro, since he brings the two injustices into something of a balance in "Skirmish at Sartoris," which is Faulkner's only treatment of the subject in his fiction?

This critical argument has been fed by Faulkner's public statements on the subject of Reconstruction, or rather by his lack of them. In interviews and in his classroom appearances at Virginia and at Princeton he has repeatedly avoided committing himself on the subject. At Princeton, for instance, he turned aside a question about how much the South had suffered in the Civil War and Reconstruction by pointing out how much literary capital it has made of it ever since.

But Faulkner has made one public statement on the subject of Reconstruction, and that an important one. This was made in Japan, in 1955, on a trip Faulkner made for the Department of State, and occurred in a message addressed "To the Youth of Japan."

A hundred years ago, my country, the United States, was not one economy and culture, but two of them, so opposed to each other that ninety-five years ago they went to war against each other to test which one should prevail. My side, the South, lost that war, the battles of which were fought not on neutral ground in the waste of the ocean, but in our own homes, our gardens, our farms, as if Okinawa and Guadalcanal had been not islands in the distant Pacific but the precincts of Honshu and Hokkaido. Our land, our homes were invaded by a conqueror who remained after we were defeated; we were not only devastated by the battles which we lost, the conqueror spent the next ten years after our defeat and surrender despoiling us of what little war had left.

Faulkner went on to say that now these things were past and that he believed the country was even stronger because of them, and compared the situation in the South during Reconstruction with that in Japan after World War II. And he apologized for bringing up the subject of the past troubles of his part of the country: "I mention it only to explain and show that Americans from my part of America at least can understand the feeling of the Japanese young people of today."[12]

It is obvious, then, that neither lack of interest, nor even of strong feelings, on Faulkner's part can account for his neglect of the troubled period of Reconstruction in his fiction. Rather, we may suppose a determination to avoid a subject which has been overworked, overtalked, overwritten, perhaps, and been used too often as an excuse to account for ills due to other, less honorable causes. I do not think we can fail to condemn such criticism which, in connection with "Skirmish at Sartoris," demonstrates literary blind spots in its partisan zeal to defend the Northern part in Reconstruction. Whatever one's feelings about Reconstruction—necessary evil, tragic mistake, avoidable error—there is no reason to assume that a literary artist must agree with one's opinion in order to write well. Yet I think there is a further lesson to be considered here, a lesson taught by Faulkner, not in what he has written, but in what he has failed to write. When we consider the fact that this major artist *has* avoided this subject, and avoided it through no lack of interest or strong feelings about it, we have the strongest kind of commentary on the problem that faces a writer of Faulkner's stature, writing as a Southerner at this time. I think that in writing "Skirmish at

[12] Robert A. Jelliffe, ed., *Faulkner at Nagano* (Tokyo, 1956), pp. 185-86.

Sartoris" as he did, Faulkner showed that he disagreed with those people who feel, as some of his critics obviously do, that the moral issues of Reconstruction were simple and that the denial of the franchise to the illiterate freedmen at that time was wholly or almost wholly wrong. I think, however, that in failing to deal with the subject again, or at greater length, anywhere in his whole body of work, Faulkner has also made a profound comment on the subject, and I suggest that he may not have wanted to wave the bloody shirt, to risk being identified with an opposite school of thought, which would hold that Colonel Sartoris was as right in what he did, as others would say that he was wrong.

No one cares today whether Shakespeare's sympathies lay with the House of York or the House of Lancaster in the Wars of the Roses; in our time the historical rights and wrongs are irrelevant to the question of the quality of his history plays. Or let us look at an example which comes a little closer to us. We are amused, and properly so, at Dr. Johnson for his eighteenth-century failure to appreciate seventeenth-century Milton's literary qualities because he could not forget that Milton was a regicide. A hundred years later, that is, the feelings engendered by the English Civil War were still strong enough to blind a great critic to a literary merit which we cannot believe Dr. Johnson would have failed to appreciate had Milton been a royalist.

We are still surprised, today, by the strength of the feelings that are yet elicited by the issues and the legacy of our own Civil War. We may say that these feelings are good, in that they demonstrate a continuing vitality in our thinking. But that they have played an important part in the peculiar and long-delayed development of a proper audience for Faulkner's work in this country is obvious; it is questionable whether we yet have that audience today. We need to remind ourselves that we have those feelings, when we are dealing with an important creative artist like Faulkner, remind ourselves that the proper perspective in which to consider him is that of a novelist. Not that we shouldn't consider his works sociologically and politically and economically and psychologically too, if we like. But if we do, let us remember that we are, for our own reasons and our own nonliterary benefit, judging him by standards other than those he has set himself to meet, judging him in a court the jurisdiction of which is at best marginal. These things are true of any creative artist, and these warnings are all old ones. My point is that these warnings are particularly necessary in the case of Faulkner because he is a Southern writer, writing at the present time about the South, and we must therefore be doubly on the alert, given the present situation, to try to avoid the faults and fallacies that beset us all, in all generations, in all countries, in trying to deal honorably with our prophets.

8

THE YOUNGEST GENERATION OF SOUTHERN FICTION WRITERS

Richard K. Meeker

William Styron, one of the most promising young Southern fiction writers, has already expressed his opinion of any critic who tries to classify and evaluate his generation:

> But don't you think it's tiresome, really, all these so-called spokesmen trumpeting around, elbowing one another out of the way to see who'll be the first to give a new and original name to twenty-five million people: the Beat Generation, or the Silent Generation, and God knows what-all? I think the damn generation should be left alone. And that goes for the eternal idea of competition—whether the new writers can beat the team of Dos Passos, Faulkner, Fitzgerald, and Hemingway.[1]

While there has been much trumpeting around, there has been very little elbowing to make a comprehensive estimate of the Southern writers of this generation. One reason is suggested by John Aldridge, a leading critic of modern American fiction.

> The chances are that we shall be deprived for some time to come of any more accurate estimate of [young writers] than can be obtained from their publishers' blurbs. One is of course free at any time to go to their books and to find there the makings of a critical judgment of one's own. But such is the state of things that for a critic, particularly a new and

A Lecture given for the Institute of Southern Culture Lecture at Longwood College, July 9, 1958.

[1] *Writers at Work: The* Paris Review *Interviews* (New York, 1958), p. 278.

untried critic, to do that before those books have been officially recognized, approved, classified, documented, explicated, and footnoted by other critics would be tantamount to professional heresy and suicide.[2]

However, since both Styron and Aldridge have successfully ignored their own warnings, it may be worth the risk for a new and untried critic to examine the output of the youngest generation of Southern fiction writers in an effort to see if the now-famous "Southern Renascence" is to be kept alive by the next generation. This is an attempt, then, to locate the future Faulkners, Wolfes, Weltys, Porters, and Warrens, and to describe their view of the modern South.

But first, what constitutes a "young Southern fiction writer"? I have made several arbitrary, but, I hope, logical decisions here. I have accepted, with a slight adjustment, the U.S. Census definition of the South as consisting of sixteen states: Virginia, Delaware, Maryland, West Virginia, Kentucky, North Carolina, Tennessee, Arkansas, South Carolina, Georgia, Alabama, Mississippi, Oklahoma, Louisiana, Texas, and Florida. I have counted only eastern Texas, however.

A glance at the birth dates of the reigning Southern fiction writers will show that they were all born around 1900. Katherine Anne Porter was born in 1894, Faulkner in 1897, Wolfe in 1900, Warren in 1905, and Welty in 1909. The appropriate birth date for the new generation would, therefore, be around 1920. Two writers, Carson McCullers and Peter Taylor, both born in 1917, obviously belong in this group, but otherwise I have held to 1920 as the earliest birth date.

In my definition, then, a young Southern fiction writer is one born in one of sixteen Southern states around 1920 who has already published at least one volume of fiction. Writers now living in the South who were so unfortunate as to be born elsewhere do not count.

First, let me sketch a typical member of the youngest generation. To him, World War I, the roaring twenties, and the depression are familiar only through fiction, song, and family legend. He was born about 1925 in a small town in, let us say, Louisiana. He grew up there and left home for the first time when he went to college. There

[2] *After the Lost Generation* (New York, 1951), pp. 201-2.

he read James, Flaubert, Joyce, Fitzgerald, Faulkner, and did some writing himself, usually on a college publication. He learned about World War II first hand after three years of military service, which took him to Europe. After the war he returned to college, sometimes to teach, but always to continue writing. His efforts won him a grant or fellowship and at least one literary prize. He has already written one novel and one volume of short stories, which have been favorably reviewed and reprinted with flashy paper covers. At present, he no longer lives in the South. Probably he lives in New York and is receptive to offers from television. He is not yet self-sustaining, but he is not living on Grub Street either.[3]

A few statistics may document my general impression. The thirty-four writers who qualify for discussion have already produced over seventy volumes of short stories and novels, plus several times that many stories published in serious periodicals. Most of them come from six Southern states: Louisiana, Georgia, Virginia, Alabama, and Mississippi. Louisiana has a slight lead over the others with six writers. Twenty-six of the group are men; only eight are women. I shall leave the interpretation of these figures for someone else.

And now let's look at the contents of the typical story by a young Southerner. It takes place in the relative present in a small Southern town. The protagonist is an earnest young man who has returned home after a long absence. He finds that he has changed in the interim while his town has not. He finds little sympathy for his predicament from his family, who represent orthodoxy and tradition. They always want him to settle down and marry in the community. This is the Hemingway-Fitzgerald-Wolfe theme of the twenties again, but the conflict is sharper, because the protagonist loves his family and his region. Unlike the disillusioned youth of the twenties, he frowns upon some Yankee or European Bohemia. He wants to live in the place of his birth, but he cannot tolerate the provincialism, racial prejudice, and worship of the past. If the conflict does not destroy him first, he sadly leaves his home.

[3] A recent description by Granville Hicks of the typical American novelist of the 1950's corresponds to my sketch at many points. It would seem that only geography distinguishes the background of the new Southern writer from that of any other young American writer. (See *Saturday Review*, April 12, 1958, p. 19.)

The differences between this and traditional Southern writing will be clearer if we notice several striking absences from recent Southern fiction. With two exceptions, there are no historical narratives. The Civil War is fought in only one novel, *Sojourn of a Stranger,* and there for only a few chapters. Almost without exceptions, the stories are set in the twentieth century. There is hardly anything of the antebellum South here, no magnolias, white columns, or darkies crooning. It is the modern South which interests the young writer. However, he does care about the past; he cares very much, but in a special way. History for him, too, "has many cunning passages"; it is full of parallels, of causes and effects. But for the young Southern writer, when history repeats itself, it is a tragedy. When the son duplicates the experience of his father, or the daughter follows in her mother's footsteps, this is counted a mistake, or even a crime.

This attitude is communicated artistically by the blending of past and present in narrative. In fact, this is one of the technical hallmarks of the new Southern novel. The story will begin in the present, but quickly shift by flashback or dream or reverie, sometimes imperceptibly—and annoyingly—to a parallel incident in the past, or to an incident which brought about the present state of affairs. The young Southern writer is a specialist in rapid transition and the juxtaposition of time levels in his story.

In short, the young Southern writer is interested in the past not to show the pastness of the present, but to show the presentness of the present. Change is in the law of the young man's universe. To frustrate change is to invite tragedy. This does not mean that the young Southerner repudiates all of the old values. He simply finds that they must be purchased at the high cost of intolerance and provincialism.

Another striking absence from recent Southern fiction is orthodox religious belief. The young protagonists never attend church willingly and tend to satirize the piety of their elders. Revivalists and liberal clergymen alike are ridiculed. One can hardly ignore the inference that the orthodox church in the South is not reaching the younger generation.

Just as there is little antebellum scenery in the new Southern novel, there are few aristocrats, except as examples of impractical or outmoded ideas. The dominant characters are middle class, or, significantly, the lower class. Increasingly in the last few decades the Negro has been treated seriously as a character in fiction, and the new Southern writer has continued this trend. There are no comic figures here, but human beings with problems the same as anybody else's, only accentuated by ignorance and prejudice. Faulkner deserves credit for exploiting the tragic possibilities of the Negro character, but it is to the credit of the younger writers that they have extended his discovery. If the white Southerner has a tragic vision unknown to other Americans,[4] what shall we call the vision of the Southern Negro if not tragic?

Several other absences from the new fiction might have been predicted. There are still very few urban settings in the South, except in the work of Peter Taylor and William Styron. Most stories are rural or small town in location. There are only one or two college settings, although many of the writers live in academic communities. Not quite so easy to explain is the relative absence of humor or satire from recent Southern writing.

Of course, no typical writer or story can indicate the range of attitudes and techniques displayed by these young writers. In order to present their view of the modern South, I have classified them into three categories:

(1) Those who describe the South, more or less favorably.

(2) Those who criticize the South, more or less unfavorably.

(3) Those who ignore the South, meaning those with themes that are irrelevant or universal.

Only about one out of four of the new Southern writers can be said to approve of the South, and most of these do so with reservations. The most obvious endorsement comes from Mac Hyman's *No Time for Sergeants* (1954), about which little need be said except that it comically dramatizes the perennial country-boy vs. city-slicker myth. By a combination of luck, physical strength, and native shrewdness, the hero, Will Stockbridge, manages to get the better of

[4] See Richard M. Weaver, "Aspects of the Southern Philosophy," pp. 15-30, and C. Vann Woodward, "The Irony of Southern History," pp. 63-79, in *Southern Renascence* (Baltimore, 1953).

city boys, Yankees, and most of the Air Force. It was inevitable that a play and a movie should be made out of this one.

An endorsement of the South arrived at after suffering is more common. Eugene Walter's *Untidy Pilgrim* (1954) is a Southern *Catcher in the Rye,* only the narrator, named Cousin, attains his salvation through a return to Mobile, Alabama, rather than through psychoanalysis. He foolishly pursues his girl, Philine, and the villain, Cousin Perrin—both of whom have been corrupted by Yankee civilization—to New York. After suffering briefly, he takes the train back home.

> Impulsively, I threw down my satchel, and pulled off my shoes without bothering to untie the laces, by dint of a hard jerk or so. Socks I ripped off in a wink, and stood there, foolishly wiggling my feet in the cool powdery dust in the shade of a blueberry thicket. . . . My heart made flipflops: I was perfectly happy, in the South again, back in the green and crazy land where I do indeed belong.[5]

However, lest we associate the narrator too closely with the author, we should note that Walter is now living in Rome.

A more sophisticated and restricted endorsement comes from Leroy Leatherman in *The Other Side of the Tree* (1954). Even the experienced Faulknerian will have trouble distinguishing past from present in this novel. In fact that seems to be the significance of the title: that the past is just over on the other side of the tree. The tree in this case in a huge, hollow live oak, in the middle of a swamp, where seventeen-year-old Jim Daigre listens to Ed Hatheway tell a long story about the romance between Ida Field and Joe Wainright. Because of the past, the Wainrights have come to stand for what is evil and vulgar, while the Fields have always stood for gentility. In the present, outside the tree, Jim Daigre is trying to decide what to do about the tantalizing and unfaithful Margaret Rainey. His dilemma is reinforced by an invitation from the Wainright family to the debut of their granddaughter. The Wainrights live in a pretentious summer place with glass walls, and their granddaughter has been educated in Europe. This is the present that assaults Jim Daigre, but he sees through Ed Hatheway's story that the conflict

[5] Philadelphia, 1954, p. 136.

between tradition and change has always existed. Finally, he decides to attend the Wainright debut, where he finds Margaret also. Thus he has reluctantly made peace with what he has considered evil.

A more painful acceptance comes in Kathleen Crawford's novel *Strawfire* (1947), in which Frances Acheson, a Richmond girl, falls in love with Paul Revkin, a talented Jewish violinist. Frances' conservative Virginia family object, and so do all her friends, except Dr. McDonough, a liberal—and unpopular—Presbyterian minister. Paul senses that Frances isn't strong enough to endure the social rejection of such a mixed marriage, so he breaks off the romance. The end is not definite, but we assume she marries the proper man eventually. A straw fire blazes brightly but is soon burned out.

By far the most powerful, and tragic, affirmation of Southern values comes in *The Innocent* (1957) by Madison Jones. After seven years of roaming in the North, Duncan Welsh returns to his father's farm in Tennessee, hungry for the traditional virtues and the uncomplicated life he remembers.

His return is spoiled by a symbolic incident. He rides into town with a sturdy old farmer and his son over a shiny new bridge which has replaced the old ferry. The father, a champion wrestler in his time, wants to match his son against a carnival wrestler. In that setting of freak shows, girlie shows, ball and marble games, and flimsy rides—where everything is tawdry and contrived—the son is killed by Tiger Sloan, whose new wrestling style neither father nor son can fathom.

Duncan finds his house unchanged; it is large, old, worn-out, and full of mementoes of past days. However, his sister has become engaged to a sociologist-minister, Hiram Garner, who stands for everything Duncan has fled in the North. His father, in the face of change, has retreated silently. A parallel scene is acted out in their Negro tenant family. Logan and Della are the only stable figures around the farm, but their boy Herman has returned from New York lazy and insolent.

As a symbol of his new feelings toward the past, Duncan decides to restore the old Mountain Slasher breed of horse, which has been replaced by the more popular Allen breed. He goes to a horse show in search of a stud and finds that the judges favor the Allen with its unnatural gait to the natural Tennessee walking horse.

All of these [Allens], he thought, for sheer elegance, for refinement of line only, probably outdid the old horse. Yet none of them, Duncan was sure, could equal him. Just what the quality was that they lacked, Duncan could not define to his own satisfaction. It was related to power, endurance, adaptability; but it was not these only, or exactly. It was a defect arisen, perhaps, out of a too deliberately calculated refinement of breeding. What was sacrificed was that perfection of balance among the horse's qualities which had in the past characterized the walking horse, at his best. In addition to being "walking horse," he had been simply "horse."[6]

Duncan finds the last descendant of Mountain Slasher in the hands of a savage old Indian, and they manage to breed him to Duncan's old mare to produce Chief. But Chief is a throwback to his ancestors, and is uncontrollable, though magnificent. He throws Duncan and is finally shot by Dicky Jordan, son of the *nouveau riche* breeders of Allens. Duncan then learns that Dicky has also seduced his wife.

Desperately, Duncan turns to Aaron McCool, a moonshiner who runs a still on his property. McCool may be interpreted as a Dostoevski-Conrad double, or perhaps a Freudian id. At any rate, he supplies an outlet for Duncan's frustrations. McCool has torn a wildcat to pieces with his bare hands for attacking his chickens and has choked a man to death for shooting his dog. McCool easily persuades Duncan to kill Dicky Jordan, and with this act the identification of Duncan with Aaron is complete. Both outlaws are now pursued and killed by the representatives of law and order.

Duncan's ideal is summed up in his horse, Chief, and with the loss of his ideal, he has no further resources, since he has already renounced progress. An ironic comment on Duncan's fate comes from his foil, Garner, who preaches, "You're afraid of change. You came here to get away from it. The world is changing. There is such a thing as progress, and we're making it. . . . You can't get away from it . . . here or anywhere."[7]

There is a powerful theme being dramatized here, both in personal and social terms. Specialization and mechanization are the

[6] New York, 1957, p. 86. [7] Pp. 265-66.

enemies of the South, just as they are the enemies of Duncan Welsh. With the loss of Chief and Duncan we see the loss of what makes the South unique.

Another symbolic lament for the loss of heroic qualities in the South is contained in *Home from the Hill* (1958) by William Humphrey. There is a good deal of structural ingenuity here, chiefly to communicate the sense of loss through a contrast of past and present. A mysterious black hearse with Dallas County plates pulls into a town in East Texas. Only at the end of the first chapter do we learn that in the casket is Hannah Hunnicutt, mother of Theron and wife of Wade, who has at last died after fourteen years in a Dallas asylum. Working backward from the funeral, we learn from the perspective of a local citizen the mystery of their three gravestones with identical death dates.

Character symbolism is very obvious. Wade Hunnicutt stands for the Old South: proud, strong, and independent. Hannah, a parallel to Wade, personifies Southern pride which refuses to admit dishonor. Albert Halstead, who mistakenly kills Wade, stands for the New South: uncertain, self-righteous, aggressive. Theron Wade is the link between the Old and the New South; his attempt to marry Libby Halstead is an attempt to bridge the gap. Symbolically, Theron kills Halstead, the middle-class image, but destroys himself too.

The reader's response to *Home from the Hill* will be something like that to *The Innocent:* regret for the loss of strength, independence, tradition, mixed with a feeling that it was inevitable. Power corrupts, and Wade Hunnicutt corrupted himself as well as those around him. The ambivalence of the Southern tradition, its good and bad, is powerfully summed up in the figure of Wade, who knew the woods and the animal world better than anyone else, but was unable to face the righteous indignation of Albert Halstead.

The external framework supplied by the curious townspeople at the beginning of the story, fifteen years after the symbolic deaths, gives us an ironic perspective on the events. To the curious crowd, the Hunnicutt family tragedy—Hannah's behavior, particularly—looks like eccentric folly. To the thoughtful reader, it "makes divinest sense."

The high point of the novel is the pursuit and killing of a wild boar, the last one in the county, by Theron Hunnicutt. Humphrey is obviously aiming at an effect like that in "The Bear," for Theron demonstrates all the traditional virtues of the hunter—strength, courage, endurance, and wisdom. However, the wild boar is no pastoral divinity like the bear; he is a symbol of uncontrolled violence and evil. Theron demonstrates what can be accomplished in the woods with these traditional virtues, but he also shows their inadequacy in conflict with twentieth-century civilization.

Elizabeth Hardwick's *Simple Truth* (1955) is set in an Iowa college town, but its theme may be interpreted as Southern. Miss Hardwick contrasts the common-sense approach of a simple Iowa jury to a campus murder with that of two college intellectuals. The intellectuals, despite their elaborate character and motive analysis, fail to understand what the jury does instinctively. However, Miss Hardwick's turgid, Jamesian approach to the story kills all but the irony in the situation. She is a better critic than a novelist.

So far, the sense of cultural loss has predominated in the fiction we have discussed, and the result is an affirmation of Southern values. A more ambiguous discussion of Southern society is presented in novels such as William Styron's monumental *Lie Down in Darkness* (1951). Like many others in this category the novel uses the decay of the Southern family as a microcosm of the decay of Southern civilization.

The time scheme in the novel is handled even more ingeniously than in *Home from the Hill.* It covers only a few hours on a hot summer's day in Port Warwick, Virginia, but by a series of interrelated episodes, Styron takes us back into the lives of Milton and Helen Loftis and their daughter, Peyton, whose coffin is arriving at the station as the story begins. There are two time sequences operating simultaneously: minute by minute we follow the hearse and limousine from the railroad station to the cemetery; at the same time, the recollections of Milton, Helen, the minister Carey Carr, Milton's mistress Dolly, and Peyton herself, give us Peyton's story from five different perspectives. The result is a story dramatized more fully than it could ever be known to one person.

The technical ingenuity of this novel is worthy of James Joyce, whose *Ulysses* must have been an inspiration to Styron, but the important question for our purpose is the novel's commentary on the South. Are we to believe that the Loftis family disintegrated because they lived in Port Warwick, or could this happen anywhere? Styron gives us no definite clue, but several characters in the novel have opinions. Albert Berger, the high priest of a New York culture den, says to Peyton, "It is symptomatic of that society from which you emanate that it should produce the dissolving family: *ah ah,* patience, my pretty, I know you say symptomatic not of that society, but of *our* society, the machine culture, yet so archetypical is this South with its cancerous religiosity, its exhausting need to put manners before morals, to negate all *ethos*—Call it a *husk* of a culture."[8]

Peyton recalls an argument with her husband, Harry Miller, and his crippled friend Lennie.

> Why, she said, were there so many bigots in the North? Why couldn't they realize certain obvious truths: that the South was benighted, maybe, and the people filled with guilt, but didn't they see that this was the very tragic essence of the land, that it was still going through its upheaval, still shattered by conflicts, that it was improving, rising from the ruins, and that when it emerged it would be a greater place for its very ordeal? Couldn't they see that? Lennie couldn't see that: how romantic can you get? he wanted to know.[9]

Despite this discussion, Styron presents the problem as not merely a Southern one. Peyton does not see herself as lost because she is Southern. In New York she finds nothing better than the family, church, and friends she had known in Port Warwick. She tends to blame it on the parents of her generation: "They thought they were lost. They were crazy. They weren't lost. What they were doing was losing us."[10]

Milton, on the other hand, blames his father, says his advice was suitable only for an age without crisis. Milton also blames Helen. Helen blames Milton, and immorality, and lack of religion. Peyton blames everybody at some time, but just before she dies she admits that she doesn't know who's to blame.

Styron may be indicating an inevitable decay in the South, a loss of something good, but a loss. And yet a subplot in this novel

[8] Indianapolis, 1951, p. 363. [9] P. 331. [10] P. 235.

makes us wonder. Parallel to the sophisticated, disillusioned clergyman, Carey Carr, we have the vibrant figure of Daddy Faith and his shouting, swooning followers. A Negro revival might easily be satirized, just as sophisticated religion is satirized, but one can hardly miss the sympathetic treatment, the color and the warmth of the Negro worshipers. Ignorant, yes, but Daddy Faith meets the needs of his flock in a way that Carey Carr fails. Ironically, we can see little likelihood of one of Daddy Faith's congregation throwing herself out of a seven-story building. The story ends with two religious services: a Negro baptism, with all its delirium and pageantry, and a white funeral service, done hurriedly, almost surreptitiously, in a dismal cemetery chapel.

Styron obviously intended his novel to have meaning outside of its Southern setting. In his *Paris Review* interview, he says, "Only certain things in the book are particularly Southern. I used leitmotivs —the Negro, for example—that run throughout the book, but I would like to believe that my people would have behaved the way they did anywhere. The girl, Peyton, for instance, didn't have to come from Virginia. She would have wound up jumping from a window no matter where she came from."[11]

Another analyst of the Southern family is Peter Taylor, whose three volumes have concentrated on the decay of the upper middle-class family. As Robert Penn Warren has pointed out, six of the seven stories in *A Long Fourth* (1948) describe the disintegration of the family unit. Warren also notes Taylor's carefully detached attitude. "If Peter Taylor is concerned with the attrition of old loyalties, the breakdown of old patterns, and the collapse of old values, he regards the process without too much distress to his personal piety."[12] The most ambitious story in the collection, *A Long Fourth,* sums up much of what Taylor has to say about the South. Here Taylor draws a clear parallel between Harriet Wilson's loss of her son to the draft and her servant Mattie's loss of BT, her son, to the city. Both boys are planning to leave the day after July 4, and there are parallel celebrations, both failures. Incidentally we learn that Negroes can suffer loss as deeply as whites. But there is a

[11] *Writers at Work,* p. 272.
[12] *The Long Fourth* (New York, 1948), Introd., pp. viii-ix.

larger point, because on July 4 both men, the black and the white, declare their spiritual independence from their parents.

The Widows of Thornton (1954), a collection of eight stories and a play, again chronicles family dissolution. Usually the death of an elderly kinsman is the incentive, and we are made to lament the passing of the old, though we see the inevitability of it. Here, too, Taylor can recall the noble sentiments and the tribal customs with reverence, yet detachment. The characters do all the mourning.

The last widow in the volume, Sylvia Harrison, acts out the struggle of all Southerners about returning to their homelands. Mrs. Harrison must decide whether to remain in Chicago, where her children have all become accepted, or to return to Cedar Springs, Tennessee, after her husband's death. The attraction of Cedar Springs is obvious. Their name means something. "There wasn't anything in the world like living in a place where there were no questions you didn't know the answers to."

And yet, Cedar Springs comes to symbolize the past as it decays on the banks of the Tennessee River. The oversized furniture and the huge paintings, which serve as her link with the South, are only subjects for jokes by her children. And so, as the last moving van is closed, Mrs. Harrison decides not to follow the furniture back to Cedar Springs. She realizes that only selfishness would lead her to take her children back to a place where *they* are as little known as *she* is in Chicago. The next morning in a bare but sunny apartment house, she plans to buy new furniture. "Everything would be according to her own taste, and even of that there would be only enough to serve the real needs and comforts of the family. There must be nothing anywhere in the apartment to diminish the effect of newness and brightness, or to remind her of the necessity there had been to dispense with all that was old and useless and inherited."[13]

Although the Nashville Agrarians no longer function as a group, they continue to influence young writers. In fact, if there are any schools in this literary generation, there is the second-generation Vanderbilt school, of which Peter Taylor is the most distinguished product so far. He has a double pedigree because he attended

[13] New York, 1954, p. 310.

Vanderbilt and later graduated from Kenyon College. Three other members of the unofficial school are Madison Jones, Elizabeth Spencer, and Walter Sullivan. Miss Spencer received a Master of Arts degree from Vanderbilt in 1943 and has been publicly praised by both Robert Penn Warren and Eudora Welty. Walter Sullivan was born in Nashville and now teaches English at Vanderbilt. Refinement of style and structural ingenuity distinguish the work of all three. Their attitudes toward the South are likewise refined; they are analytical rather than didactic. All their preaching is done within a narrative framework.

Two of Miss Spencer's four novels to date will show the artful ambiguity of this group. Her second novel, *This Crooked Way* (1952), describes a Southern Gatsby named Amos Dudley, who invades the peaceful town of Yocona, Mississippi. Dudley is a climber who succeeds in marrying Ary Morgan, the proud daughter of the ruling family. He builds his empire until Dudley becomes the name of a town on the railroad, but he fails to make a permanent mark because his only son dies. Miss Spencer has neatly contrasted the Morgans and the Dudleys. Dudley, the outsider, is in many ways a symbol of evil, but he is strong and aggressive and materially successful. The Morgan family represents a peaceful, ordered, established society, but it is also decaying.

In her novel, *The Voice at the Back Door* (1956), Miss Spencer again contrasts the new and the old order. The new order in this case is represented by Duncan Harper, the new sheriff of Winfield County, Mississippi. He makes it plain that under his administration, law will supersede custom. That means no more bootleg whisky and no more mistreatment of the Negro. Unfortunately, Duncan is overcome and finally killed as a result of his efforts. The town will probably return to its *status quo* after this brief interlude.

Beck Dozer, the Negro whom Duncan protected, is less of an idealist than he. Beck says early in the novel, "I'm not trying to help anybody but me. I said that when I came back down here to live after the war was over. Any Negro with little enough sense to choose to come back to Mississippi to live had better hew his own row and not look to right nor left."[14] Beck is the New Southern

[14] New York, 1956, p. 127.

Negro. During the war, he had a child by a white woman in England, and now he wears an English tweed jacket, ordered to measure from Sears, Roebuck.

Marcia Mae Hunt represents the transitional Southerner; she is caught between two traditions. Describing her unsuccessful marriage to a handsome Yankee, she says, "He might have been a creature from Mars. He had no consciousness of families, small towns, roots, ties, or any sort of custom. I expected lightning to strike him."[15] On the other hand, when she tries to get Duncan to run off with her, she insists, "We couldn't stay in the South and be free. In the South it's nothing but family, family. We couldn't breathe even, until we left."[16] Miss Spencer's final comment on the problem is Duncan's conclusion: "She had left him [Duncan] because he would not run away with her and be free from the evil she saw in her family and the whole South. . . . He did not believe that the Hunts were worse than anybody else, or that you escaped from anything when you left Lacey and the South."[17]

Walter Sullivan's first and only novel, *Sojourn of a Stranger* (1957), achieves perspective on the melodramatic theme of miscegenation by means of an antebellum setting. Allen Hendrick, son of a New Orleans octoroon and a white artistocrat, is denied the hand of Kate Rutledge, because of his mixed blood. He goes off to the Civil War, hoping to earn the right to marry her. After the war, when all obstacles have been removed, he realizes that his determination to marry Kate was inspired partly by a desire for revenge against her family. Nobly, he leaves her. Hendrick's relatively quick reversal of feelings at the end avoids one cliché at the cost of another. Even in nineteenth-century terms, his inner triumph seems artificial.

Doris Betts at twenty-six has already produced two volumes, *The Gentle Insurrection* (1954) and *Tall Houses in Winter* (1957). Her first book is a collection of twelve short stories describing "gentle insurrections" in the lives of the well-meaning central characters. This theme of human isolation is a universal one, but *Tall Houses in Winter* contrasts Northern and Southern culture through Ryan Goodwin, a middle-aged New England college teacher, who re-

[15] P. 179. [16] P. 176. [17] P. 183.

turns home to Stoneville, North Carolina, with throat cancer. Though he expected to hate Stoneville, he makes his peace with it and with himself before he returns to a Northern hospital for a possibly fatal operation. The novel is technically ambitious, but Miss Betts just does not think like a middle-aged man.

In *A Sound of Voices Dying* (1954) Glenn Scott has obviously tried to sum up everything he learned in his freshman year at Washington and Lee. His protagonist, Reid Carrington, does most of his learning out of class and off campus in lengthy bull sessions with campus intellectuals and lengthy parking sessions with a married woman. The story could have taken place at any small liberal arts college, but there is some regional significance in that the leading influences on Reid's intellectual life are Yankees. Occasionally, Reid feels called upon to defend his homeland against attack, but nothing serious is ever said for or against the South. Despite its earnestness, this is one of the weakest novels by the youngest generation; it is suitable only for college freshmen.

Earl Hamner's *Fifty Roads to Town* (1953) is rather hard to label. He is obviously exploiting the eccentricities of Southern Virginia country people, but there is no perceptible theme. He begins in the Erskine Caldwell tradition by introducing Otha, a fanatical faith healer, to the town of Edensville. The novel could have been an exposé of religious fanaticism, but Hamner takes us off to several families in town to witness their degeneration. Our sympathies are meant to be with Otha, mad as he is, because his intentions are honest. At the end he is so confused that when he wakes up in a cave, he thinks he is the risen Christ and tells a local boy that, if anyone asks for him, he has gone to Galilee. The only normal people left by that time wisely plan to move to Richmond.

With William Hoffman's *The Trumpet Unblown* (1955), we shift from an ambivalent treatment to an implied condemnation of the Southern tradition. Tyree Shelby's romantic name corresponds with his upbringing, and his difficult adjustment to the crude realities of army life seems partly due to his idealistic background. His company commander, Captain Coger, accurately diagnoses his trouble. "You're a tilter of dragons and the world doesn't have any more use for dragon tilters. . . . I used to be a tilter of dragons myself. . . . I know all about the dragons."[18] The captain confesses that he once wanted to be an architect and design beautiful houses; instead he sold pumps and made a lot of money.

As the captain predicted, Shelby is defeated as a dragon tilter. After he has been brought back from Europe suffering from "battle fatigue," the doctor at the Battle Creek Sanatorium asks sympathetically,

> "You're from Richmond?"
> "That's right."
> "Old family maybe. Lots of ideals and family sentiments."
> "Something like that."
> "I can see where it could be tough."
> "It's got nothing to do with them. It just won't work any longer."
> "I know. Me, I was born in Chicago. Chicago is realistic."
> "You're lucky."[19]

Before this, the novel traces the gradual destruction of Shelby's idealism at the hands of the sadistic Blizzard, the hypocritical Sergeant Putney, the cynical Captain Coger, and the opportunist Petras. The chief agent of destruction, however, is Shelby's experience in Ward 4, the preoperative shock ward, the messiest in the whole field hospital.

A man with a soul would obviously have a hard time surviving all these assaults, but Shelby never gives in to Blizzard or betrays a trust or asks for transfer from Ward 4. However, he catches gonorrhea, lets an SS officer die, and runs from shellfire, before he eventually cracks up.

Around him, he sees others struggling to survive by different codes. Captain Coger soaks up his bitterness in cynicism and alcohol, and Moody drinks himself to death. Only Petras has a working solution: be an independent. His is the law of the jungle, adapted to the twentieth century. After he has almost killed Blizzard, he deserts rather than face trial, but he gives this parting advice:

> "Just hang on Shelby. That's all that matters."
> "Oh, sure."
> "Aim to survive. That's the whole secret."
> "Anything else?"
> "It's the secret of my success. I learned it early. You'll never learn it.

[18] New York, 1955, p. 84. [19] P. 243.

You should have been a Greek or a Jew or a nigger. They learn early and never forget."[20]

Symbols of Shelby's useless ideals are his great-grandfather's ring with the family coat of arms and an electric shaver which he determinedly carries with him, though it will not work on European current. Shelby offers to trade his ring for the favors of a prostitute but finds that she prefers penicillin. The useless electric shaver serves a better purpose; it buys schnapps to comfort his alcoholic friend Moody.

Hoffman's second novel, *Days in the Yellow Leaf* (1958), which he actually wrote first, is only vaguely a criticism of the South, but it has the familiar themes of the dissociated sensibility and the dissolving family.

Like Roderick Usher, J. Alfred Prufrock, and General Archbald, the hero, Tod Young, is a mass of exposed nerves, which quiver at man's cruelty to his fellow man. He is, as his friend, Grant Wolfe, claims, a "bleeder," meaning that he suffers vicariously for his fellow men. Further, he realizes that his father is a "killer," meaning that he has always trampled on people to get what he wanted. Yet, Mr. Young represents the old agrarian spirit. "His idea of a vacation was to take a tent, an ax, and a rifle into the woods and live for two weeks by his wits. He felt that if civilization ended right then, he would have been able to make out. It was a good feeling."[21]

Tod's attempts to relieve other people's suffering and to atone for what he considers his father's killings indirectly destroy his marriage, most of his relatives, and the lives of his wife and best friend. The final irony is Tod's trial for murder, in which his father uses his killing power to free him. As usual he succeeds, but Tod has long before lost all desire to live. His days are more "in the yellow leaf," than Byron's ever were.

Like Styron, Humphrey, Spencer, and other young writers, Hoffman has used the multiple viewpoint to allow each character to justify himself. However, the result is a stalemate, in which nobody understands why everything has gone wrong, including the average reader, who would like to sympathize with Tod but finds his cosmic

[20] Pp. 211-12. [21] New York, 1958, p. 69.

guilt complex too much to bear. Tod is a victim rather than a hero.

James Ballard's *But a Little Moment* (1950) is another presentation of family decay. Adam Allen, the father, has left his Kentucky farm and family to build bridges in the Midwest. Bridge building is a way of making his dreams tangible and visible. However, partly because he must spend so much time traveling, his family dissolves, until we are left with Jack Allen.

Half of the novel takes place in a CCC camp in West Virginia where Jack attempts to find himself. At this point, the novel shifts into its second theme, the search for identity. We hear long, pompous dialogues between Jack and Duncan Duquesne, a frustrated poet, on art, philosophy, ethics, politics, and music. These dialogues continue when Jack meets Mr. Sertus, the camp director and his daughter, Geneva, whom Jack finally marries. At the end of this rambling, pretentious novel, Jack leaves his pregnant wife, Geneva, to join the Merchant Marine in Norfolk, where presumably he will complete his voyage of self-discovery.

Three other novels of family dissolution are *The Naked Heart* (1953) by John Lee Weldon, *The Ruined City* (1956) by Clay Putman, and *The Ghostly Lover* (1945) by Elizabeth Hardwick. *The Naked Heart* tells the painful story of twenty-year-old Christy Livingston, youngest son of a burly Birmingham steel worker. *The Ruined City* is the depressing story of a young man who has abandoned his family in Oklahoma to live as a displaced person in New York. *The Ghostly Lover* explores the mind of a frustrated young girl in a middle-class Kentucky family.

While the decay of the family is the major social theme in new Southern fiction, an equally significant theme is the problem of the Negro. Although there are no Negro writers in this group, many stories have Negro characters, most of them more sympathetically presented than Miss Spencer's Beck Dozer.

Lonnie Coleman's *Escape the Thunder* (1944) describes a Porgy-and-Bess situation in Montgomery, Alabama. The hero marries the villain's rejected girl friend, who shows her gratitude by destroying the villain. Despite the stereotyped story and characters, the novel is worth reading for its sympathetic picture of the Negro world on Day Street. Incidentally, Coleman is the most prolific of all the younger generation. At this date he has six novels and a short story collection to his credit, of a uniformly high level of craftsmanship.

The best novel with a purely Negro focus is Jefferson Young's *A Good Man* (1953). Young has found a situation just as rich as Hemingway's *The Old Man and the Sea* in which to dramatize the Negro's upward struggle. Albert Clayton's dream of painting his house white is here made to symbolize the Negro's yearning for dignity and respect. His failure is just as tragic and ennobling as the old man's loss of his fish. A similar story is *High John* (1948) by John W. Wilson. This novel describes the struggle of Cleveland Webster against all the elements. Defeated, he loses his land but not his soul to the white plantation owner.

Two other novels explore the consciousness of the Negro in a striking way. Walter B. Lowrey's *Watch Night* (1953) is largely a first-person narrative by a young Mississippi Negro, condemned to be executed for rape. During the night, he tries to explain to himself why his life must end this way. *Debby* (1950) by Max Steele is a touching character study of a mentally arrested Negro woman who is taken from a delinquent women's home to work as a maid.

Day of the Harvest (1952) by Helen Upshaw manages to avoid the melodrama implicit in the love of Philip Farrel for a beautiful Negro servant, Noel. A similar crisis takes place in Lonnie Coleman's *Clara* (1952), where an outraged wife discovers that her husband has had a child by their Negro maid. These liberal treatments of such relationships would have been unthinkable before the publication of Lillian Smith's *Strange Fruit.*

A third category of new writers can be made of those whose themes are not essentially Southern. Paradoxically, this group contains some of the best and best-known Southern writers. For example, Truman Capote has singlehandedly created the vogue for Louisiana Gothic, a subspecies of Southern Gothic, and his publishers have fostered the notion that Capote's world is one of swamps, snakes, mold, and perversion. At twenty-four, he became the boy wonder of Southern literature with *Other Voices, Other Rooms.*

To this general impression, we must oppose several revealing facts. Ever since his first novel, Capote has steadily widened his scene from the South to the North to the West Indies to Europe and with his last volume to Russia. Also, Capote is now a resident of Brooklyn Heights and before that lived in Europe for eight years, two of them on a mountain top in Sicily. Moreover, Capote does not now regard himself as a Southerner. In his *Paris Review* interview, he said, "I like cities, and New York is the only real city-city."[22]

Capote's impressive output of six volumes makes it plain that his themes as well as his setting extend far beyond the South. *Other Voices, Other Rooms* (1948), for all of its miasmic nightmares, is essentially a spiritual odyssey, a search for a father. Joel Sansom, the thirteen-year-old hero, is literally and spiritually without a father. His real father is totally paralyzed and can only drop red tennis balls to signify his needs. Like a serpent hypnotizing his victim, Joel's cousin Randolph lures him to Scully's Landing, a decaying plantation, then gradually becomes mother, father, and lover all in one. Before succumbing to Randolph, Joel has only two opportunities for real love, but both are doomed from the beginning. He is rejected by Idabel Thompkins, a tomboy trying to cast off her approaching womanhood. Then Miss Wisteria, a frustrated female midget, destroys the rest of Joel's normal instincts by pursuing him at night through a haunted house.

Joel's corruption is inevitable in such surroundings. While gazing into the fireplace of a rotting resort hotel, Joel sees a face in the flame.

> Are you someone I am looking for? he asked, not knowing whom he meant, but certain that for him there must be such a person, just as there was for everybody else: Randolph with his almanac, Miss Wisteria and her search by flashlight, Little Sunshine remembering other voices, other rooms, all of them remembering, or never having known. And Joel drew back. If he recognized the figure in the fire, then what ever would he find to take its place?[23]

While the theme is universal, it is expressed in such terms that we may call Joel a symbol of the present South, who is seduced by Randolph, a symbol of its decadent past. But beginning with his next volume, Capote began his escape from those other voices, other rooms. *The Tree of Night* (1949) contains four short stories with a

[22] *Writers at Work*, p. 292. [23] New York, 1958, pp. 137-38.

Southern setting and four with a New York setting. The Southern stories are comic and easygoing; the Northern stories are cold, bitter, and nightmarish. The most Southern story is "Children on Their Birthdays," describing the effects of Miss Lily Jane Bobbitt from Memphis, Tennessee, on the teen-agers in a small Southern town. Her sophistication changes the whole tone of the neighborhood, but her sophisticated philosophy is her undoing. She prays to the devil as well as to God, because the devil is too powerful to make an enemy of and may grant small favors which are not worthy of God's attention. The devil helps her to win a talent contest, and also answers her prayer for an escape from this provincial town by having the six o'clock bus from Mobile run over her.

The Northern stories are the more ambitious. "Master Misery" is a psychological fantasy about a girl who sells her dreams to a man named Mr. Revercomb. Too late, she realizes that she has been selling parts of her soul. "The Headless Hawk," the longest and most ingenious, is, like the others, a mixture of dream and reality. The main character is an art dealer who is described as "a poet who had never written poetry, a painter who had never painted, a lover who had never loved (absolutely)—someone, in short, without direction, and quite headless."[24] He is pursued by a girl with green eyes in a green raincoat, who is also headless, or insane. Capote is plainly not recommending Northern culture over Southern in this volume.

In *The Grass Harp* (1951), Capote returns to his search-for-identity theme in a Southern setting. The hopelessness of the search is made plain by the five people who retreat from organized society to a tree house. The story is narrated by Collin Fenwick, a teen-aged orphan. Eventually all five are forced to descend from the tree and to face real life, but before that, a seventy-year-old retired judge, who has been looking for a person to whom everything may be said, asks, "Am I an idiot to want such a thing? But, ah, the energy we spend hiding from one another, afraid as we are of being identified. But here we are, identified: five fools in a tree. A great piece of luck provided we know how to use it: no longer any need to worry about the picture we present—free to find out who we truly are."[25]

Thomas Hal Phillips is another writer whose preoccupation is not

[24] New York, 1949, p. 181. [25] New York, 1951, p. 44.

necessarily Southern, though Mississippi farms and woods are essential to his stories. The hero of all five of his novels is, like Joel Sansom, in search of a spiritual father. As in *Other Voices, Other Rooms,* homosexuality lurks in the background. *Bitterweed Path* (1950) and *The Loved and the Unloved* (1955) have heroes who are driven to ambiguous relationships by intolerable family conditions. *Search for a Hero* (1952) is probably the best of these searches for an ideal love.

We have already seen that the search for a father or the search for an ideal love extends beyond the South. Carson McCullers is another major Southern writer who has made the search for love her theme. Her stories are peopled by lovers whose love is unrequited. There is no mutual love, only one active and one passive lover, or one active lover with no one to love.

The striking thing about Mrs. McCullers' work is that she seems to take this unrequited love for granted. In *The Ballad of the Sad Café* (1951), she has tried to rationalize it in this way:

> First of all, love is a joint experience between two persons—but the fact that it is a joint experience does not mean that it is a similar experience to the two people involved. . . . Often the beloved is only a stimulus for all the stored-up love which has lain quiet within the lover for a long time hitherto. And somehow every lover knows this. He feels in his soul that his love is a solitary thing. . . . So there is only one thing for the lover to do. He must house his love within himself as best he can; he must create for himself a whole inward world—a world intense and strange, complete in himself.[26]

Mrs. McCullers uses this rationale to explain the strange relationship between adults in *The Ballad of the Sad Café* and *The Heart Is a Lonely Hunter* (1940); to describe the adolescent longing of Mick Kelly and Frankie Addams; and to justify the cosmic yearnings of the drunk in "A Tree, A Rock, A Cloud" and of Jake Blount in *The Heart Is a Lonely Hunter.*

Biff Brannon's meditation in his restaurant at the end of *The Heart Is a Lonely Hunter* may be Mrs. McCullers' ultimate statement. He is playing with a zinnia.

> He plucked the soft, bright petals, and the last one came out on love. But who? Who would he be loving now? No one person. . . . Then sud-

[26] Boston, 1951, p. 24.

denly he felt a quickening in him. His heart turned and he leaned against the counter for support. For in a swift radiance of illumination he saw a glimpse of human struggle and of valor. Of the endless fluid passage of humanity through endless time. And of those who labor and of those who—one word—love. His soul expanded. But for a moment only.[27]

An instant later he realizes that he is actually suspended between radiance and darkness, between the past and the future, between fear and faith. This Joycean epiphany is all that is granted even to Biff Brannon as he waits for the morning sun.

The Heart Is a Lonely Hunter has its Southern themes too. The struggle to organize labor in the South and above all the struggle of the Negro to achieve social equality are dramatized here. Dr. Copeland drives himself to an early grave trying to minister to the physical and spiritual needs of the Negroes. Sadly, he watches his own people desert him and fall into the trap that the whites have set for them. He is carried off to die of tuberculosis in a mule cart by the stereotype of the humble old darky whom he has been trying fruitlessly to elevate. We must also admire the struggles of Jake Blount, the Marxist reformer, but their zeal, their pity for human misery are not enough. Patience and humility must be added to love.

There is a characteristically strong emphasis on family in Mrs. McCullers' stories. The Addams family in *The Member of the Wedding* (1946) is so closely bound together that Frankie cannot bear to lose her brother to another woman outside the family. Mick Kelly's family rallies against the common enemy in *The Heart Is a Lonely Hunter,* and this makes their poverty bearable. John Ferris in "The Sojourner" feels detached and empty because he has left his family in the South. "The Domestic Dilemma" might not have happened if the Meadows had not been transplanted out of their natural environment. To all of these characters and many others in Mrs. McCuller's stories, family and place give a sense of belonging. Those who long for faraway places, as Frankie does for Alaska, are soon cured of their folly. Mrs. McCullers seems to be saying that those who cut themselves off or are cut off from family and region are lost; the only safe place is home, where love is most easy to find.

Yet the outside world still exists for her. "Wunderkind" is set in

[27] Boston, 1940, p. 497.

Cincinnati, "The Jockey" at Saratoga Springs, "The Sojourner" in New York, "A Domestic Dilemma" in New Jersey, and "Madame Zilensky" in a small college town. Only the first and last stories in Mrs. McCullers' collected work have unmistakably Southern settings.

Like Mrs. McCullers, Shirley Ann Grau resists easy classification. On the surface, she looks like a pure regionalist, one of a vanishing race in the South. Both of her published volumes, *The Black Prince and Other Stories* (1954) and *The Hard Blue Sky* (1958), have deep Southern settings, and her characters are as Southern as could be. Moreover, there is no crusading or preaching in her work, no obvious social or antisocial attitude expressed. Instead, she achieves a sympathetic projection which enables her to understand equally an adolescent country boy, a young upper-class white girl, a mature white woman, an adolescent Negro girl, and an ex-convict. This universal sympathy is matched by her sharp eye and quietly lyrical style. Like Eudora Welty, she is a regionalist who has not succumbed to provincialism. In technique, she is the closest young competitor to Miss Welty.

One of the most controversial Southern writers is Flannery O'Connor, whose two volumes, *Wise Blood* (1952) and *A Good Man Is Hard to Find* (1955), have baffled many readers, including her own neighbors in Milledgeville, Georgia. On the surface, her world is peopled by cripples, morons, misfits, and perverts. A good man is indeed hard to find in her stories. There are two heroes in *Wise Blood;* one is the evangelist Hazel Motes, who preaches, "There was no Fall because there was nothing to fall from and no Redemption because there was no Fall and no Judgment because there wasn't the first two. Nothing matters except that Jesus was a liar."[28] The other hero is his first disciple, Enoch Emery, who spends much of his time watching girls swimming in the park pool and drinking chocolate malteds at the Frosty Bottle. A similar character is the Bible salesman in "Good Country People," who offers the heroine a hollow Bible, containing whisky, cards, and contraceptives. When she resists him, he steals her wooden leg. The misfit in *A Good Man Is Hard to Find* is a worthy companion for these people, because

[28] New York, 1952, p. 66.

while he methodically kills off a whole carload of strangers, he remarks, "If [Jesus] did what He said, then it's nothing for you to do but throw away everything and follow Him, and if He didn't, then it's nothing for you to do but enjoy the few minutes you got left the best way you can—by killing somebody or burning down his house or doing some other meanness to him. No pleasure but meanness."[29]

However, Miss O'Connor has made it plain that like Faulkner, she is often writing an inverted moral allegory. In Granville Hicks's symposium, *The Living Novel* (1958), she defends the distortion and grotesqueness in her work,

> My own feeling is that writers who see by the light of their Christian faith will have in these times, the sharpest eye for the grotesque, for the perverse, and for the unacceptable. . . . The novelist with Christian concerns will find in modern life distortions which are repugnant to him, and his problem will be to make these appear as distortions to an audience which is used to seeing them as natural; and he may well be forced to take ever more violent means to get his vision across to this hostile audience.[30]

Her theme, then, is positive, Christian, and universal.

William Styron's *The Long March* (1956) is another brilliantly conceived microcosmic situation on the order of Jefferson Young's *A Good Man.* The participants in a Marine Corps forced march act out the eternal theme of free will versus authority. Lieutenant Culver, the center of focus, and Lieutenant Mannix represent modern man subjected to laws he does not understand or admire. The originator of the march is Colonel Templeton, who is symbolically treated with Godlike dignity and restraint. Godlike, he gives orders which are incomprehensible, but, Godlike, he assumes that they will be obeyed.

Culver and Mannix demonstrate two intellectual responses to "divine" commands. Culver, despite bitterness, gives in to the inevitable, while the courageous Mannix refuses to submit. For Culver, the moral struggle in which he resigns his freedom of will has already taken place before the march, but we watch the tragedy of Mannix taking place; we see him gradually humbled by the Godlike Templeton and his disciple, Major Lawrence.

[29] New York, 1955, p. 28. [30] New York, 1957, pp. 162-63.

Styron draws an ironic contrast between the free will allowed men in the outside world and the utter submission to authority required in the Marines. But this is not an attack on the Marines; rather it is a sober observation that free will or political freedom can be held only at great cost today. Submission to some authority —a machine, a society, a government, or God—is one of the facts of twentieth-century life.

In his *Paris Review* interview, Styron prepared us for such a universal theme by saying, "Frankly, I don't consider myself in the Southern school, whatever that is. *Lie Down in Darkness,* most of it, was set in the South, but I don't care if I never write about the South again, really."[31] Suiting the word to the deed, Styron, after his return from Europe, settled first in New York and then in Connecticut. His next novel, *Set This House on Fire,* is to be about Americans abroad.

William Heath's *Violent Saturday* (1955) is on the surface merely a very skillful melodrama about an unsuccessful bank robbery in Morgan, Alabama, presented from the composite viewpoint of a half dozen of the participants. But Heath's character analysis raises the situation above the melodrama and achieves a universal theme. The story is actually about fear, and Heath shows that instead of good and bad people there are really only strong and weak people. The strong ones admit their fears and fight to control them. The weak ones are overcome by their fears. One of the strong ones is Shelley Martin. His car is stolen as a getaway car, and he is tied in a barn, but instead of lying still and waiting for the whole thing to pass over, he says, "No, I ought to at least try. A man ought to do what he can."[32] Thus Shelley becomes a hero in spite of his fears.

Yet another kind of universality has been achieved by those young Southerners who put their military experiences to literary use. Styron and Hoffman have already been discussed, but three others have used foreign as well as local settings. George Garrett's *King of the Mountain* (1958) is a collection of nineteen stories ranging from the Florida Keys to the Mediterranean and back to Greenwich Village. They extend thematically from father-and-son conflicts to bloody German occupation stories. *Time Moving West*

[31] *Writers at Work,* p. 272. [32] New York, 1955, p. 163.

(1947) by Lonnie Coleman presents a cross section of the crew of a Navy transport in the Mediterranean during World War II. Finally, *Two Soldiers* (1956) by Paxton Davis consists of two novelettes about the American army in Burma during World War II.

Probably the least Southern of the youngest generation of writers are Speed Lamkin and Calder Willingham. Lamkin in two novels and Willingham in five novels and a short story collection have a decidedly Yankee attitude. Lampkin's farewell to the South was his first novel, *Tiger in the Garden* (1950), in which he pretty obviously draws upon his own family background in Monroe, Louisiana. *The Easter Egg Hunt* (1954) is a shameless imitation of Fitzgerald's *The Great Gatsby,* with a Hollywood setting. The South in this novel is a symbol of mediocrity and conformity from which the narrator is proud to have escaped.

Calder Willingham is not likely to be taken up by the graduate schools or the literary quarterlies, but he is the only satirist in the group. A list of his books will reveal the range of his interests. *End as a Man* (1947), a slightly disguised analysis of life at the Citadel, reached a wide audience as a play and movie. *Geraldine Bradshaw* (1950) is an exposé of life in a Chicago hotel from the bellboy's point of view. This is the crudest of the lot; even Nelson Algren, a specialist in Chicago low life, was disgusted by it. *Reach to the Stars* (1952) is almost as bad a novel about life in a Hollywood hotel. *Natural Child* (1952) is a razzle-dazzle account of two lively teenage romances. *To Eat a Peach* (1955) shifts to the Southern woods and offers the usual Willingham formula: one-third sex, one-third satire—in this case of boys' camps—and one-third accurate journalism. When last heard from, he was living in New Hampshire.

There you have a sampling of the output of our young Southern writers. And now, do the writers of this generation in any way alter the established Southern literary tradition? Two recent critics, Louis Rubin and Hugh Holman, have recognized these traditional characteristics:

(1) A love of rhetoric and a sense of style.
(2) A deep awareness of the past.
(3) A belief in man's innate depravity.

(4) Pride in family and race.
(5) Regional pride.[33]

If we assume that these thirty-four young writers comprise the next literary generation in the South, we must revise slightly the prevailing concept of the Southern literary tradition. The love of rhetoric and the sense of style continue. The consciousness of evil remains. However, racial and family pride clearly and significantly diminishes, as does pride of region. Also, the awareness of the past no longer includes the Civil War. In short, the tragic vision has been replaced by a guilt complex.

The result is a Southern literary tradition which is more in line with the prevailing American tradition than before, and there is good reason why this should be so. The young Southern writer has by travel and education lost many of his regional characteristics. Furthermore, these regional characteristics have always depended upon a cultural gap between the South and the rest of America. So long as race, place, and family are essential to the Southerner, there will be a distinctive Southern literature, for the artist thrives upon the incongruities produced by the impact of one culture upon another. But if, as sociologists tell us, the cultural gap between the South and the rest of America is closing, then we must expect that in the future Southern literature will be less distinctive, though not necessarily less distinguished.

Heeding the sociologists, John T. Westbrook has already hailed "the twilight of Southern regionalism." He predicts, "The writer of tomorrow must take into account another South, a South already born and growing lustily, a rich South, urban, industrialized, and no longer 'Southern,' but rather modernized, Europeanized, cosmopolitan."[34]

Perhaps Westbrook is premature and overenthusiastic. After all, Allen Tate has been predicting the end of the Southern Renascence since 1935, but even if he is eventually right, the end of Southern

[33] See C. Hugh Holman, "Ellen Glasgow and the Southern Literary Tradition," p. 123 of this book; and Louis D. Rubin, Jr., "Thomas Wolfe in Time and Place," *Southern Renascence,* pp. 290-305.

[34] "The Twilight of Southern Regionalism," *Southwest Review,* XLII (Summer, 1957), 234.

regionalism will not be the end of good writing in the South. The youngest generation is continuing the Southern Renascence, but in universal terms. The first novels of McCullers, Capote, and Styron are better, I think, than the first novels of Glasgow, Faulkner, and Warren, and I believe we shall have more like them before this generation is finished.